Interpreting the 20th Century: The Struggle Over Democracy

Part III

Professor Pamela Radcliff

THE TEACHING COMPANY ®

PUBLISHED BY:

THE TEACHING COMPANY
4151 Lafayette Center Drive, Suite 100
Chantilly, Virginia 20151-1232
1-800-TEACH-12
Fax—703-378-3819
www.teach12.com

ISBN 1-56585-888-3

Pamela Radcliff, Ph.D.

Associate Professor, Department of History,
University of California, San Diego

Pamela Radcliff was born in Passaic, New Jersey, and grew up in Clifton, New Jersey, and Escondido, California. She received her B.A. in history, with membership in Phi Beta Kappa, from Scripps College, one of the five Claremont Colleges, then spent a couple of years traveling around the world before beginning graduate education at Columbia University. She studied modern European history at Columbia, where she received her M.A. and Ph.D. degrees, completed in 1990.

Since the conclusion of her graduate work, Professor Radcliff has been teaching at the University of California, San Diego, in the Department of History. She teaches undergraduate courses on 20th-century European history, modern Spanish history, the history of women and gender in modern Europe, and 20th-century world history. She has received two awards for undergraduate teaching, one granted by the university faculty and another by the students of her world history course.

Professor Radcliff's historical research has focused on Spanish history in the 20th century, with particular emphasis on popular mobilization and the long-term struggle to establish a democratic system of government. She has published articles and books on these issues, including *From Mobilization to Civil War: The Politics of Polarization in the Spanish City of Gijón, 1900–1937*, which received the Sierra Book Award from the Western Association of Women's Historians in 1998. She also co-edited (with Victoria Enders) a collection of articles on the history of women in modern Spain, *Constructing Spanish Womanhood: Female Identity in Modern Spain*. Her current book project focuses on the construction of democratic citizenship during the transition from an authoritarian to a democratic regime in Spain in the 1970s, and her latest article on this topic is "Citizens and Housewives: The Problem of Female Citizenship in Spain's Transition to Democracy," appearing in the fall 2002 issue of the *Journal of Social History*.

Professor Radcliff also served as an associate editor for the recent multivolume *Encyclopedia of European Social History* and belongs to a number of professional associations, including the American

Historical Association and the Society for Spanish and Portuguese Historical Studies.

Professor Radcliff lives in Solana Beach, California, with her husband, Bill Perry, and their two children.

Table of Contents

Interpreting the 20th Century:
The Struggle Over Democracy
Part III

Interpreting the 20th Century:
The Struggle Over Democracy

Scope:

The 20th century transformed the world in ways few could have imagined in 1900. Making sense of this transformation is the challenge of this 48-lecture course. Because one course could never provide a history of every corner of the globe, our focus will be on how the different regions and countries interacted with each other. It is through this interaction that we can discern the common themes that allow us to talk about the history of the world.

One of the key themes was precisely how the growing interaction between regions would operate. By 1900, the process of Western expansion and imperialism had created a level of global interdependence that would only get stronger as the century progressed. But the interdependent world order created by Western imperialism was a fundamentally hierarchical one, based on Western leadership or domination of the non-Western world. The 20th century was defined by the various efforts to transform this connection into a more democratic relationship between Western nations and the rest of the world, or between the developed and less developed regions of the northern and southern hemispheres. In the first two-thirds of the century, these efforts focused on the struggle for independence from colonialism, while in the latter part, Third World nations pursued the more complex search for prosperity and stability.

The struggle over democracy was also a key theme in the Western, or developed, world. Most Western nations had some form of representational political systems in 1914, but they were not democratic. Furthermore, the process of democratization was neither automatic nor harmonious. Until almost the end of the century, the democratic ideal had to compete with powerful challengers, especially fascism and communism. The fascist alternative was defeated with the Second World War, while the communist challenge lasted until 1989 and the collapse of the Soviet bloc. Parallel to these challenges, there were ongoing debates about the nature and practice of democracy that did not end in 1989. Although democracy emerged at the end of the century as the unquestioned political ideal, the parameters of a truly democratic world order are still vigorously contested. Thus, the struggle over democracy frames the end, as well the beginning, of the 20th century.

The first lecture in this course sets up the framework of struggle over liberal democracy and a broader set of ideas associated with it, what we will call the "Enlightenment project." The remaining two lectures in Section 1 explain why this new era began in 1914 rather than 1900, with the outbreak of the First World War and the "crisis of meaning" it precipitated.

Section 2 explores in more detail this "crisis of meaning" of the interwar years, in which a generation of Western artists and intellectuals questioned all the certainties of the Enlightenment project and the cultural and social order in which they lived. Section 3 focuses on the political manifestation of the interwar crisis, in the form of alternative political ideologies and regimes that challenged liberal democracy's claim to offer the best form of government and society. In Lectures Twelve through Fourteen, we will look at what these ideologies promised and why they attracted so many people; in Lectures Fifteen and Sixteen, we will focus on what happened to communism and fascism in power in the USSR and Germany.

Section 4 shifts the locus of struggle to the non-Western world, where the competition among liberal democracy, communism, and fascism took shape in the first serious anti-imperialist movements of the century. Each of the four case studies, China, India, Mexico, and Japan, illustrates a different kind of imperialist influence and a distinct path to national independence in the decades leading up to World War II. Section 5 analyzes the Second World War as a mid-century watershed that marked the culmination and defeat of the fascist challenge but also the end of an imperialist world order based on European domination. Section 6 explores the new world order that emerges out of the Second World War, one dominated by the clash between democratic and communist systems and by the stalemate, that is, the Cold War, between two new superpowers. In particular, we will look at the contested origins of the Cold War and its impact on American society and its democratic system.

Section 7 shifts again to the non-Western world, where the Cold War realignment helped set the stage for the process of decolonization. Although this process created dozens of independent nations, it also generated a new set of problems and challenges for the developing world, or what became known as the *Third World*. Through the use of case studies once again, these lectures will chart alternative paths to development and the successes and pitfalls of communist, liberal democratic, and mixed models. Section 8 looks at a series of challenges that undermined the Cold War order, from Western-based social movements that questioned the democratic credentials of the "free world," to Eastern-bloc dissidents who cast doubt on the socialist credentials of the USSR, to a new political movement based on religious fundamentalism that rejected many of the values on both sides. The section ends with a lecture on the demise of the Soviet bloc after 1989, which analyzes how and why the communist challenge finally collapsed. The final lectures of Section 9 will speculate on the post-Cold War world since 1989 and the prospects and challenges for a democratic world order in the 21st century.

Lecture Twenty-Five
The Holocaust

Scope:

The scope of Nazi ambitions provides a context for analyzing the extermination of Jews carried out by the regime, although the genocidal program deserves independent analysis. This lecture describes the implementation of the "final solution," then reviews and evaluates some of the debates over why and how the Jews were exterminated. It considers the argument between so-called intentionalists and functionalists over how the "final solution" was arrived at, as well as the debates over why "ordinary" Germans collaborated in such a horrific process. Finally, the lecture considers the broader international failure to stop the genocide as a culmination of the crisis of meaning that erupted with the First World War.

Outline

I. Even within the context of Hitler's racial world order, the Holocaust was a unique horror that deserves special attention.

    A. As a case of genocide, it was not, unfortunately, unique. From the Turkish campaign against Armenians in the early 20th century to the more recent killings of Tutsis in Rwanda and of Croats and Muslims in Bosnia, some historians have argued that genocide has become one of the marks of the 20th century.

    B. The reason we remember the Holocaust as a unique horror is not simply the deaths of 6 million people, but the way in which they were killed.

        1. Never had there been such a lethal combination of technology, science, and bureaucratic efficiency, three of the modern achievements of Western civilization.

        2. The gas chamber and all it symbolized made it impossible to return to naïve links among "modernization," "progress," and Western civilization.

        3. Following so closely on the First World War, the Holocaust made it clear that "progress" had a dark side that couldn't simply be explained away by blaming the actions on one evil man.

II. But why were the Jews exterminated and how did the process unfold?

    A. The question of why and how has occupied many scholars, who have formed diverging schools of thought.

        1. On one side are the *intentionalists*, who focus on Hitler as the main "perpetrator."

        2. The other school, the *functionalists*, see the "final solution" as part of an evolving and incoherent Jewish policy that turned to genocide only when other expulsion options fell through.

        3. Why is this debate interesting? It connects directly to larger debates about the nature of the Nazi regime.

        4. For intentionalists, the Holocaust was a perfect example of a totalitarian system in action, where all policies were the expression of a single will.

        5. For functionalists, the Nazi state was a more complex arena of actors, institutions, and changing circumstances.

        6. In recent years, some scholars have made convincing efforts to bring both models together.

    B. Whether the decision was made in 1924 in *Mein Kampf* or in the summer of 1941 after the invasion of the Soviet Union, the facts of extermination are the same.

        1. After years of escalating harassment, expropriation, terror, and isolation, systematic killing began in the summer of 1941, when the infamous memo sent from Field Marshall Goering called for a "final solution" to the Jewish problem.

        2. The killings in Soviet territory were carried out "on the ground," that is, by military units called *Einsatzkommandos* following behind the advancing front lines, but with varying amounts of local collaboration.

        3. At this point, the method of killing was not institutionalized and there were a number of local variations, but most Russian Jews were killed where they lived.

        4. In 1942, the first extermination camps were built, partly because existing methods "wasted" too many bullets and partly because of the reported strain on the executioners of killing people one by one.

5. Nevertheless, some 40 percent of the total killings occurred before the first camp was built.

C. The six death camps were built between December 1941 and June 1942, and their operation opened a new phase in the organization and method of killing, what one historian called the "bureaucratization of mass murder."

    1. The fact that Jews needed to be shipped from all over Europe to camps in Poland required an elaborate transportation network.

    2. Planning for this task took place at the Wannsee Conference in January 1942, at which officials made a list of 11 million Jews from 20 European countries slated for eventual evacuation and murder.

    3. Once Jews were shipped to the camps, the technology of mass murder had to be perfected.

    4. After trying various methods of mass asphyxiation, a product called *Zyklon B*, which contained enough gas in a hand-sized canister to kill a large room of people, became the standard.

    5. The final numbers of dead are staggering: 67 percent of the almost 9 million Jews in Europe perished.

    6. Furthermore, they perished in a system of mass murder that required 100,000 to 500,000 direct participants and many more who passively acquiesced.

III. One of the most debated questions has been why so many people collaborated and what their motives were.

A. One answer argues that the "bureaucracy of mass murder" kept the brutal reality hidden from the vast majority of actors, who could perform their discrete tasks but never had to pull the trigger, so to speak.

B. For those who did pull the trigger, there have been a number of other explanations, from fear to peer pressure, cowardice, conformity, or vicious anti-Semitism. It's hard to know whether a banal motive or blinding racism is the more chilling explanation.

C. The active or passive collaboration of millions of Germans goes beyond individual motives to demonstrate the devastating success of Hitler's "racial revolution." By systematically breaking down the human bonds between

Germans and Jews over the course of a decade, when Jews were finally carted off, it was something happening to "other" people.

D. Beyond German collaboration, why did no one else try to stop the mass murder, when Allied governments had information about the camps by at least June of 1942?

  1. The official answer was that all resources were being put into defeating the Germans.

  2. Whether this was a militarily sound response or not, it is devastatingly true that no other country focused the kind of energy on saving the Jews that the Nazis focused on killing them.

E. This broader failure to prevent the systematic, bureaucratized murder of six million people represented a larger indictment of European civilization: that at a crucial moment of crisis, all of its laws, religious institutions, great scientific knowledge, and political freedoms were either helpless or complicit.

  1. These failures required not only a physical but a moral and political reconstruction of European society after the war.

  2. At the same time, it was the challenge and horror of fascism that helped Western civilization regain the sense of good and evil lost in the First World War.

  3. The combination of shame and a renewed moral purpose provoked a somber but ultimately creative effort to rebuild the Enlightenment project, but with important modifications.

Essential Reading:

Leslie Derfler and Patricia Kollander, eds., *An Age of Conflict: Readings in 20th Century European History*, chapter 8, "The Holocaust."

Lucy Dawidowicz, ed., *A Holocaust Reader*, Goering's memo, July 31, 1941; minutes of the Wannsee Conference, January 20, 1942; memos from Generals Gienanth and Himmler on the conflict between war aims and the final solution; memos from the death camps; pp. 72–82, 101–120.

Supplementary Reading:

Christopher Browning, *The Path to Genocide: Essays on Launching the Final Solution.*

———, *Ordinary Men: Reserve Police Battalion 101 and the Final Solution in Poland.*

Questions to Consider:

1. In recent years, the debate over "German guilt" has increased following the publication of a high-profile book, Daniel Goldhagen's *Hitler's Willing Executioners*, which argued for the existence of a widespread "eliminationist" anti-Semitism in Germany that preceded the Nazi era. Do you think Goldhagen's claim has merit?

2. Even after the experience of abandoning the Jews to their fate in the 1940s, the practice of genocide in the world seems to have increased rather than decreased. What factors can explain this shameful feature of 20th-century life?

Lecture Twenty-Five—Transcript
The Holocaust

Even within the context of Hitler's racial world order that we talked about in the last lecture, the Holocaust was a unique horror that deserves special attention. As a case of genocide, it was not, unfortunately, unique. From the Turkish campaign against Armenians in the early 20th century to the killings of Tutsis in Rwanda and of Croats and Muslims in Bosnia at the end of the century, some historians have argued that genocide has become one of the marks of the 20th century.

The identification of genocide with the 20th century might make sense if we think of the totalitarian potential of mass society to organize such a new level of killings against a single people. But, unfortunately, this does not explain everything because most of these cases had little to do with the organization and technology of mass society; for example, if you think of Turks in the early 20th century, or Rwanda in the late 20th century. In fact, the case that most clearly does illustrate the tools of mass society being harnessed to genocide is precisely the Nazi murder of the Jews. It is partly for this reason that we remember the Holocaust as a unique horror. Not simply because of the death toll, but because of the way in which the Jews were killed. Never had there been such a lethal combination of technology, science, and bureaucratic efficiency, three of the supposed qualities of advanced modern civilization. Once again, you see that kind of paradox of the benefits of modern civilization having this barbaric underbelly. Think about the organization it takes to round up 6 million people, to process them individually, to keep minute records on them, to organize transportation that keeps thousands of people a day flowing from one place to another. Of course, in the perfection of systematic mass murder on a scale never before conceived, the greatest benefits of modern industrial civilization were being used for the most barbaric ends. If the machine gun in the First World War provided the first shock, the gas chamber made it impossible to revive naïve notions about the links among "modernization," "progress," and Western civilization.

But why were the Jews exterminated and how did the process unfold? Everyone agrees that the genocide of the Jews was a shocking and horrible thing; scholars are divided in their interpretation of why it happened. What are the origins of what became known as the "final solution," the decision to murder the Jews?

On the one side are the so-called *intentionalists*, who focus on Hitler as the main "perpetrator." They argue that the decision arose from his long-nurtured plan for the physical annihilation of the Jews, which he had laid out in *Mein Kampf,* and that as soon as Hitler took power in 1933, he was simply preparing the ground for the right moment to carry out his plan.

The other school, the so-called *functionalists,* see the "final solution" as part of an evolving and less coherent Jewish policy whose main goal was, in fact, getting rid of Germany's Jews, but in which the actual decision to kill them and European Jews was not made until late 1941 after other kinds of expulsion options fell through. So, those are the two positions.

Why is this debate interesting? I think it connects directly to larger questions about the nature of the Nazi state. In the view of the intentionalists, the final solution was a perfect example of a totalitarian system in operation. After years of preparation, the Jews had been terrorized and demoralized into submission while the German population had either been terrorized or convinced that the Jews were subhuman.

In this narrative, Hitler was able to harness all of the resources of the German state and population using a combination of coercion and consent to carry out his plan. It was through Hitler's long ideological commitment, his complete control of anti-Jewish policy, and his role as master of the Third Reich that he bears the weight of responsibility for the Holocaust. As a corollary, of course, totalitarian control explains both why few Jews resisted and why many, if not most, Germans either passively or actively contributed to the genocide.

For the functionalists, however, Hitler's ideology became only one factor in a more complex state in which there is an interaction between changing circumstances—particularly the changing circumstances of the war, different governmental institutions competing with each other, the role of rank and file perpetrators, and finally Hitler, himself. In other words, for the functionalist, there is some complicated interaction between all of these factors.

While Hitler's anti-Semitic obsession was clearly important in radicalizing racial policy, the argument here would be that there was no fixed, coherent anti-Jewish policy from the very start that was simply carried out. What evolved was a series of ad hoc responses to changing circumstances on the part of a splintered and disorganized government. In particular, functionalists argue, that it was the failure of the *blitzkrieg* invasion of the Soviet Union that really turned the tide from an expulsion policy to an extermination policy. When local Nazi leaders in the occupied territories of the East could no longer cope with vast numbers of Jews being transported, they initiated systematic killings on a local level, which were then approved from above and expanded to a general policy, according to this argument. Rather than totalitarian will or the implementation of a single agenda, the functionalist argues for a less monolithic but equally frightening version of the Nazi state.

One of the interesting things about the functionalist version is that there is much more room for other actors than simply Hitler. A few people have even gone so far to argue that Hitler never even gave an order for the "final solution," and it is true that no document exists with his signature on it ordering the murder of the Jews. Most people don't go this far; that is, most people don't relinquish Hitler's responsibility. Still, acknowledging that Hitler was involved and certainly approved the functionalist view opens up the question of who actually participated and what their motives were. If they are not simply terrorized or faceless bureaucrats, then who were they and why did they kill?

In recent years, a number of historians have made convincing efforts to bring these two models together, to find a compromise between the functionalist and the intentionalist models. On the one hand, this compromised position agreed that it is crucial to see the role of local adaptation and local initiative in the development of the "final solution." The image of a kind of Hitler-driven totalitarian state is simply too monolithic to describe realty. Despite Hitler's clear anti-Semitism, he rarely—in all levels—contributed to specific policies, and he tended to let his underlings fight it out and have policies emerge from the bottom.

On the other hand, though, the compromised position said it is equally important to see Hitler's major role in setting the vicious tone within which initiatives from the bottom took place. So, his bombastic and hate-filled rhetoric legitimized and encouraged even the most extreme measures. You have to see both of these things at the same time. Whether you buy the argument that the decision was made in 1924 in *Mein Kampf* or in the summer of 1941 after the invasion of the Soviet Union, the facts of extermination are the same, as is the escalation of anti-Semitic policies from the early 1930s to 1941.

If we begin with the first stage, between 1933 and 1936, a series of laws were passed that increasingly pushed the Jews out of the mainstream of German society. We have already talked about the *Gleichshaltung*, the coordination, of social life that pushed the Jews out of German social interaction, while other laws disqualified them for professional and government jobs, prevented intermarriage with non-Jews, expelled them from universities, and so on. After 1938, we have systematic attacks on Jewish property and forced expropriations. Finally, in 1939, plans were made for the expulsion of Jews from Germany. In preparation for this measure, they were forced into ghettos, and the first plans for relocating Jews to occupied territories were made. The first plan was to take them out of Germany and put them somewhere else. One of the options considered briefly was to send them to Madagascar, overseas, but this was rejected because of logistical difficulties. Systematic killing begins with the invasion into the Soviet Union in 1941. Most historians agree, at this point, that the final decision to annihilate the Jews has been made. There is an infamous memo sent from Field Marshall Goering to General Heydrich, who was the chief of the security police in July 1941, in which he asked for a plan showing: "the preliminary organizational substantive and final measures for the execution of the intended final solution of the Jewish question." It is here that we get the term "final solution" and a clear message from the top that it is asking for a plan.

The killings in Soviet territory were carried out "on the ground"; that is, they were carried out by military units called *Einsatzkommandos*, who followed behind the advancing front lines, as it was a rear-guard action of these police units, and they did this local killing with various degrees of collaboration by local Polish or Ukrainian inhabitants. At this point, the method of killing was not institutionalized, and there were a number of local variations, but what is important to emphasize is that most Russian Jews were killed where they lived; they were not moved to camps.

One of the most common procedures was that Jews were told to gather outside of the town where they lived and then forced to dig trenches, take off their clothes and their possessions, and stand beside the trenches while they were machine-gunned and then buried in those trenches. In two days—October 29 and October 30 of 1941—33,771 Jews were killed this way in Kiev, Russia. There were also plenty of local variations depending on the local units carrying out the killings. One soldier described a mass killing in Bialystok, another Russian city in July 1941 in which 700 Jews were herded into their local synagogue, which was then set on fire while the battalion surrounded the building to shoot anyone who managed to escape out of the windows. This ad hoc killing lasted until the first extermination camps were built in 1942, that is, extermination as opposed to concentration camps, which had existed since 1933.

This kind of "on the ground" killing was given up partly because it wasted too many bullets and partly because the strain on the executioners became too great, it was argued, having to kill people one by one. But before more efficient methods developed, virtually all of the Russian Jews died this way, as well as a good proportion of Polish Jews. By the end of 1941, the death toll estimates are at about 2 million or 40 percent of the Jews had been killed before the first death camp had been built. I think that first phase reminds us and demonstrates, as with the later killings in Rwanda and Bosnia, that bureaucratic efficiency and organization are not essential to mass murder. To put it another way, genocide does not require a totalitarian state. To replace this killing method, the Nazis opened the first permanent death camp in December 1941 in Chelmno, Poland, and in the next few months five more were built; the last one was opened in June 1942 at Auschwitz. The death camps signal a new phase, not only in the method of killing but also in its organization, what one historian called the "bureaucratization of mass murder." I think it is at this point, in this phase, where we really get the harnessing of the tools of mass society to the genocidal process. Instead of commando units moving through and killing Jews as they went, now, Jews are shipped from all over Europe to central locations. At a conference held in January 1942 called the Wannsee Conference, Nazi officials made a list of 11 million Jews from more than 20 European countries that were slated for eventual relocation and evacuation to these camps. Once the camps were built, the technology of mass murder still had to be perfected; that was not automatic either. They tried various methods of mass asphyxiation, from plugging in truck exhaust fumes to using prussic acid, but eventually they perfected a technique of efficiently gassing people with a product called *Zyklon B*, which was contained in small canisters that could fit into one hand and kill a large room full of people in about 15 minutes.

Once this technique of killing was perfected, rates of killing quickly surpassed what had been achieved through the commando units and mass graves. At Auschwitz alone, 1,765,000 men, women, and children were gassed between April 1942 and April 1944. By October 1943, 5 million Jews were murdered by the summer of 1944—another million—most of them Hungarian and Romanian Jews who had been partially protected by collaborationist regimes. The final results, most of you probably know, out of 8.8 million Jews in all of Europe, 67 percent of them were murdered. In some countries like Poland, the Baltic countries, and Germany, their communities were virtually wiped out—up to 90 percent.

Furthermore, they perished in a system of mass murder that required between 100,000 to 500,000 direct participants and many more who passively acquiesced. One of the most debated questions has been why so many people collaborated and what their motives were.

At first, Germany tried to isolate the Holocaust as something perpetrated by a handful of fanatical Nazis, and that most Germans were either ignorant of the camps or terrorized into silence. This fits nicely with the intentionalist's totalitarian model in which it is really just Hitler and a few of his fanatical cronies who were responsible for the Holocaust.

Most historians now reject this attempt to marginalize the Holocaust and instead pose the serious question of why millions of Germans collaborated or accepted, to some degree or another, this process. There have been different answers put forth to this question. On the one hand, there is an argument that focuses on the bureaucratization of mass murder as the answer. For them, the key to the Holocaust was the impersonal bureaucratic organization of mass murder in which each person did their little job, but most of them did not have to pull a trigger any more. The example often given in this model was a train switchman who every day had to pull a lever, allowing cattle cars full of Jews to pass through his station on their way to extermination camps. One historian interviewed such a man, a train switchman, who simply said that he sort of knew but did not want to face the truth, and that because he was not faced with having to actually pull the trigger, so to speak, that he did not have to face the reality. There must have been thousands of others whose small jobs contributed in some bureaucratic way to the effort needed to relocate hundreds of thousands and millions of Jews, who could pretend not to know the full implications. How much responsibility we, in turn, place on them depends on how we evaluate their level of fear, denial, and so on.

What about those who actually did pull the trigger, who pushed those Jews into the synagogue and watched them burn alive; how do we understand them? One potential answer is fear and intimidation; the totalitarian state had really taken away their individual will and made them terrified—the power of the Nazi state to coerce. Another potential answer is that they were convinced that the Jews were, in fact, subhuman so that they could kill without remorse or guilt. In this position, one of the debates is whether this hatred of the Jews existed before 1933, or if it was created afterwards. There have been some powerful studies done of so-called ordinary Germans, that is, not Nazi fanatics who killed Jews—Germans who had been police officers before the war, or reserve army personnel. There was a controversial book published by Daniel Goldhagen called *Hitler's Willing Executioners*, which focuses on an organization called the "Order Police," comprised of between 100,000 to 300,000 men—policemen, Nazi Party members, people who had joined the army even before 1933. What he demonstrates convincingly in this book is that these men had the choice not to kill Jews; that is, before they went out on operations their officer would say if anyone does not want to go with us, you can say no. Virtually none of them took the option not to kill. Goldhagen also demonstrates that they often went beyond the orders to kill the Jews and subjected them to torture, often expressing enjoyment with their tasks. One of the men watching the Jewish synagogue burning exclaimed: "Let it burn; it is such a nice little fire. It is great fun." What explains this behavior, Goldhagen argues, is a pervasive—and here is his word—"eliminationist" anti-Semitism, which was endemic among Germans whether they were Nazis or not. Goldhagen has been in a lively debate, and here is the controversial part of his book, he has been in a lively debate with another historian, Christopher Browning, who studied the exact same battalion as Goldhagen did and came to different conclusions. What Browning argues is that instead of the single motive of blinding anti-Semitism, that there were a range of seemingly benign motives like peer pressure, the fear of being thought a coward by one's colleagues, simple conformity, and the ambition to want to get ahead in the military—all of which, he argues, played a part, especially when placed in the brutalized context of the war on the Eastern front.

In other words, in a sense, Browning's conclusions point to the horrific deeds that any human being might commit if placed in the proper context. Browning makes explicit links with some of the psychological studies that were done after the war, in the United States. Some of you may be familiar with the Stanley Milgram experiment at Yale in 1960-1961, in which he found that subjects were willing to administer what they thought were painful electric shocks to victims if they were told by the authority figures that it was okay to do that. So, there's this idea that people can be brutalized into committing acts of violence against other human beings. It is difficult to know whether a benign motive like accepting authority or whether what Goldhagen calls "eliminationist anti-Semitism," it is hard to know which is the more chilling explanation.

The active or passive collaboration of millions of Germans goes beyond individual motives, to demonstrate the devastating success of the "racial revolution" implanted by the Nazi state. In and of itself, the genocide of the Jews does not necessarily tell us how far the racial revolution penetrated into German society. If you blame the Holocaust simply on a few fanatical Nazis, it does not really say anything about the rest of German society. But if we accept that hundreds of thousands and millions at least passively acquiesced, then this demonstrates the full impact of the Nazi racial revolution. By systematically breaking down the human bond between Germans and Jews over the course of a decade, when Jews were finally carted off, it was really something happening to "other" people.

Beyond the facts of German collaboration, why did no one else try to stop the mass murder? The Allied governments had information about the camps by at least June of 1942, so why did none of the other governments step in? Really, with the exception of a few Jewish organizations, no official government organization outside Germany did much to stop the Holocaust. In particular, the remaining Western democracies—the United States and Britain—

both passively stood by even when there was significant information about what was going on. Thus, it was not until December 1942, when most of the Polish Jews were already dead, that Allied governments finally issued a statement condemning extermination of the Jews—five months after they had received their first notice of it. Even after this acknowledgment, little action was taken to rescue the Jews, such as bombing the rail lines, for example, or even bombing the gas chambers.

The British Foreign Office responded to such requests by Jewish political leaders with a polite refusal based on what they called "technical difficulties," and in the United States, Roosevelt refused to order it. The official answer from both the United States and Britain was that all resources were being put into defeating the Germans militarily. Whether this was a militarily sound response or not, it is devastatingly true that no other country focused the kind of energy on saving the Jews that the Germans focused on exterminating them.

Furthermore, few countries were willing to take Jewish immigrants even if they could be rescued. The United States was very reluctant, and Britain refused to let Jews into Palestine, where Zionists wanted to set up a new Jewish homeland. This broader failure to prevent the systematic, bureaucratized murder of 6 million people represented, I think—and I think many Europeans felt it at the time, afterwards—something more than the evil of Hitler and his Nazis. Instead it becomes the ultimate symbol of the crisis of European civilization: that all its laws, its religious institutions, great scientific knowledge, and political freedoms were either helpless or complicit and could do nothing to stop the open murder of millions of people. Anti-fascist Europe does eventually win the war, but the machine gun and the gas chamber had made it impossible to go back to the status quo ante.

A liberal democratic Europe that had failed to prevent such horror would need to undergo a complete moral as well as physical and political reconstruction, and even then, it would never recover the naïve optimism in unending progress that had characterized Europe in 1914.

However, at the same time, it was precisely the challenge and the horror of fascism that helped Western civilization regain its sense of good and evil, that sense of good and evil that had been lost in the First World War. So, the Europe that emerges out of the Second World War is full of paradoxes. On the one hand, the victory of the Allies signals the death of fascism and the rebirth of liberal democracy; thus, it was precisely during the war that liberal democracy regains its momentum, its faith, and its confidence. It is no longer the anachronistic past; it is now the future once again. Ironically, it was the very challenge posed by the fascist regime that in the end forced the democratic West to recover the strength and sense of moral purpose it had lost.

So, the challenges that had seemed to threaten the existence of liberal democracy in the 1920s and 1930s actually proved to be the spark that revitalized it.

In the postwar period, the combination of shame and a renewed moral purpose provoked a somber but ultimately creative effort to rebuild the Enlightenment project, but with important modifications so they could win the loyalty of the kinds of people who had earlier turned to fascism and communism as alternatives. Out of this creative process, came the postwar consensus and a new era in Western democracy.

Lecture Twenty-Six
Existentialism in Post-War Europe

Scope:

Although the war marked the final defeat of the fascist challenge in Europe, it was also the final nail in the coffin of a world order based on European supremacy. For many Europeans, Auschwitz came to symbolize the end of this era, a devastating mark of failure that was now a part of European history. One of the best expressions of this pessimistic postwar mood was the popularity of the existentialist movement in the late 1940s and early 1950s, which offered a bleak but dignified way for individuals to survive in a post-Auschwitz world. We will discuss existentialist ideals, as articulated by Jean-Paul Sartre, and their expression in Samuel Beckett's *Waiting for Godot*. By the late 1950s, economic and political recovery and the fading of war memories ended this period of intense self-reflection, but Europe never returned to its world power status.

Outline

I. Although Europe would rebuild itself along new lines, the "30 years war" had destroyed the 19th-century European world order for good.

    A. Why didn't final victory over fascism bring a return to the old optimism?

    B. Partly, it was the impact of two devastating European civil wars.

    C. Partly, it was the special horror of the Holocaust and the Nazi system that produced it, both of them now a shameful addition to European history.

    D. More broadly, Auschwitz was both a symptom and a culmination of the larger process of European decline.

    E. The tide had begun to shift from Europe to other regions after World War I, but an apparent return to economic normalcy had hidden this reality.

    F. But in 1945, the empire was in a shambles, Europe was a wasteland, and the United States had emerged as the new leader of what will become known as the *free world*.

II. The postwar mood in Europe was nicely expressed in the popularity of existentialism in the late 1940s and early 1950s, while significantly, this movement never took root in a supremely optimistic America.

   A. Existentialism had long intellectual roots but became the dominant intellectual stance in the first postwar decade.

      1. Like some of the post-World War I movements, existentialism was an attempt to come to terms with an absurd world. Or, situated in the new context, how do we go on after Hiroshima and Auschwitz?

      2. Existentialism crystallized as a movement in the 1920s, but it was the war that popularized it.

      3. Its most famous proponent was Jean Paul Sartre, along with his companion, Simone de Beauvoir, and his friend Albert Camus.

   B. How do we define existentialism?

      1. It is not a set of doctrines but more an attitude toward coping with an uncertain world.

      2. Life, in simple terms, has no preexisting meaning or essence. Instead, the task for individuals is to create meaning for their own lives through their choices: Existence precedes essence, in shorthand.

      3. The notion of "no preexisting meaning" should sound familiar, from Nietzsche and the dadaists, who all rejected the idea of some objective "meaning" out there.

      4. Given the reality of disorder, the existentialists argued that man had to stop yearning for objective signposts: "nothing beyond…no need for more."

      5. If there is no meaning "out there," then the individual has no special role to play either. We were not placed on this earth for a purpose, as Christians would claim. Instead, we are another of the random accidents of the universe.

      6. How, then, do we find meaning in a universe indifferent to our existence?

      7. If we imagine each person as a blank canvas, then the person is not only the canvas but the painter. As Sartre said, "man exists, and only afterwards defines himself."

      8. Each individual is faced with the awesome responsibility of defining himself or herself through the accumulation of choices made. If this is true, the least we should expect of ourselves is to be fully aware and take those choices seriously.

9. If this is our life's work, then it is something we must pursue alone, because no one else can provide meaning for us.

C. Although the image of solitary beings in a meaningless universe may sound bleak, the idea was to provide dignity in a post-Auschwitz world without falling into either despair or the nihilism of the dadaists.

1. Instead of either extreme, humans could live serious lives in an absurd world.

2. It was also a way to rescue the individual from the dangers of 20th-century life—the threat of totalitarianism or the homogenizing effects of mass society—by placing the highest value on individual choice.

3. Thus, you are a product of all the choices you have made up to this moment, nothing more, nothing less. Instead of passively allowing unconscious choices to shape our lives, we should take an active role in shaping our destinies.

4. The focus here is on choice itself, not on content: Existentialism does not clarify what is right and what is wrong, except for a general rule that each person should consider what would happen if everyone acted the same way.

D. One of the offshoots of existentialist thought was an artistic movement called the *theater of the absurd*, whose most eminent practitioner was Samuel Beckett.

E. To express the absurdity of the world in theater, the playwright put characters in implausible settings, wrote illogical plots, and left the audience with unresolved tensions.

F. Samuel Beckett lived the exemplary existentialist life.

1. Like many existentialists, he worked for the Resistance during the war.

2. He had an ambivalent attitude toward life but never gave in to despair; as one of his characters put it: "you must go on, I can't go on, I'll go on."

G. The most famous play in the theater of the absurd genre is *Waiting for Godot*, written in the late 1940s.

1. It is a play about two tramps waiting for a character named Godot, who never arrives.
2. They (and we, the readers) don't know why they're waiting for him, but they have a vague sense that they will know what to do when he arrives.
3. As they wait, the characters' waiting turns into simply living, the petty existence of too small boots, carrots or turnips, and so on; all these are the stuff of life.
4. Instead of waiting to be enlightened by some nonexistent savior, Beckett seems to be saying, we should focus on the daily struggle that is the essence of who we are.

H. Thus, in a European civilization that had reached rock bottom, existentialism offered a path for individuals to survive with dignity. Its popularity began to wane in the late 1950s as Europe recovered and the memory of war and Holocaust faded, but the movement serves as an elegiac swan song for a European civilization that would never again claim to lead the world.

Essential Reading:

Jean-Paul Sartre, "Existentialism," in Stephen Priest, ed., *Jean-Paul Sartre: Basic Writings*, pp. 20–57.

Samuel Beckett, *Waiting for Godot*.

Supplementary Reading:

Anthony Cronin, *Samuel Beckett: The Last Modernist*.

H. Stuart Hughes, *The Obstructed Path*.

Questions to Consider:

1. One of the criticisms against existentialism was that its focus on "choice" made no value judgements about the content of those choices, that is, about what is "right" and "wrong." Would you agree with this criticism?
2. The only signpost the existentialists offered was the obligation to consider the consequences of your actions if everyone felt free to make the same choices. Do you think this a workable criterion for existence?

Lecture Twenty-Six—Transcript
Existentialism in Post-War Europe

In the last lecture, we talked about the paradoxical impact of the Second World War on Europe, in which the war acted as both a destructive and also a restorative force. While Europe would rebuild itself after the war, it will not be the same Europe as existed in 1914. That Western Europe that stood at the top of an imperial world order, with a confidence in itself at the peak of civilization, had been destroyed for good.

What we will talk about in this lecture is the intellectual response to this new reality in Europe in the form of existentialism. So why didn't victory bring a return of the optimism and confidence of the 19th century? Partly, it was the accumulation of crises: first, the First World War; then, the Depression; then, the Second World War. Each crisis eroded another corner of that old optimism and self-confidence. But partly, also, it was the special horror of this Second World War. Despite the defeat of fascism, Europe was left with the memory of the Holocaust, that Holocaust that it had done nothing to stop and the totalitarian system that had produced it.

Rather than resolving the crisis of meaning, the Second World War and the Holocaust in some way enhanced this crisis in Europe. As the playwright, Bertolt Brecht, put it: "After Auschwitz and Hiroshima, there could be no poetry." In fact, of course, Auschwitz was both a symptom and a culmination of the larger process of European decline. What the war had finally revealed was that European world domination was over, that Europe as a region was declining in power. The tide had begun to shift from Europe to other regions after the First World War, but an apparent "return to normalcy" had hidden this reality after the First World War. But now, in 1945, Europe was a shell of its former self, and the war had finally exposed this fact for everyone to see. On a material level, Europe was faced with a physical devastation that went well beyond that of the First World War. Cities had been destroyed. Economies had been bled dry through occupation policies, and people were homeless and hungry.

Furthermore, in the far reaches of the world, the colonial empires were in full revolt, forcing European imperial powers to either fight to regain their colonies, or to stage a humiliating retreat. Finally, for the second time in 30 years, a new Western power had come in to rescue the Europeans from yet another civil war. While that Western power had only reluctantly entered the war, in fact, it had only reluctantly entered each war. By 1945, it was clear that it could not go back to its previous isolation. That power was the United States, which will displace (in the postwar period) Europe as the leader of what will soon become known as the *free world*. For Europe, then, there was no going back to that 19th century of optimism and world power.

Perhaps the best expression of the postwar mood in Europe was the popularity of an intellectual movement known as existentialism. The philosophy had long intellectual roots, but only in the 1940s and 1950s does it become the dominate intellectual stance in Europe. The fact that it never really took off during this period in the United States is a perfect demonstration of the growing split between American and European culture in this period. As America takes on the new role of world power, it also takes up the standard of liberal democracy with as much enthusiasm and optimism as Europe once had.

Europe becomes the twisted cynic questioning the old values and looking down on the Americans as naïve and gullible. Existentialism was a movement that fit this mood perfectly. Like the intellectual movements that came out of the First World War, existentialism was one more attempt to come to terms with what was perceived to be an absurd world. Only now the question was slightly rephrased to paraphrase Brecht, how do we go on in a world after Hiroshima and Auschwitz? Existentialist ideas can be traced back to the 19th-century philosophers, philosophers as different as Kierkegaard and Nietzsche. But it crystallized as a movement in the 1920s and early 1930s, and still not again until after the Second World War does it really become a widespread popular movement.

Once again, the war made these ideas resonate for many people, and it was no accident that the most famous proponent of existentialism was Jean Paul Sartre and his lifelong partner, Simone de Beauvoir, as well as his friend, Albert Camus, and that all of them lived in Nazi-occupied France during the war. It was the wartime experience that really crystallized these ideas. All three of them had a tremendous impact on this postwar generation, partly because they captured the tone of the time, but also because all three wrote, in addition to abstract and obscure tones about existentialism, they also wrote popular plays, novels, poems, and so on that helped make existentialism accessible to a broader audience.

How, then, do we define existentialism? It is a little bit difficult to define because it is not a doctrine or set of beliefs; you cannot lift a set of things that existentialism believes in. What it is more is an attitude towards the world, a method for living in a world where man has little certainty to hold onto. Existentialists started from the assumption that the universe was devoid of any inherent meaning or truth. As a result, our lives as individuals had no inherent meaning. So, the task, then, for each individual was to create meaning for his own life through the choices he made. In shorthand, the existentialist model was: Existence precedes essence. The initial assumption of a world without objective meaning should sound familiar because this goes back to the same assumption of both Nietzsche and the dadaists and surrealists that we talked about in the post-World War One period; that is, the existentialist rejected the idea that there is some sort of master plan out there in the universe that provides a stable anchor for us to hold onto, that Christian cosmos in which not a sparrow falls from his nest without God noticing it, that kind of master plan.

Instead of this, the universe is made up of random and disorderly phenomenon; the best evidence that they could put forth for this idea, of course, was the Holocaust. How could a master plan make sense of the Holocaust? Given the reality of disorder, the existentialist argued that man had to stop yearning for some sort of objective signposts to guide us. They were not "out there." Instead, their slogan was: "nothing beyond...no need for more." As Sartre said, "there is nothing in heaven, man will be what he will have planned to be." In other words, there is nothing beyond our immediate existence and no need to yearn for it.

It is important to make the distinction with the dadaists and the surrealists of the early generation in that existentialists were not happy about this; there was no joy in flinging oneself into the void as the dadaists and surrealists talked about. But, it was simply a reality that people had to face. So, for the existentialist, it was a joyous but sober reality. As a result of this reality, individual life had no inherent meaning, so if the world "out there" is absurd and meaningless, the corollary for us as individuals is that we have no assigned role in that universe, which makes sense. We are not placed on this earth for a purpose. Instead, we are another of the random accidents of the universe, so man has no nature to fulfill, no purpose to carry out. Given that lack of individual purpose within the universe, then, what is left for human beings? How do we find meaning in a world that is indifferent to our existence? That is, of course, the essential question, and that brings us to the center of the definition.

The task then for each individual was to create meaning for his or her own life; that was essentially one's life work. The need to create meaning implied that it is not something we discover; it is something that we make, that we manufacture. As Sartre wrote, "man exists, and only afterwards defines himself." To use a metaphor, imagine that each person at birth is a blank canvas, but that person is also the painter as well as the canvas. The task of each person's life is to paint one's own canvas, in a sense, to define who they are, what Sartre called the thrust towards existence, that existence is an active; it is the result of action, not just something that you are.

This process is what existentialism sought to help people do. If we are faced with a meaningless, absurd world, then how do we go about doing that? How do we create meaning for ourselves? How do we create our identity?

In simple terms, each individual is faced with the awesome responsibility of defining himself or herself through the choices we make. The individual is constantly faced with choices, the existentialist would say. Our life, in fact, is consumed by choices, whether we are aware of them or not, and that is a key point: the choice from what you should wear when you get up in the morning, what you should have for breakfast, to larger decisions about whether you should leave your job or move to another city. Some of these choices seem petty, but if you add them all up, they are what define us.

In a sense, you can see existentialism as an extreme response to totalitarianism, an intense focus on life as choice to take back the autonomy of the individual from the dangers of totalitarianism. Thus, you are a product of all the choices you have made up to this moment, nothing more and nothing less. People can deny that they have choices, but the existentialist will say you have them whether they are denied or not; you are making choices whether you know it or not.

The problem is that most people deny that they have choices, or they are not conscious of them, or they don't take them seriously. They float through life doing what is expected of them: what their boss says, what their parents say, what their church says, what the experts say. They listen to what everyone says, and so instead of taking the responsibility of their choices seriously, they rely on the advice of others. For the existentialist, the bravest thing that we can do is to realize the complete responsibility that we have for our lives. Again, in Sartre's words, "man is condemned to be free; once thrown into the world, he is responsible for every thing he does." More than brave, accepting this idea of choice allows us to lead the most authentic life we can, a life made by ourselves, made by our own choices, and not by some automaton following orders or what they think they should do. Instead, then, of passively allowing unconscious choices to shape our lives, we need to take an active role in shaping our destiny. Notice here that the focus is on choice, that is, it is on the need to take action; it is not focused on the content of that choice. So, existentialists don't really talk about what is true or false in terms of the choices you make, but simply on the act of choice itself. The only larger context of judging right and wrong within existentialism is the basic principle that you must consider what would happen in the world, as a whole, if you make this choice; that is what gives you the broader context.

Although we do make these decisions in a broader context, if self-definition is one's life work, then it is something we must pursue alone. It is something that no one else can do for us: not parents, friends, or partners. No one else can provide meaning for us. No one can save us from the lack of meaning "out there." What that means within the existentialist world is we are all solitary beings, essentially, shaping our individual destinies in a meaningless universe. In this universe, love and friendship can offer some solace, the comfort that we are all facing the same task together. But when it comes down to it, we each face our own destiny alone. This condition is expressed nicely in the poignant relationship between Estragon and Vladimir who are the two tramps in Samuel Beckett's great existentialist play *Waiting for Godot*. At one point, Estragon has a nightmare that he wants to tell Vladimir about, but the latter refuses to listen. Estragon replies, "It is not nice of you, Didi, who am I to tell my private nightmares, if I can't tell them to you?" to which Vladimir replies, "Let them remain private. You know I can't bear that." Despite the fact that they are friends, they cannot share the private nightmares that belong to them alone. They are drawn together in their loneliness and their despair, but deep down, their friendship cannot really transcend that loneliness and despair.

While this image of solitary beings in the meaningless universe may sound bleak to us, the idea was to provide a sense of dignity in a post-Auschwitz world without falling into either complete despair or nihilism. In other words, either committing suicide because the world was bleak, or simply throwing one's hands up and saying nothing matters, are the two extremes that the existentialists were trying to avoid. They offered a different route; they argued that people can still live serious, meaningful lives even if we accept the irrationality of the world. We must go on with our lives the best we can and not get bogged down in the bleakness around us. Samuel Beckett poignantly expressed this in the last line of another work, a novel called *The Unnamable*. He says: "you must go on, I can't go on, I'll go on." So, existentialism was a way to go on in a world that appeared to be hurdling itself towards a self-induced apocalypse. It was a way to create meaning and dignity within this world. It was also a way, as I implied before, to rescue the individual from the dangers of 20th-century life and the threat of totalitarianism, and also the homogenizing effects of mass society. I think it is significant that postwar existentialists have come of age during the era of fascism and Stalinism, and that they fought in the Resistance. This was the reality of the world that they grew up in. In the increasingly homogenous world of mass society, where everyone consumed the same mass culture, existentialism cried out for individuals to break away from the mass and reassert their own identity. In a world in which the state's power to control individual lives had been on the rise, existentialists placed the highest possible value on individual choice.

For existentialists, then, totalitarianism was the ultimate evil, the ultimate nightmare. Not only did it destroy our freedom, it destroyed our identity by controlling our choices. If we define our identity through our choices, and if totalitarianism takes away those choices, then it literally takes away our existence.

Furthermore, totalitarianism produced the kind of conformism that allowed the Nazis to murder 6 million Jews, with almost no opposition. So, if people really wrested their individual lives back from the mass, it was possible to prevent a future Holocaust in their minds. Existentialism was also a weapon against totalitarianism.

One of the offshoots of existentialist thought was an artistic movement defined at the time as the *theatre of the absurd*, of which Samuel Beckett was clearly the most eminent practitioner. Beckett, himself, lived the exemplary existentialist life. He was born in Dublin in 1906, but he spent most of his adult life in Paris. He published his first poem, called "Whoroscope," in 1930 and continued to write poetry, short stories, and novels even during the war, when he was actively involved in the Resistance like Sartre and Camus. He worked undercover during the war as a farm laborer, with his female companion delivering messages for the Resistance. As with many other existentialists, he saw joining the Resistance as an important individual moral act, the individual choosing to stand up for what he believed. So, the war, once again, was a perfect environment for breeding the existentialist mentality of the importance of choice as an effective weapon against totalitarianism.

Aside from the war, one of the crucial turning points in Beckett's life was when one day he was walking down the streets of Paris and was stabbed by an assailant; this happened in 1938. When he later went to visit his assailant in jail to ask him why he had done that, the man simply shrugged his shoulders and said, "I don't know." That, for Beckett, summed up the randomness of life in which you could really count on nothing. You could be walking down the street one day, and someone could stab you for no reason at all.

As an individual, Beckett developed an ambivalent attitude toward life, which had to be endured but could never be truly joyful. His general mood was expressed well by one anecdote in which he was walking through the park on a beautiful spring day with a friend who remarked that this was the kind of day that made one glad to be alive. Beckett responded, "I would not go that far." Although he was ambivalent about life, he never gave in to complete despair, and that was what existentialism was trying to achieve. One of the best expressions of this commitment to life in the face of ambivalence is this poignant statement of his: "There is nothing to express, nothing from which to express, no power to express, no desire to express, together with the obligation to express."

In the theatre of the absurd, the playwright sought to express the absurdity of the world by putting the characters in implausible settings, writing plots that defied logical analysis, and leaving the audience itself with unresolved tensions. The most famous play in this genre was Beckett's *Waiting for Godot*, which I mentioned earlier, which was written in the late 1940s. It was his second play, and it was first performed in Paris in 1953, just towards the end of this postwar decade of mourning and soul-searching. The play got mixed reviews, with some critics raving and others dismissing it without comprehension (particularly in the United States where it did not go over well; it did not do well in its first opening act at the Coconut Grove Play House, where it was billed as a comedy starring Bert Lahr, of cowardly lion fame, playing Vladimir. The play is about two tramps, Vladimir and Estragon, who spend the entire play waiting for a character named Godot, who never arrives. The tramps aren't sure why they are waiting for him, but they have a vague sense that they will know what to do when he arrives. They see him as some sort of savior that is going to tell them what to do; he is going to give them a sense of where they should go. Naturally, at the end of the play, the audience is also left with this unresolved tension since Godot never shows up; so, the audience is left wondering who he is and why he has not come, and the audience leaves the theater with that tension of not knowing what they were waiting for. They know that they were waiting for Godot. They thought that the play was going to be about when he arrived, and the play actually ends up being about something else. In the process of watching the play, the audience experiences the same things that the characters do, waiting for something unknown and the tension that produces.

As the characters wait, their waiting turns into simply living, which I think is the message, the petty, struggling existence of these two tramps and its focus on things such as boots that are too small, whether we should eat carrots or turnips, the diversions of other passing figures who go through the story. All of these petty events, Beckett seems to be saying, are the stuff of life; these are the actions and choices that make us what we are. Instead of waiting for Godot, who seems to symbolize an outside source of meaning in their lives, of waiting for him to come and tell them what to do, we need to realize, as the tramps never do, that there is nothing else out there, nothing that is going to rescue us from our existence, no grand plan that will make our lives seem somehow grander and more worthwhile. I think it is significant that Beckett chose two very common ordinary tramps to make this message; it only emphasizes the lack of transcendence that any of our lives has.

So, what is it, then, that makes our lives worthwhile? Is there something to live for even if Godot does not show up? The tramps talk about hanging themselves, but they don't. So, what you have is the perfect existentialist dilemma: You must fight. You must go on. You cannot give up on life, and yet, life is a constant struggle. Again, to go back to Beckett's line: "you must go on, I can't go on, I'll go on." So, the tramps do go on with both humor and pathos, embracing each other and pushing each other away, never satisfied and yet always going on. Their friendship provides them with solace, but of course, it cannot do anything more than that if you go back to the story of the private nightmare; you cannot really go into the personal solitude of each individual. This, Beckett is saying, is the human condition: "nothing beyond…no need for more."

There is a funny story in which a reporter once asked Beckett who Godot was, and Beckett responded, "If I knew, I would have said so in the play." In other words, what he was saying with that line is that the playwright himself cannot transcend that human existence either. The playwright is not there in some sort of all knowing outside force, who really secretly knew who Godot is. He is not there to lead the way to some transcendent paradise; he simply is working out his own destiny, as we all must work out our own. Beckett refuses to let us see him as a savior; he is not going to tell us the secret of the universe because there is no secret, and we are all on our own. This was the message of *Waiting for Godot* and of the existentialist movement that thrived in the decade after World War Two in a devastated Europe, a Europe in which its sense of itself, its sense of self-confidence, its sense of being at the pinnacle of civilization had been destroyed by a series of powerful events in the early 20th century. In a European civilization that had reached rock bottom, existentialism provided a path for individuals to survive with dignity. If the big picture was collapsing around them, the individual could still make a meaningful, serious life for himself or herself.

The popularity of existentialism waned in the late 1950s as Europe recovers and as a new generation of material prosperity makes the memories of the war fade, but the movement serves as a kind of elegiac swan song for a European civilization that would never again claim to lead the world, and would instead focus on taking responsibility for its own individual existence.

Lecture Twenty-Seven
Origins of the Cold War

Scope:

With the end of the Second World War, a new world order took shape. Instead of a world united under European rule, it was a world separated into liberal democratic and communist spheres, each led by a new global power, the United States and the USSR. This lecture discusses how this new Cold War order emerged out of the rubble of World War II and what the conditions were that maintained it. It analyzes American and Soviet visions of their own national missions and of the nature of the enemy. Finally, we consider the contested question of responsibility, which continues to divide scholarly and popular opinion.

Outline

I. One of the consequences of the new, divided world order was an endemic conflict between the two spheres over which side would dominate world politics and the economy. This conflict came to be called the *Cold War.*

   A. With this new world order, the struggles over democracy are put into a different context.

      1. Most obviously, the existence of a non-democratic superpower posed a constant military and ideological threat to the democratic world.

      2. The competition between superpowers also injected an added element of confusion in newly decolonized nations' attempts to define their independence.

      3. But more subtly, the Cold War created a new struggle for democracy inside the heart of the democratic world.

      4. Critics of U.S. policy argued that, in the course of fighting the Cold War, America was sacrificing its own democratic ideals, while defenders argued that defeating the USSR was the most important democratic goal.

   B. What were the origins of this dramatic transformation in world politics?

      1. In broad terms, the Cold War depended on three elements.

2. First was the existence of two superpowers.
3. Second was the reality of nuclear weapons on both sides after 1949, which made direct "hot" war between superpowers unthinkable.
4. Third was each side's claim to world domination, not in the older sense of empire, but in the sense of a mission to lead the world. Further, each side had to believe that its opponent had a mission to lead the world.
5. Thus, nuclear weapons made real war unthinkable, but competing world missions made real peace impossible.
6. It's important to note that there were plenty of "hot" wars fomented by the Cold War standoff but not directly between the two superpowers.

C. How did the United States come to feel that it had a world mission?
1. The mere existence of a "world mission" was a new development for a traditionally isolationist nation.
2. U.S. intervention in both world wars was reluctant and occurred only after direct attacks on American interests.
3. But by the Second World War, U.S. participation had begun to shift attitudes among the population and the political elites.
4. As Europe fell into a postwar depression, the United States was flush with the victory of having saved the world from fascism, and many began to argue that America needed to take on a new world role befitting this status.

II. With this impetus, postwar leaders formulated a new vision of American leadership.

A. Henry Luce, in his 1941 book *The American Century*, made one of the earliest and strongest appeals for a move from isolationism to *internationalism*.

B. In his argument, America had four valuable things to bring to the world: free enterprise, technological expertise, good Samaritanism, and her devotion to the great principles of Western civilization.

C. What's important to note is the sense of universalism about the American way of life.

D. In this sense (but not others, of course), American universalism was another version of the European "civilizing mission," that is, the desire and confidence to transform the world in its own Western image.

III. This vision of American ideals and prosperity brought to the four corners of the earth was powerful enough, but what made it seem urgent was the existence of an enemy whose sole goal was to destroy this way of life.

    A. The result was a powerful mix of idealism and fear, which was enough to mobilize a previously isolationist American public.

    B. *What to Do When the Russians Come*, published as late as 1984, articulated the fearful consequences of what life under Soviet occupation would be like.

IV. How was the Soviet enemy defined?

    A. During the first few years after the war, American policy makers shifted from defining the USSR as an enemy to being the major threat to what became known as the free world.

        1. In 1946, Soviet expert George Kennan wrote an influential report that called the USSR an irrational, sociopathic power.

        2. The most important document, however, was NSC-68, a National Security Council report written in 1950 by Paul Nitze, National Security Adviser for the Truman Administration.

        3. In the memo, Nitze warned that this was a battle for the future of civilization.

        4. The adversary was a ruthless enemy pursuing worldwide totalitarian domination.

    B. Was this a fair evaluation of the Soviet threat?

        1. Few questions have been more debated by historians than the origins of the Cold War and who was to blame. Even with the opening of Soviet archives, opposing opinions remain.

        2. However, the "revisionist" position that accused the United States of fabricating the threat seems untenable in the face of new archival sources.

3. The most balanced position on Soviet motives in 1945 would be to see them as multifaceted.

4. On the one hand, there is no doubt that the USSR supported and promoted worldwide communist revolution.

5. On the other hand, it appeared to have had no master world revolutionary plan for invading either Western Europe or the United States.

6. American policy makers assumed the existence of such a plan and, moreover, interpreted all Soviet actions through its lens.

7. Instead, Soviet policy reflected a mixture of interests, including fears about the security of its own borders after the devastating impact of German invasion.

8. Whatever the balance, it is clear that U.S. policymakers did not recognize the existence of multiple concerns.

V. At the same time, the USSR interpreted all American behavior through a single lens.

A. Thus, Stalin viewed all foreign economic aid as an attempt to spread the capitalist system and strangle the Soviet economy.

B. In Marxist ideology, it was capitalism that was inevitably warlike and destructive and controlled political decisions in supposedly democratic societies.

C. Soviet interpretation of the Marshall Plan provides a good example of these ideological blinders.

D. Was the Soviet view of the Marshall Plan total paranoia?

E. Partly, but not entirely. It did pursue a global free-market economy dominated by the dollar and anchored by the U.S. economy, and it was not unreasonable to see this as a threat to the closed spheres of a socialist economy.

VI. Why did both sides simplify the motives of the other side?

A. Partly, the answer is ideological blinders, simplistic notions about the inevitable course of warlike capitalism or world communism.

B. But partly, it suited each superpower to have a super-enemy to get their people behind the idea of a world mission.

C. Because scholars argue about origins, they also argue about what constituted the opening act of the Cold War and who was responsible.

   1. From the American point of view, it was the Soviet occupation of Eastern Europe in 1945–1946.

   2. From the Soviet point of view, it was the Marshall Plan of 1947.

   3. What can we conclude about responsibility for starting the Cold War?

   4. While the opening acts are ambiguous, most historians today would place greater blame on the Soviets.

   5. By 1950, however, both sides are equally invested in maintaining the Cold War, and it becomes the central political reality of the new world order.

Essential Reading:

Robert McMahon and Thomas G. Paterson, eds., *The Origins of the Cold War: Problems in American Civilization.*

Supplementary Reading:

John Lewis Gaddis, *We Now Know: Rethinking Cold War History.*

Melvin Leffler, *The Specter of Communism.*

Josef Stalin, "Economic Problems of Socialism in the USSR," in Bruce Franklin, ed., *The Essential Stalin*, pp. 467–473.

Paul Nitze, "NSC-68: United States Objectives and Programs for National Security," in Katherine A. S. Sibley, ed., *The Cold War.*

Questions to Consider:

1. While our perspective on the Cold War is usually a critical one, it's also important to understand why it "worked" on some level for such a long time, 43 years. What do you think explains such long-term popular support for maintaining the Cold War on both sides?

2. Do the continued debates over the Cold War's origins have any relevance today outside of academic circles?

Lecture Twenty-Seven—Transcript
Origins of the Cold War

We have been talking about the Second World War as another breaking point in the 20th century. What this means is that with the end of the Second World War, a new world order was taking shape. The essence of this new world is that it is divided into two separate spheres. In other words, instead of the 19th-century world united under European rule—united in a somewhat hierarchical single sphere with its liberal ideology and far-flung colonies—we have a world divided into liberal, democratic, and communist spheres. Each of these spheres is led by a superpower, a new global power, the United States and the USSR.

One of the consequences of this new divided world order was an endemic conflict between the two spheres over which side would dominate world politics and the economy. The name given to this permanent conflict is the *Cold War*. Thus, the Cold War becomes the essence of the new world order that emerges out of the devastation of the Second World War.

What I want to talk about in this lecture is how the Cold War evolved. The next time I want to focus on the consequences, particularly in American society. With this new world order of the Cold War, the struggles over democracy were put in a different context. Most obviously, the existence of a non-democratic superpower posed a constant military and ideological threat to the democratic world. While the fascist alternative had been defeated with the Second World War, the war strengthened, in some ways, the communist alternative and its sphere of influence. Moreover, the competition between communism and democracy and between the two superpowers injected an element of confusion into the process of decolonization that begins right after the war. As dozens of new countries attempt to define their post-colonial identities, the two superpowers offered conflicting models on the best political path to follow, the best political system that would lead them to prosperity.

Democracy now has to compete directly with communism for the hearts and minds of the Third World, the non-Western world. But more subtly than this global struggle between democracy and communism was that the Cold War opened up a new struggle over democracy within the heart of the democratic world, that is, inside the United States. On the one hand were those who identified with the voice of official American Cold War policy that argued that the struggle for democracy had now fundamentally become about defeating the Soviet Union. So, the struggle for democracy was the defeat of the Soviet Union and preventing it from spreading its anti-democratic ideals elsewhere, including in the United States.

On the other hand were the critics who argued that in the course of fighting communism, that the United States had lost sight of many of its own liberal democratic ideals that it sought to defend. In the words of one historian citric, "As the Cold War progressed, the enemies became more like each other; their hostility forced them into a collision course of convergence." From this perspective, the undemocratic means used to defeat the Soviet enemy made it difficult to argue that the United States was defending democracy.

At the heart of this debate was really the age-old philosophical debate over ends versus means. Both supporters and critics acknowledge the undemocratic means: from assassination, to covert wars, to suppression of civil rights. But supporters of these policies argued that these means were necessary to achieve the noble end of protecting democracy. In contrast, critics argued that the United States should be held to a different standard than the Soviet Union, and that it had to fully practice the democratic ideals it propounded. From one perspective, the alternative was being posed as America versus the Soviet Union, and in this paring of American versus the Soviet Union, America emerged the clear moral victor because compared to how the Soviet Union behaved, there was no comparison.

From the other critical perspective, the alternative was being posed as America versus model democracy. In this comparison, America fell short; America was not the moral victor. These are the two different perspectives that are being used to analyze the United States in the Cold War. These distinct poles of reference continue to define debates about the United States and the Cold War even among scholars and politicians today.

Where did the Cold War come from? What were the origins of this dramatic transformation in world politics? In very broad terms, the existence of the Cold War depended on three major elements. The first was the existence of two superpowers. The second was the reality of nuclear weapons; the USSR developed the atom bomb in 1949, so both superpowers had the capacity for nuclear explosions. What the existence of nuclear weapons meant was that any real war between the superpowers could end in the annihilation of both sides. Neither side wanted to risk fighting on the battlefield, neither wanted to risk a final confrontation or showdown on the battlefield. The result was the replacement of ordinary "hot" war with a new kind of Cold War, which meant that you could wage a war through indirect methods that did not involve direct confrontation of the superpowers. These methods could range from propaganda, to military support of third parties, to economic assistance, to the support of proxy wars, and so on.

It is important to note that this did not mean that there were no ordinary "hot" wars during this period. There were plenty of ordinary "hot" wars, but they were not fought between the two superpowers; they were fought between other peoples. So the Cold War defined this kind of relationship between the two major powers.

The third element that made the Cold War possible is the most important, and that was each side's claim to world domination. I don't mean world domination in the 19th-century sense of imperial domination, but in the new sense of each side having to have a mission to lead the world. It was this claim that provided the motive for fighting a Cold War with the opposing superpower. Not only did they have to believe that they had a mission to lead the world, but each side had to believe that the other side had a mission to lead the world. In other words, both sides had to be convinced that if they did not lead the world, the other superpower would. The result of all of these elements was that the Cold War nuclear capacity made real war unthinkable, but competing world missions made real peace impossible, thus, the Cold War.

How did the United States define its "world mission"? The mere existence of a world mission was a new thing for the United States. Remember, for the century before the Second World War, United States policy had been isolationist. It had been defined by securing her own borders through Western expansion, manifest destiny and maintaining independence on global issues. Even her intervention, as we mentioned before, in both World War I and World War II, was reluctant. It took the bombing of American territory at Pearl Harbor for the Americans to get involved in the Second World War, even in the face of the fascist threat in Europe.

After 1945, there is a real transformation in American attitudes. It began with the important role that the United States played in the war itself in the sense that the United States had almost single-handedly rescued Western civilization from the European civil war, and it had defeated fascism. Out of the flush of pride over this victory, many Americans began to argue that the United States needed to take on a new world role that was more befitting her status as Europe sunk into a postwar depression. With this impetus, postwar leaders began to formulate a new vision of American world leadership. The American publisher, Henry Luce, in his 1941 book *The American Century*, made one of the earliest and strongest appeals for a move from isolationism to what he called *internationalism*. Now, first, when he wrote this book in 1941, he was trying to create momentum for joining the European war. But the major impact of the book was after 1945. In this book, Luce argues that America has four things to offer the world: first, free enterprise; secondly, technological expertise; third, good Samaritanism as he calls it, that is, the famous American generosity; and finally, fourth: devotion to truth, justice, and the American way, in other words, the American ideals of democracy. These things would be, for Luce, the cornerstones of American internationalism; they would be the goals that America would promote in new her role as global power. In his own words, he concluded, "America as the dynamic center of an ever-widening sphere of enterprise; America as the training center of the skillful servants of mankind; America as the Good Samaritan really believing, again, that it is more blessed to give than to receive; and, America as the powerhouse of the ideals of freedom and justice. Out of these elements surely can be fashioned the division of the 20th century, to which we can and will devote ourselves in joy, and gladness, and vigor, and enthusiasm."

What's important to note here in this quote is the sense of universalism about the American way of life, the security that the rest of the world will embrace and welcome this way of life. In this sense, American universalism was another version of the European "civilizing mission" in the 19th century, that is, the idealistic desire and confidence to transform the world in its own Western image. Listen again to the statement of Luce's, which sounds much like a

19th-century British imperialist talking about bringing civilization to the rest of the world. Here's Luce: "It now becomes our time to be the powerhouse from which the ideals of Western civilization spread throughout the world and do their mysterious work at lifting the life of mankind from the level of beasts to what the Psalmist called 'a little lower than the angels." Again, that could be out of the mouth of a 19th-century British imperialist.

This vision of American ideals and prosperity brought to the four corners of the world was pretty powerful as a motive in and of itself. But there was another element that made this mission not only desirable, but seemingly urgent. Here is where we deviate from the 19th-century European civilizing mission. That other element was the existence of an enemy whose sole goal was to destroy that American way of life, and that sense of urgency, that enemy, did not exist under the European 19th-century world order. In other words, the conviction that there was an enemy with its own powerful world mission working to bring its totalitarian way of life to the rest of the world. The scope of this fear (that is, so you have idealism and fear combined in this world mission) is nicely illustrated in a book that was published as late as 1984, called *What to Do When the Russians Come – A Survivors Manual*, which laid out a dismal portrait of what life would be like in Soviet-occupied America: from rapes and summary executions to the nationalization of property and labor camps. The combined result of this fear with the idealism of the American way of life was a powerful mix, the idealism of wanting to spread American values around the world and the conviction that there was a nefarious enemy that would do anything to stop this. This combination was enough to mobilize a formerly isolationist American public around a new more assertive dramatic world mission for the United States.

How was the enemy defined? In the first five years after the war, American policy makers increasingly defined the Soviet Union not merely as an enemy but as the major threat to what became known as the free world. The first influential report was written in 1946 by the Soviet expert, George Kennan, who called the USSR a malignant, irrational power bent on world domination and who thus should be treated as a sociopath. Perhaps the most important document is the memo NSC-68, a National Security Council report written by Paul Nitze, who was the National Security Advisor for the Truman administration in the 1950s. Nitze expressed, in the strongest terms yet, the extreme urgency of the Soviet threat, as he said, "The integrity and vitality of our system is in greater jeopardy than ever before in our history. The issues that face us involve the fulfillment or the destruction not only of this republic but of civilization itself." Thus, Nitze described a mortal battle being waged over not only the future of the United States but, also, the future of civilization itself, again, the world mission part of it.

The adversary in this battle was a ruthless enemy completely amoral without any scruples who waged war on the United States in the free world, without any limits except the limits imposed by expediency. The Soviets fought dirty; they used any means they could to achieve their goal, and what was their goal? Nitze left no doubt that the Soviet goal was world domination. As he says, "The Kremlin is inescapably militant because it possesses and is possessed by a world wide revolutionary movement because it is a totalitarian dictatorship. Persistent crisis, conflict, and expansion are the essence of the Kremlin's militancy."

Was this a fair evaluation of the Soviet threat in 1950? Few questions have been more debated in the 50 years of the Cold War than the origins of the Cold War, who was to blame, and even with the opening of the Soviet archives in 1991, there are still opposing positions on this question.

However, some things seem clearer today with the opening of the Soviet archives; that is, it seems clear that the "revisionist" position that was proposed by some critical scholars in the West—which accused the United States of basically fabricating the Soviet threat— it seems that position has been disproved. There is enough evidence with the Soviet archives that demonstrate the existence of some kind of threat. Perhaps the most balanced perspective would be one that sees complex motives on the Soviets' side; that is, it seems clear that the Soviet Union did support the idea of worldwide communist revolution and pursued this goal through various strategies.

Furthermore, Stalin clearly wanted to extend Soviet influence and control in Eastern Europe from the beginning. On the other hand, it also seems clear that there was no clear master plan for world domination that Stalin had in 1945 to take over the world, or even to take over Western Europe—a plan that United States analysis thought directed all Soviet actions. Instead of operating according to a master plan for communist world revolution, the USSR was also concerned with its own survival—so, that is the other part of a complex set of motives. In 1945, the USSR had a powerful military force but not nearly as powerful as the West imagined. In addition, it was a devastated nation in 1945. Its economy had been destroyed by the war; it had lost 20 million people, and German occupiers had pillaged its resources. There was a strong sense of vulnerability within the Soviet Union, of the need to secure its borders and to prevent another invasion in the future. So, much of Soviet policy after the war was, thus, a confused mix of the desire to protect the Soviet Union from ever being vulnerable again and the desire to spread communist revolutions around the world and to spread Soviet influence.

Scholars argue about which of these concerns took priority at different points, but what seems to be clear is that the United States policy makers never acknowledged the other motive; they never acknowledged the sense of vulnerability that the Soviet Union had. Instead, the United States focused on the threat of expansion as the sole Soviet motive and used that threat as a way of mobilizing the American public around United States global intervention. At the same time, the Soviet Union was doing the same thing in its interpretation of American foreign policy; that is, it was interpreting all American behavior through its own narrow ideological lens. In particular, every American action was interpreted as the attempt of Western capitalism to destroy the Soviet Union. Thus, in an essay on the economic problems of the Soviet Union, Stalin expounded on his conviction that the capitalist powers led by the United States would greedily expand their markets and their influence in an effort to strangle the Soviet Union. He followed Lenin's earlier ideas on the inevitable war-like tendencies of capitalism. He wrote much the same thing about American capitalism that Nitze had written about Soviet communism—the inevitable war-like tendencies, the inevitable expansionist tendencies.

The Soviet Union accepted Marxist ideas that democratic politics were simply a cover for the protection of capitalist interests. To provide an example of this lens—of how it was used—when the United States proposed the Marshall Plan, which was an enormous financial aide package to help rebuild the Western European economies, Stalin interpreted this aide as an attempt to ensure capitalist control of Western Europe and as an attempt to strangle the Soviet economy.

In the United States, this package was seen and widely perceived as an illustration of good Samaritanism, that generosity that Henry Luce described. In fact, the Marshall Plan was a key factor in Western Europe's economic rebuilding after the war, and Europeans continued to remember the Marshall Plan as a great generous act of the United States.

So, was the Soviet interpretation pure paranoia then? Partly, but not entirely. What was true was that American aide emerged from an ideological commitment—not just to democracy, but, of course, to capitalism—to a global free-market economy tied to the dollar. The Soviet perception that this dollar-centered, free-market economy would be a threat to their model of a protected socialist economy was not completely wrong. In other words, we have—in a sense—a kind of reprise of the conflict between the United States and Japan over the Open Door policy in China in the late 19th and early 20th centuries; that is, the United States is proposing, in a sense, an Open Door policy in Western Europe, which its powerful economy could control through the free market. It didn't need domination, and it didn't need protected markets; whereas, the Soviet model of Europe was a protected market; it wanted protected markets in Eastern Europe within a socialist model.

The United States foreign policy was promoting capitalism as well as democracy, and it is not surprising that this would be perceived as a threat by the Soviet Union. So, the conflict between the two superpowers was not a mere fabrication. On the other hand, the motives on both sides were more complex then war-like capitalism versus world communism.

Why did each government prefer a simpler interpretation? Party, it was because of the ideological assumptions that each side had about the truth of their side versus the lies of the other side. But, partly also, the existence of the super-enemy was useful. It was useful for both governments in their attempts to mobilize their population in this world mission.

This complicated set of motives has led scholars to argue about when the Cold War actually began, and who was responsible. From the American point of view, the Cold War began when the Soviets occupied Eastern Europe directly after the war in 1945–1946. In contrast, from the Soviet point of view, it was the Marshall Plan of 1947 that was the first provocative act of the Cold War, American war-like capitalism asserting its power. In fact, of course, as I intimated before, each of these two acts was more complicated. The Soviet occupation came out of the fear of invasion and the desire to create a buffer zone between it and hostile Western capitalist countries, as well as to expand communist influence.

However, again, Stalin had no grand plan for the absorption of Eastern Europe until the Marshall Plan of 1947, which made him realize that he had to close off, completely, the Eastern European boundary in order to protect a socialist, economic sphere of influence. Again, the other part of the American motive, the desire to help struggling democracies get back on their feet, was completely lost on the Soviets.

After these initial acts, which were viewed by both sides as provocations, each side began to escalate the conflict in what became a self-fulfilling prophecy. Both sides contributed to fanning the flames, while increasingly apocalyptic rhetoric and aggressive actions served to escalate the conflict. In the United States, President Truman issued the Truman Doctrine in March 1947, in which he pledged the United States to help fight communist movements all over the world, including—by implication—in Eastern Europe. In the Soviet Union, Stalin moved from temporary occupation to the assertion of full political control over the buffer states of Eastern Europe in 1947 and 1948. Thus, in Poland, Hungary, and Czechoslovakia, Stalin overturned pluralist postwar regimes and installed single-party, Soviet-dominated regimes. Soon after that, the Korean War broke out in 1950, which signaled the extension of the Cold War to the rest of the world.

What conclusions can we come to about this question of the responsibility for starting the Cold War? While the opening acts of the Cold War are ambiguous, most historians would now accept that the Soviets carried more of the blame. While both the United States and the Soviet Union did want to expand their sphere of influence, and both were articulating as early as 1946 that the world was divided into two irreconcilable camps of good and evil spheres, American universalism was clearly more benign than Soviet universalism, especially in these opening acts in Europe. Thus, the impact of the Marshall Plan cannot be compared with the impact of the Soviet occupation of Eastern Europe, which must be considered a more proactive act. Even if, as historians now argue, that occupation was not the result of a master plan, but an ad hoc "Sovietization" that was being carried out on the ground, Western officials did not know this.

Once the Cold War starts, both sides become equally invested in maintaining it, and it becomes, then, the central political reality of the new world order.

Lecture Twenty-Eight
The Cold War in American Society

Scope:

More than a framework for international relations, the Cold War profoundly affected life at home. This lecture considers the impact of the Cold War on American domestic and foreign policy, especially in the 1950s and 1960s. It raises the question posed by scholars of whether the United States undermined its own liberal democratic principles in the course of waging the Cold War or whether the methods used to fight the communist enemy were justified by the nature of the threat. With this question in mind, we will focus on the domestic phenomenon of McCarthyism in the 1950s and on the international presence of the United States in a variety of conflicts, from Latin America to Asia, including Korea and Vietnam.

Outline

I. The challenge of fighting the Cold War presented the American government with certain moral dilemmas, articulated directly in Nitze's NSC-68 memo.

   A. In the memo, he outlined two complementary strategies for defeating the enemy. The first was the power of American ideals to attract the rest of the world.

   B. If the USSR really was a sociopathic power, however, Nitze did not think this idealistic attraction was enough. If the Soviets could be expected to use dirty, underhanded methods, then the United States was obliged to respond in kind.

   C. What this two-pronged strategy created was a moral dilemma, in which national security could be used to justify the short-term practice of suspending American ideals, at home and abroad.

II. One of the best case studies of this moral dilemma in practice was the phenomenon of *McCarthyism*, which brought the fear of the Soviet threat to Americans' own backyard.

  A. The context for this fear was a wave of spy cases and growing suspicion that the Soviets had access to American government documents.

  B. In response to this fear, the Truman administration passed the Federal Employees Loyalty Act in 1947.

  C. The most prominent spy cases were those of Alger Hiss and the Rosenbergs.

  D. Senator Joseph McCarthy entered the fray with a speech in February 1950, in which he argued that the United States was being undermined by communist sympathizers inside the country.

   1. Although his "list" of card-carrying communists in the State Department did not exist, his speech sparked a groundswell of anti-communist fear, a *Red Scare*.

   2. The Red Scare was certainly not caused by one man, but McCarthy clearly articulated the fears of many.

  E. Historians have argued about the truth of these accusations and the dangers of internal subversion, as well as the justification for the government's response.

   1. Critics argue that even the existence of Soviet spies did not justify the broader violations of civil rights.

   2. The House Committee on Un-American Activities (HUAC) was set up to find and purge communists from prominent positions, and it called hundreds of suspects to testify on their own or others' communist sympathies.

   3. Significantly, suspects were defined, not by criminal actions, but by beliefs and attitudes, which were supposed to be protected under the law.

   4. Historians have recently argued that, in addition, members of marginalized groups, such as racial minorities or homosexuals, were more likely to be targeted.

   5. The most famous HUAC investigations targeted Hollywood.

   6. HUAC was aided by the FBI and the CIA, which gathered thousands of secret files on Americans who had criticized government policy or engaged in other suspicious activities.

7. Many institutions outside the federal government established loyalty acts, firing employees considered subversive and banning books considered "un-American."

8. In 1950, Congress, over President Truman's veto, permitted communists to be rounded up in concentration camps in a national emergency.

9. As a result, thousands of professors, government officials, and others lost their jobs and status, leading to professional ruin for many and social marginalization for all.

10. These civil rights violations in no way compared to the purges of the USSR, and defenders argue they were a necessary price to pay for protecting democracy, while critics argue that the United States failed to live up to its own democratic standards.

F. By the late 1950s, the Red Scare had died down and McCarthy fell out of political favor, but the underlying message shaped government policy into the next decade; that is, that the requirements of national security "containment" could override the right to political pluralism and individual freedom of belief.

III. A similar sort of moral dilemma shaped American foreign policy during the Cold War.

A. On the attraction side, the United States pursued a generous policy of foreign aid and strategic alliances that funneled billions into Third World nations' coffers.

B. If nations refused to remain in the American sphere, however, the United States (like the USSR) adopted various coercive strategies to force them to do so.

C. These could include proxy wars, in which military aid was funneled into an opposition group, or direct intervention by U.S. armies.

D. This militarization of the Third World was apparent in the first non-European theater of the Cold War: Korea.

1. At times, American-supported forces were more anti-communist than democratic.

2. This put the United States in the position of supporting authoritarian regimes, from the Shah of Iran to Spain's Franco.

3. For the same reason, it was difficult for the United States to understand popular revolutions in poor countries as something other than cogs in the Soviet's world plan, that is, as expressions of local conflicts and grievances.

4. The United States explained its support for authoritarian regimes by arguing that they were a lesser evil than the alternative totalitarian Soviet system.

IV. Now that the Cold War is over, how do we come to terms with these contradictions? On the one hand are those who continue to defend the necessity of these morally ambivalent actions on the grounds that they, in fact, helped us to win the Cold War; in other words, the victory in the Cold War justified a temporary deviation from our principles. On the other hand are those who argue that the sacrifices were too great, that the end of making the world safe for democracy was lost in the undemocratic means with which the Cold War was fought.

Essential Reading:

Edward Pessen, *Losing Our Souls: The American Experience in the Cold War*.

Supplementary Reading:

Thomas Reeves, *The Life and Times of Joe McCarthy*.

Arthur Herman, *Joseph McCarthy: Reexamining the Life of America's Most Hated Senator*.

Questions to Consider:

1. The continued relevance of this question is apparent in the similar debate opened up between the defenders and detractors of the Patriot Act. How would you frame the relationship between national security and civil rights?

2. The moral question of the "ends justifying the means" has a long and contested history, which makes it unlikely that the Cold War debates will be resolved in the near future. What is your position?

Lecture Twenty-Eight—Transcript
The Cold War in American Society

In the last lecture, we discussed the origins of the Cold War and the framework for international relations, or for a new world order based on competing superpowers. Of course, the Cold War was much more than a blueprint for superpower relations; it had profound impact on all the players involved, especially the two superpowers.

While the impact of the Cold War on the Soviet Union has not raised much debate, its impact on the United States continues to be a source of controversy, both political and academic. Even if we assign the USSR greater responsibility for starting the Cold War, the debate still wages about how the United States fought the Cold War. The origins of the Cold War are not the same debate as how it was waged, particularly in the United States because of the way it raised issues about the practices of democracy. Once again, experts and scholars have been divided about whether the United States had to use undemocratic means to wage the Cold War, or whether these means undermined democracy itself. Because the Soviet Union was not a democratic state, these issues did not even come up. That is why the debate really focuses on the United States as opposed to the Soviet Union.

The United States government realized from the outset that the challenge of fighting the Cold War presented it with certain moral dilemmas. If we return to Nitze's NSC-68 memo that I mentioned in the last lecture, which outlines the strategies for fighting this war with the Soviet Union, he lays out two complementary strategies. On the one hand, he says, America should fight the battle for the pure power of her ideals. As Nitze says at one point, freedom is the most contagious idea in history. Thus, he assumes and hopes that many peoples will simply choose to follow American ideals by being convinced of their moral superiority. On the other hand, there was clearly a dilemma. If the Soviet Union was really an evil and irrational sociopath empire that Kennan had described, then Nitze did not think that this idealistic attraction was enough. If the Soviets could be expected to use every dirty, underhanded means to undermine America, then, he argued, America was justified in using those same means to defend itself and the American way of life. As he said in what became a famous phrase, "a means to be employed must be proportional to the extent of the mischief." So, the Soviet threat justified not only the use of democracy as a model, but also the use of undemocratic methods to further American objectives.

What this two-pronged strategy created was a moral dilemma, in which national security could be used to justify the short-term sacrifice of American ideals, at home and abroad. On the one hand, Nitze glorified a free society of America, which tolerated not only diversity but also those who would use their freedom to destroy it. Conversely, his position implies that the immediate means of what came to be called "national security" could override other intermediate and long-term goals. When a judge sentenced a nuclear scientist, J. Robert Oppenheimer, for his criticism of United States nuclear policy, he said, "There can be no tampering with national security which in time of peril must be absolute and without concession for reasons of admiration, gratitude, regard, sympathy, or charity." So, national security becomes an independent value that could override democratic practice.

The issue here is not whether the new priority of national security made the United States more repressive or more undemocratic than the Soviet Union; that is not the issue. No one is arguing for any kind of conflation between McCarthyism and the gulags. What is at issue is whether the United States should have been held to a different standard than the Soviets, or whether the Cold War had made this impossible. That is the heart of the debate.

It is in this framework that we can talk about McCarthyism as a case study of this moral dilemma and practice. *McCarthyism* was named after a Wisconsin senator, Joseph McCarthy. He began playing on the fears of Soviet threats by arguing that Soviet communism was infiltrating the United States. On this basis, he opened up a full-scale campaign to root out communism within the borders of the United States. McCarthyism and the *Red Scare* of the 1950s represented the transference of the Soviet threat abroad to the internal threat on the home front.

The plausible context for this threat was created by a wave of spy cases that gained publicity in the late 1940s and early 1950s. With these spy cases, comes the growing suspicion that the Soviets had gained access to American government documents. In March 1945, government agents found numerous classified documents in the offices of an allegedly pro-communist magazine in New York, called

Amerasia. A year later, a Canadian investigation led to the arrest of 22 men and women for passing classified United States documents to the Soviets.

The conviction that the Soviets had somehow gained access to the government led to calls for a broader investigation and a purge of all communists from sensitive jobs. J. Edgar Hoover, the head of the FBI, declared that the disloyalty of American communists is no longer, as he put it, a matter of conjecture. President Truman established a federal employee loyalty program in March 1947, which called for the dismissal of any federal employee if "reasonable grounds exist for belief that the person involved is disloyal." The Truman administration also pursued a high-profile trial against 11 communists accused under the Smith Act of 1940, which punished anyone conspiring to advocate and teach the violent overthrow of the United States government. The Supreme Court upheld the constitutionality of the Smith Act in its 1951 ruling, *Dennis v. the United States.*

Within the context of this plethora of cases of Soviet spies, perhaps the most talked about loyalty case was that of Alger Hiss, a former democratic aide to Franklin Roosevelt, who was accused in August 1948 by the editor of *Time Magazine* of having passed classified documents to him in 1938. Hiss denied the charges and was granted a mistrial, but in a second trial he was convicted of perjury and sentenced to five years in jail. Shortly after his conviction, the FBI arrested Ethel and Julius Rosenberg on charges of having conspired to pass nuclear secrets to the Russians. After a two-week trial in 1951, a judge who called their crime "worse than murder" because it furthered the cause of "godless communism" convicted the Rosenbergs. In June 1953, they were executed. McCarthy enters into this frame with a speech he gave to a Republican Women's Group in West Virginia in February 1950, when he argued that the United States was being undermined by communist sympathizers within our borders. As he said, "The reason why we find ourselves in a position of impotency is not because our only powerful enemy has sent men to invade our shores, but rather because of the traitorous actions of those who have been treated so well by this nation."

While rhetoric about communist infiltration was not new, the innovation of McCarthy's speech was that he claimed to have proof of this infiltration. So, he claimed to have a "list" of 205 members of the Communist Party, who worked in the United States government—particularly in the State Department, which he said was infested with communists. McCarthy actually had no list, and he kept changing the numbers—later he said there were 57 instead of 205 Communist Party members in the government. However, his lack of hard evidence did not matter because his speech came at the right moment. It touched a fear that many Americans were already beginning to feel, and it helped to spark a ground swell of anti-communist fear, a *Red Scare* that affected all levels of society, from elite businessmen and politicians to uneducated common voters. Over the next few months, McCarthy received more than 2,000 invitations to speak around the country—more than all of the other senators combined. He did not create the Red Scare, and sometimes the focus on him and the use of the word *McCarthyism* puts too much emphasis on him as an individual and distorts his role. But he certainly did articulate the fears of many. So, anti-communism in this period becomes the American obsession, as a *Life Magazine* article put it, "The fellow traveler (communist sympathizer) is everywhere, in Hollywood, on college campuses, in government bureaus, in publishing companies, in radio offices, even on the editorial staff of eminently capitalist journals." So, there was this sense that communists were somehow everywhere, hidden and infiltrating and subverting the American government—and more broadly even, the society.

Historians have long debated the justification for this fear of domestic communism, of how many American communists were really spying for the Soviets, and what kind of threat did this internal subversion really have. Once again, the opening of the Soviet archives has provided us with more information. It does seem to support the existence of at least 100 high-level government spies who worked for the Soviets, including incriminating evidence against Alger Hiss and the Rosenbergs. Defenders of the Red Scare and defenders of the anti-communist policies of the period point to these statistics and say they were justified because, in fact, communist spies did exist.

On the other hand, critics still argue that even the existence of Soviet spies failed to justify the larger violation of civil rights that emerged with the anti-communist scare. After the Truman administration's Federal Employees Loyalty Act in 1947, a congressional committee was set up—the House Committee on Un-American Activities (HCUA). This committee called hundreds of suspects to testify before Congress as to their own communist sympathies, or the communist sympathies of people they knew, people who had information, in other words, they were asked to give information on themselves and others. Suspects included, not only people who were known members of the Communist Party, but also anyone who had criticized the government, expressed sympathy for leftist viewpoints, even whether they were communists. Many civil rights activists were summoned because as one Loyalty Review Board member said, "The fact that a person believes in racial equality does not prove he is a communist, but it certainly makes you look twice, doesn't it?" A broader net had been thrown around people who had shown some sort of dissidence against American government policy. Even groups with no political identity, like homosexuals, were automatically dismissed as security threats, simply because they were considered marginal groups. HUAC was aided by the cooperation of the FBI and the CIA, which gathered files on thousands of Americans who had been known to participate in what was defined as "suspicious activity," again, that was defined as criticism of the government. The CIA, which had been set up to spy on other countries, was now turned to the surveillance of the American population.

Perhaps the most famous of the HUAC investigations was that carried out in the entertainment industry in Hollywood. Why did they focus on the entertainment industry? As one committee member said, "Large numbers of moving pictures that come out of Hollywood carry the communist line." So, the committee called in screenwriters, actors, directors, and so on and asked them to supply the names of suspected communists. A small group of screenwriters, the so-called "Hollywood Ten" served prison terms for refusing to answer these questions. Following this movement, the major studios began to blacklist actors and directors who would not publicly denounce communism. Beyond the federal government and Hollywood, universities, local governments, school districts, libraries, and other organizations instituted loyalty acts similar to that of the Truman Federal Employees Loyalty Act of March 1947, in which they had to publicly declare that they were not communists. Employees were fired who were considered subversive, and books were banned that were considered "un-American," and this had a broader impact even beyond people who worked for the federal government or in Hollywood.

In 1950, Congress also passed, over Truman's veto, an internal security act that permitted rounding up communists in concentration camps in a national emergency. As a result of this broader witch hunt, thousands of people—professors, government officials, actors, and other professionals—were blackballed and unable to find work either for expressing radical opinions, or for being members of the Communist Party, or for being suspected of being communists. They were blackballed not for any specific crimes they committed, but for their beliefs. Many of these people were professionally ruined, and all were marginalized from American society.

If we take the scope of these civil rights violations and compare them with the repressive purges of the Soviet Union in the 1930s, there is no comparison with the millions of people carted off to the gulags and summarily executed. But, if the point of reference is not the USSR but a democratic society in which diversity of opinion was protected, then you can see the moral dilemma. Then, McCarthyism sent a rather undemocratic message that toleration of diversity had been trumped by national security. People were being judged not by their criminal actions but by their non-conformist beliefs.

By the late 1950s, the intense period of McCarthyist persecution had died down and McCarthy, himself, fell out of political favor. But, debates over the primacy of national security, over democratic rights, continued. In fact, it is interesting that a similar sort of moral dilemma emerged again recently—an American political debate in the context of the support and criticism of the Patriot Act, which brings up a similar set of issues about the impact on civil rights versus the threat of terrorism. Again, the debate is formulated in very similar terms.

A similar sort of moral dilemma shaped American foreign policy during the Cold War. On the one hand, the United States sought to promote democracy and development abroad through a generous package of foreign aide and assistance to a number of countries. This was the first part of Nitze's strategy of bringing the model of democracy and capitalism to the rest of the world.

By the 1960s, America was sending foreign aide, both military and economic, to more than 100 countries. The first major foreign aide projects were the Marshall Plan of the late 1940s in Europe, funneling 12 billion dollars into 16 nations, and then a similar aide package to Japan, which helped rebuild the Japanese economy after the war. I think those aide packages to Western Europe and Japan were really both the center of United States aide and the major success stories of that aide.

On the other hand, the United States was committed to preventing the spread of communism abroad, and to this end, it formed numerous security alliances; this was the military side of it. The most important was NATO in 1949. By 1956, America had signed defensive alliances with 42 states in strategic locations, from Europe to Asia, all designed to bring other nations into the struggle against communism. To back up these alliances, by 1967, America had 700,000 soldiers stationed around the world.

The problem came because these two goals of spreading democracy abroad and preventing communism were not always congruent. In the name of preventing communism, the United States waged a number of wars, occasionally with its own troops but usually what were called proxy wars, where they funneled military aide to support one side of a war against troops that were often supported by Soviet military aide. If you consider these proxy wars on a basic level, they worked against the establishment of stable democratic regimes, both because they dramatically militarized the Third World, Soviet, and United States military aide coming in, and because so much of the foreign aide was channeled into guns instead of bread—into military aide instead of development aide. This militarization of the Third World was brutally apparent in the first non-European theater of the Cold War, which was Korea. Korea had emerged from the Second World War scarred by decades of Japanese occupation. Furthermore, at the end of the war, Korea had been divided, like Germany, into a northern communist sphere and a southern non-communist sphere, and they had been absorbed into the Soviet and American spheres of influence.

When the American and Soviet armies left in 1949, the well-armed North Korean army invaded the south, and opened a new period of warfare for the Koreans, easily defeating the South Korean forces. Documents released after the opening of the Soviet archives revealed that the Soviet Union actually had no role in this invasion; they were not pushing the North Koreans to invade. What the Americans assumed was that this invasion was part of a Soviet plan to extend communist influence into Asia. They interpreted the invasion as a Soviet maneuver; although, we know now that was not the case, they did not know that.

Already nervous by the fall of nationalist China in 1949 and worried about the spread of communism in Asia, the Truman administration decided to intervene, bringing a vote to the United Nations and getting approval for troop deployment. From 1950 to 1953, United States troops fought in a bloody civil war, at first nearly conquering all of North Korea, but then pushed back by the entrance of 400,000 Chinese troops who came in to aide the North Koreans. Fearing even greater escalation, the United States finally had to settle for negotiated peace, which protected the independent south but essentially went back to the status quo. In the process, almost 37,000 American soldiers died and 100,000 were wounded. Meanwhile, the Koreans lost 1 million people, and another 3 million were left homeless in a shattered economy.

Whether or not the South Koreans were better off for United States' intervention is certainly an important question. But looking at the 1 million to 3 million people who were left homeless or were killed in the war revealed—in a very direct way—what it meant to be a pawn in superpower reveries.

Adding to the moral dilemma for the United States was that the local forces supported by the United States were usually more anti-communist than they were democratic, as was the case in Korea.

As a result, the United States ended up supporting many openly undemocratic regimes simply because they were willing to operate in the American sphere of influence. In 1953, a United States backed coup in Iran propped up the authoritarian Shah of Iran, who was eventually overthrown in an Islamic fundamentalist revolution 25 years later.

Likewise, the United States made friends with Spanish and Portuguese dictatorships because they were firm in their support of anti-communism. Finally, the United States government let in known Nazi war criminals because of their usefulness in providing ant-Soviet information.

Furthermore, because of the black and white vision of the world—divided into communist and anti-communist spheres—it proved difficult for the American government to distinguish between local grievances and the expansion of communist revolution, to distinguish local grievances from Soviet threats, to understand that popular revolution could be something other than a Soviet-manipulated regime.

For example, in 1954, the CIA organized a small invasion force to overthrow the populist president of Guatemala when he talked about taking land from the United Fruit Company to give to the peasants. But he was neither communist nor a Soviet puppet. In 1965, America sent 20,000 marines into the Dominican Republic to quash a popular rebellion against a military dictator. Again, in 1973, the CIA helped sponsor the overthrow of a social democratic government in Chile, which was replaced by the military junta under Pinochet.

As a result of these kinds of policies, America created a reputation, especially in Latin America, of supporting repressed dictators and of being the enemy of populist social progressive regimes.

During the Eisenhower administration, then, Vice President Nixon took a tour of Latin America, and he was greeted with such hostility at every stop, that the Eisenhower administration actually had to step back and reconsider what kind of reputation the United States was building in Latin America.

One attempt on the part of the State Department to justify these policies and the support for these dictatorships came from Jean Kirkpatrick, a former UN ambassador who justified the support of what she called authoritarian regimes as a "lesser evil," but condemned what she called "totalitarian regimes," which was a code word for communist, which the United States would never support, making that distinction between authoritarian and totalitarian. In the long-term pursuit of a world free for democracy, Kirkpatrick argued, it was justifiable in the short run to support certain kinds of undemocratic regimes as long as they were authoritarian as opposed to totalitarian.

The Cold War that justified these policies is now over, and moreover, the West certainly emerged victorious in this war. For many, the victory itself of the West was the final vindication of the policy that focused on the defeat of what Ronald Reagan called the "evil empire." For this camp, the democratically ambivalent actions were necessary to fight against an enemy without democratic scruples. They would argue that democratic values emerged even stronger at the end of the Cold War, including a wave of democratic transitions in Latin America.

For detractors, however, the victory in the Cold War was marred by the sacrifice of the very democratic principles the United States claimed to defend, whether at home or abroad. They would argue that final victory does not erase the harm done to democracy along the way.

Since the debate feeds off a moral dilemma much older than the Cold War—that is, this philosophical debate about ends versus means—it is a debate, I think, that will unlikely be resolved anytime soon..

Lecture Twenty-Nine
Science and the State in Cold War America

Scope:

This lecture continues to examine the impact of the Cold War on American society, through a close look at the transformation of scientific research and development. Beginning with the state-directed program to build the atom bomb in the 1940s, atomic physics evolved from an industry based on individual free enterprise to a government-run national science industry, similar in many ways to its counterpart in the USSR. We examine the nature of this evolution, from the Manhattan Project of the 1940s, and consider how massive federal funding, monopolization, and the channeling of research into government projects created a new relationship between the state and private industry that challenged classic liberal economic principles. Finally, we consider the implications of this new relationship in the context of the Cold War.

Outline

I. The result of having a government-run national science industry was that, once again, in fighting the Cold War, the United States ended up sacrificing some of the liberal ideas it was defending: in this case, the sacred principle of private free enterprise. To illustrate this point, we will focus on a single case study, that is, the development of the field of nuclear physics in the years during and after the war.

   A. Historians have argued that the growing relationship between nuclear physics and the American government represent the extension of Cold War national security priorities over what had been a classic liberal enterprise of individual research programs.

   B. Again, the question of whether this transformation was justified by a clear and present danger has been debated.

   C. What did scientific research look like before the war?
   1. The central figure was the classic "lone scientist," tinkering in the lab, designing his or her own research projects, and with little interest in government involvement.

2. Funding came from a variety of sources, a small percent from the federal government.
3. There were no government institutions to coordinate research and no national science research policy.
4. In other words, scientific development operated according to a classic liberal laissez-faire model.

D. What changed this picture was the Second World War and the threat posed by fascism.
   1. This threat convinced many important scientists, even the pacifist and socialist Einstein, to collaborate with the government on weapons research for the war effort.
   2. The threat also began to push the government into considering new ways of harnessing civilian research toward military goals.
   3. In 1940, the first national institute, the Office of Scientific Research and Development, was established to coordinate defense-related projects.
   4. By 1941, 75 percent of the most eminent physicists in the United States were employed in defense work.
   5. The government also set up its own labs, defined specific research projects, and dramatically increased funding.

E. The most dramatic example of these wartime shifts was the successful project to build the atom bomb, the *Manhattan Project*.
   1. The initial discovery of nuclear fission was made before the war by individual scientists, but it was the federal government that brought the money and organization to produce the bomb.
   2. The project involved the coordination of research at existing university labs, as well as the construction of a special government-run lab at Los Alamos, New Mexico, which employed more than 2,000 scientific and technical staff.
   3. The intense concentration of resources produced results: only seven years after the discovery of nuclear fission, the first bomb was tested, on July 16, 1945.
   4. If we compare the machine gun with the atom bomb from an organizational perspective, the contrast is clear.

II. What made this new relationship between science and the state more than a temporary alliance was the Cold War, which turned the wartime sense of urgency into a permanent condition.

    A. If technological superiority was essential to winning the Cold War, then research into nuclear physics was in the direct interest of the government and should be harnessed to national security imperatives.

    B. What were the characteristics of a nuclear physics industry harnessed to national security?

        1. The most obvious consequence was the domination of federal funding, most of it funneled through the Atomic Energy Commission and the Department of Defense.

        2. A related consequence is that because the majority of this federal funding came from the Defense Department, the government took an active role in channeling research toward military applications.

        3. Why did scientists agree to this new relationship with the state? The combination of money, prestige, and patriotism must have been a powerful attraction for young scientists.

        4. As a result of this attraction, by 1951, two-thirds of all engineers and scientists in the United States worked in defense-related research.

        5. Another characteristic was the concentration of research into large projects employing teams of researchers and costly equipment.

        6. Finally, these large projects were more likely to focus on applied research rather than basic research, particularly applied weapons projects.

        7. The result has been a range of impressive weapons projects, from ICBMs to smart bombs and thermonuclear warheads, which clearly advanced the overall goal of technological military superiority.

    C. What are the broader consequences of the close relationship between science and the state during the Cold War period?

        1. It seems clear that individual scientists working in this field had much less autonomy in 1960 than they did before the war; that is, the state had encroached further into the realm of individual choice.

2. However, the encroachment of the state into individual lives is not a product of the Cold War. Since the early 20th century, the state has increasingly made more demands of individuals at the same time that it has taken more responsibility for helping them.

3. The Cold War reinforced a tradeoff between individual autonomy and national security, which justified the expansion of state power into the realm of scientific research.

III. Once again, we are left with the same unresolved question of whether this process was ultimately necessary or even positive, justified by ultimate victory or criticized as imitating the enemy's national defense industry. Whichever position is taken, it is important to recognize that a shift did take place as a result of the Cold War and that this shift involved a tradeoff between the practice of the "American way of life" and the goal of winning the war.

Essential Reading:

Dan Kevles, *The Physicists*.

Supplementary Reading:

Gregg Herken, "The University of California, the Federal Weapons Labs and the Founding of the Atomic West," in Bruce Hevly and John Findley, eds., *The Atomic West*.

Questions to Consider:

1. While the percentage of scientists working in defense industries has dropped since the 1950s, the larger issue of federal funding and the way it shapes research priorities remains an important one. Would you agree?

2. It would be impossible to return to the old model of the lone scientist tinkering in his or her lab, but what role should the scientist play in a world in which science, money, and politics are inextricably linked?

Lecture Twenty-Nine—Transcript
Science and the State in Cold War America

This lecture continues to examine the consequences of the Cold War on American society, through a close look at the transformation of scientific research and development. In particular, we will follow the transformation of nuclear physics that led to the creation of so-called "big science" in the decades after World War Two.

Beginning with the state-directed program to build the atom bomb in the 1940s during the war, atomic physics evolved from an industry based on essential individual enterprise to a government-led science national industry, similar in many ways to its counterpart in the Soviet Union. The result was that, once again, in fighting the Cold War, the United States ended up trading off some of the liberal ideas it had been defending: in this case, the sacred principle of private free enterprise. To illustrate this, we are going to focus on this single case study of the field of nuclear physics in the years during and after the war.

Historians have argued that the growing relationship between nuclear physics and the American government represented the extension of Cold War national security priorities over what had been a classic liberal enterprise of individual research programs. Once again, the judgment over whether this was a necessary transition, that is, a response to a clear and present danger represented by the military threat of the Soviet Union, is debated by scholars and pundits.

What we are going to focus on in this lecture is not that judgment, but on the details of the transition—the development of big science and the kinds of tradeoffs that it involved.

Although the Cold War is over, the general issue about the relationship between the state and private enterprise in scientific research and development still generates debate and controversy, even today. So, it is useful, I think, to have a clear sense of the origins of this relationship in this postwar period.

Let's begin by going back to the operation of prewar science as a point of departure. In simplified terms, the central figure in the world of prewar science was the "lone scientist" tinkering in his lab, pursuing his or her individual research, the classic liberalism entrepreneur you might say. In this world, the government played a very small role. Funding came from a variety of sources including the federal and state government, but, altogether, the federal government contributed only about 20 percent of all research and development money. Furthermore, even when they did contribute, they played little role in dictating what kind of research would be carried out. There was no single federal institution to coordinate research efforts, or even to link the research efforts of the military branches to civilian labs. There were no national science policies and no national scientific institutions to coordinate such a policy. Government contributed some funding, but it had no control over the content of that research—again, the classic liberal laissez-faire model, with scientific research being carried out by hundreds or thousands of essentially independent entrepreneurs. One of the few exceptions to this small-scale model of prewar science was the Lawrence Berkeley Lab, which was set up in Berkeley by the physicist, Ernest Lawrence, in the early 1930s. He developed the cyclotron particle accelerator and developed a lab to build more sophisticated versions of the machine. The goal of the machine was to smash the atom and discover its parts. This lab was to be a later model for the big national research laboratories that are built during and after the war, and Lawrence, himself, becomes a key figure in this process in helping to develop these labs. But, in the 1930s, it had few peers, and even this large-scale operation—which was unusual for the 1930s—was funded by a variety of sources, with the federal government playing a fairly minor role. So, 20 percent of the operating costs came from Washington, and another 40 percent came from the state of California, while 40 percent of the operating costs and 80 percent of capital costs came from private investment. Even the Lawrence Berkeley Lab was essentially a large private business. Furthermore, in this prewar period, scientists show little interest in cooperating with the government and working on scientific research and development. They pursued what they called "pure science," which they did not want to have invaded by any kind of political motives. Many scientists especially resisted being drawn into the national security research, and they maintained an isolationist attitude toward the relationship of science and politics. In general, scientists clung to their independence and their private tinkering.

What begins to change this situation is the Second World War, which begins to convince both scientists and the government to establish a closer relationship with each other. Of course, the reason for that was that both sides realized that the democracies were entering some sort of death struggle with fascism. The threat changed the attitudes of scientists because the overt evil that was represented by Hitler convinced many scientists to soften their isolationist stance and to drop their disdain for national security considerations. Even the socialist and pacifist Einstein saw no alternative to rearming the democracies. So, scientists—along with the rest of the population—were drawn out of their isolationist stance and into the war on fascism.

By 1941, 1,700 physicists were employed in defense work; this constituted 25 percent of the entire profession, but 75 percent of the eminent names in the field. The fascist threat also began changing government policy toward scientific research; that is, the United States government began to ask how civilization science could be harnessed to defense needs. The result was the first major attempts by the government to coordinate scientific research. By 1940, it established a national organization, the Office of Scientific Research and Development, the OSRD, to coordinate scientific research in defense-related projects, and to bring scientists into weapons projects. It also greatly increased funds for any research and development programs with military applications. By 1945, the government was providing 83 percent of all research and development money for scientific research. That is a huge jump from the 18 percent in 1940. By the end of the war, research and development was virtually federally funded.

The government also set up its own labs funded and run by the military branches, but operated by civilian scientists, to work on specific research projects that could be expected to produce weapons and technology that would be useful in the present war. In other words, the goal of this research and development was short-term to develop weapons that could be used immediately. One of the biggest of these labs was nicknamed the "Rad Lab" at MIT, which worked on improving radar technology. In fact, the improved radar that came out of this lab turned out to be one of the crucial technological edges of the Allies in the Second World War in Europe. All of these shifts from federal funding to the creation of research projects, to the building of government labs, are illustrated in the biggest and most famous science project of the war, which was to build the atom bomb, the so-called *Manhattan Project*.

The idea for the bomb emerged out of the private research of independent scientists; it emerged out of the old laissez-faire model. But it was government money that built the bomb itself—that brought it to fruition. In 1938, independent scientists discovered the process of nuclear fission and began to discuss the potential for releasing nuclear energy, particularly in the form of an explosive. With the outbreak of the war, the government began to show interest in this research and this idea. In the summer of 1941, scientists got authorization to research whether a bomb could be developed for use in the current war. By the summer of 1942, things looked so good that scientists got the green light for a full-scale effort to build the atom bomb.

The Manhattan Project involved the cooperation of a number of existing labs at the University of California, Berkeley; the University of Chicago; Columbia University; as well as the construction of a new lab for the construction and testing, and that was the lab in Los Alamos, New Mexico, 75 miles north of Albuquerque. By 1944, there was more than 2,000 technical and scientific staff at Los Alamos, among the several eminent noble-prize-winning physicists. The entire project was operating on an intense deadline mentality. They were trying to get this weapon developed in order to use it in the current war. This crash program produced amazingly, within only seven years from the discovery of nuclear fission in 1938 to the production of the first atom bomb in 1945, only seven years had passed—which was a remarkable feat. Less than a month after the testing of the first atomic bomb in New Mexico on July 16, 1945, the two bombs of the American arsenal were dropped on Nagasaki and Hiroshima. The dramatic lesson of the Manhattan Project was apparent to everyone, that is, that dramatic lesson of what happened when you put so many resources into a single project and what could actually be produced. Almost more impressive than the weapon itself was the organization that had produced it: the awesome power of scientific research harnessed to national security imperatives. As the White House said, the atom bomb was the greatest achievement of organized science in history.

Despite the fact that many scientists and many of those who were involved in building it turned away from atomic research after witnessing what the bomb produced in Hiroshima, there was no going back. The bomb had opened a new era in the relations between science and the state. Furthermore, it pointed to a new relationship between science, military technology, and national power. In the post-Cold War period, national power is going to be linked closely to military technology and superiority in military technology.

If we compare the atom bomb with the machine gun from the First World War, we can see the contrast in the relationship between science and military technology and the state. The machine gun, which as we recall had transformed the First World War, was a classic product of laissez-faire liberalism; it was designed and invented by that lone scientist tinkering in his lab, a man named Hiram Maxim, and it was sold and distributed on the market. But the atom bomb came out of a government blueprint that harnessed the energies of several thousand scientists and billions of dollars to produce a weapon that was owned by the government and not sold on the open market. The production of those two weapons demonstrates the drama of the change.

The implications of this contrast are tremendous. If you think about it the bomb was a scientific discovery that was produced neither for the market of scientific ideas, nor for the more conventional economic market. Instead, it was produced as part of the national security apparatus of the state. So, the bomb really signals a shift from individual free enterprise to national security as the engine of scientific research, and with the state as the new driver of that engine.

What made this new relationship between science and the state something more than a temporary alliance was the Cold War? During all wars, there is a greater tendency to push national security over other priorities, as governments harness their forces to defeat the enemy. After 1945, the heating up of the Cold War turned that temporary wartime into a permanent one, that this was a permanent threat not a temporary one. It makes it seem imperative to continue this shift from a laissez-faire science policy to one dictated by national security. As the Director of the Bureau of the Budget said to President Truman in 1950, "The emphasis which the increasing responsibilities of the United States in world affairs places on the relationship between strategic plans and scientific research and development made national coordination essential."

One of the fundamental assumptions of Cold War politics was that America had to maintain technological superiority in order to protect herself and the free world from the Soviet threat. What that superiority meant in a post-Hiroshima world was atomic weapons. As a result, scientific research into nuclear physics became the direct and permanent interest of the government. Thus, the Cold War helped create a permanent, institutionalized relationship between the state and the scientific community, particularly in the field of nuclear physics, and with a central role played by major universities.

What were the characteristics, then, of this new nuclear physics industry that was harnessed to national security? The most obvious characteristic was the trend towards federally funded science. This trend, which had begun during the war, was reinforced and maintained. After the war was over, the government set up funding channels largely through the newly created the Atomic Energy Commission (AEC) and through the Department of Defense (DoD), which made the state the principal patron of research and development in the sciences. So, the government paid for research in private industry labs and the universities as well as running labs of its own.

For example, in the late 1940s, 85 percent of MIT's research budget came from DoD and AEC sources, as well as 25 percent of Bell Telephone's research budget. By 1951, DoD and AEC contracts accounted for nearly 40 percent of all scientific research projects. After a slump in the 1970s, the Reagan administration increased federal research and development monies again so that by the mid-1980s, a full 70 percent of the country's research and development budget came from the federal government.

The first characteristic of the new kind of science was massive dependence on federal funding. The government is expanding in what used to be the realm of private industry. Furthermore, it is important to emphasize the source of this federal funding; that is, most of it came from the DoD. For example, in 1960, of all federal money going to research and development, 80 percent came from defense agencies. This means that 80 percent of the scientific research funded by the government is being focused into national security issues. It is not only that the government is funding more science; it is that the government is focusing on what kind of science is done, as well. There are two separate processes—the channeling and focusing of research.

The obvious upshot of this channeling of this money was to increase military and weapons research, both in private industries and in universities. For example, after the war, labs dedicated only to weapons research were set up at Cal Tech, a jet propulsion lab; at John's Hopkins, the applied physics lab; and at the University of California, the Los Alamos weapons lab. At the time, some scientists, like J. Robert Oppenheimer, were shocked. In 1948, he asked how the University of California could be a great liberal university that manufactured—under contract with the government—atomic bombs, and he compared the paradox to monks manufacturing liquors in their basement.

What is the upshot of this funding pattern? There were two separate, but related processes here. First, the government makes a conscious decision to take an active role in funding and shaping scientific research—a decision that could have taken a number of directions. The government could have decided, for example, to use a lot of money to fund mass transport programs, or to fund toxic waste cleanup, or to fund any number of things. But, because of the Cold War and the focus on national security, the decision was made to focus on military strength. Because of this decision with the dollars to back it up, the government succeeds in directing much of the energies of the scientific community into military research.

Why did scientists get drawn into this relationship? In simple terms, the rewards were tremendous in terms of money and prestige, especially in the late 1940s through the 1950s, and again in the 1980s, when defense money was flowing generously for those who worked on defense projects. They got the best technology; their requests for more funds were rarely denied, and they had the best lab space, more research assistance—all of these things made it very attractive to work on these projects. In some ways, the privilege status of a physicist during the Cold War period was akin to that of their counterparts in the Soviet Union, who in the Soviet Union were treated to material luxuries denied the rest of the population. An interesting intangible factor was the new high status of being a physicist. In a poll taken in 1964, respondents rated physicists the third most prestigious profession, up from number 15 in 1947.

So, the result of the attraction of working in defense projects was that many of the young, bright physicists who were coming out of graduate school in that period went into nuclear physics. In 1951, two-thirds of all the nation's engineers and scientists in the United States worked in defense-related research; that is an extraordinary figure. Later, this percentage declined somewhat. In 1980, it was down 30 percent to 40 percent. But, still, what this meant was that a big chunk of the country's technical elite had a personal, if indirect, stake in the Cold War.

Another characteristic of big science was the concentration of scientific research into large, expensive operations with costly equipment and teams of researchers. As President Eisenhower said when he left office, "The solitary inventor tinkering in his shop has been overshadowed by task forces of scientists in laboratories and testing fields." So, Eisenhower was noting this change that the postwar scientists was the team scientists, no longer those individual tinkerers.

In other words, big science has witness a climb of the small competitive entrepreneurs and the growth of the few monopoly businesses that win exclusive contracts. Government involvement in scientific research contributed to this trend by funding a small number of large projects at a few elite institutions, whether they are industries or private businesses. Again, just to give you an idea of the figures, in 1980, of all federal research and development money given to private industry, half of that money went to only eight firms. Likewise, of all federal research and development money given to universities, 90 percent went to eight universities, including the University of California. They funneled a lot of the federal money into these large projects, both in private and academic settings.

Since most research money, in general, came from defense agencies, that means that this unevenly distributed federal funding had a deleterious effect on competition. One could argue that the result was the reinforcement of this kind of monopoly science industry and the erosion of market competition.

Another aspect of this new relationship between science and government was that inevitably basic research was slighted for the benefits of applied projects that could be shown to be useful to the Defense Department.

As the Secretary of Defense, Charles Wilson, put it bluntly in the mid-1950s: "Basic research is when you don't know what you are doing." In other words, the Defense Department was much less eager to fund projects with no weapons applications or at least political usefulness in the Cold War, like the space race that—although was not direct weapons—had a broader political interest for the Cold War.

Of the defense research budget in 1980, for example, only 5 percent went into basic research, with the rest of it being designated for applied research and testing.

The result of this focus was an impressive list of military products that were produced—a range of weapons: ICBMs (intercontinental ballistic missiles), smart bombs, nuclear-powered submarines, surveillance satellites, thermonuclear warheads—all of which were produced with federal monies out of big projects.

The less obvious consequence of this strategy for research and development funding is that it narrowed the scope of scientific research. The development of a weapons program is the result of a limited targeted research project, not the offshoot of general advances in the basic scientist. If you look at the contrast, if you remember the atom bomb, the origins of the discovery of nuclear fission actually came out of this basic research, which was not directed towards any particular end and had no clear purpose in the 1920s when it was first being explored. With the advent of big-government-funded science based on these Cold War priorities, applied research took priority over the kind of broad experimentation that had once defined what scientists once called "pure science"; the consequence has been a focusing of scientific research. In order to get federal dollars, you must show certain usefulness to what the federal agencies are interested in having researched.

What are the broader consequences of this close relationship between science and the state during the Cold War period? It certainly seems clear that individual scientists in the 1960s had much less personal autonomy than their counterparts in the prewar period; that is, the state had encroached further into the realm of individual choice for scientists, with a resulting decline in the liberal principle of free enterprise. Of course, the best symbol of this contrast is that tinkering scientist of the prewar period, and the team scientist of the postwar period who works as part of a larger project not designed by that individual scientist.

Nevertheless, it is important to emphasize that the Cold War itself did not start the trend of state encroachment into individual autonomy, which is a process that begins already in the late 19th and early 20th centuries. Since that time, the state has increasingly made more demands of individuals, as well as taking more responsibility for helping them. This has been an ongoing process of the 20th century. What the Cold War did specifically is to reinforce a specific tradeoff between individual autonomy and national security, which justified expansion of state power into the realm of scientific research. Once again, we are left with the unresolved question of whether this process was ultimately necessary (or even positive) because it led to the victory of the Cold War, or whether it should be criticized as imitating the enemy's national defense industry—back to that question of ends versus means, again.

Whichever position is taken, however, it is important to recognize that a shift did take place, to acknowledge the shift and that it took place as a result of the Cold War and that this shift involved a tradeoff between what had been the practice of the "American way of life" and the goal of winning the war.

Lecture Thirty
The Welfare State

Scope:

Although the Cold War may have undermined liberal democratic practice in certain ways, it also provided the backdrop for a dramatic democratization of liberalism that came to be known as the *welfare state*. The postwar construction of the welfare state continued pre-World War II trends but also developed as an alternative to socialist economics, a democratic response to the communist critique of capitalist inequality. This lecture compares and contrasts the northern European welfare state, spearheaded by Social Democratic parties, and the American model, constructed on the foundations of Roosevelt's New Deal in the 1930s. The lecture concludes with a consideration of the significance of this development in the expansion of democratic citizenship rights from the political to the social realm.

Outline

I. The postwar construction of the welfare state continued pre-World War II trends but further developed as an answer to the socialist critique of capitalist inequality and as an attempt to better integrate the masses into a liberal democratic system.

   A. The welfare state that blossomed, first, in Western Europe during its reconstruction and, later, in the United States during the 1960s had its roots in prewar developments.

      1. As we discussed earlier, the Depression dealt a huge blow to the liberal confidence in a "self-regulating" market and a weak state presence in the economy, because millions were left unprotected by the crisis.

      2. In contrast, the states with booming economies during the Depression were fascist Nazi Germany and the communist USSR, both of which funneled massive state funds into production and exercised various levels of control over the economy.

      3. The case for state intervention was made in Western Europe, as well, by Social Democratic parties, which had

been pushing for social security measures to protect workers from the vagaries of the capitalist market.

B. In more theoretical terms, the Depression had inspired a major rethinking of liberal economic ideas by British economist John Maynard Keynes.

1. He argued that there was a middle ground between classic liberalism and a planned economy, where both government and private enterprise could work together.

2. If leaders wanted to save capitalism from Bolshevism, they needed new more flexible strategies, Keynes argued.

3. The key to flexibility was creating a greater role for government intervention, not simply to pursue development but to soften the impact of crises on individuals, what came to be known as a *safety net*.

4. The two roles came together in Keynes's analysis of unemployment.

C. In the 1930s, the only liberal country that began to adopt some of Keynes's ideas was the United States, with its New Deal.

1. The New Deal was a panoply of programs rather than a coherent scheme, but all programs shared the idea that government could help an ailing economy and that it should help people suffering its effects.

2. One set of programs aimed to provide economic assistance for those who were unemployed and impoverished.

3. The other set of programs aimed to jumpstart the economy through massive public spending, which was meant to put people back to work and boost consumer spending.

4. The success of the New Deal continues to be controversial today; both Keynesians and neo-conservatives refer to it to provide evidence for their opposing views about welfare, but either way, it marked a dramatic new path that postwar European states continued to follow.

II. While the New Deal marked a departure, after 1945, it was Western Europe that was the major testing ground for these ideas.

   A. One of the keywords of reconstruction was *cooperation*, between European countries and between formerly warring classes, as well as between business and labor.

   B. The problem of class warfare, which had led to both communist revolution and fascist reaction, was to be diffused through a generous social welfare system that provided health care, unemployment insurance, pensions, subsidized housing, and education.

   C. In postwar citizenship theory, the British sociologist T. H. Marshall defined three levels of citizenship that had been gradually achieved: in the 19th century, civil rights; in the early 20th century, political rights; and now, in the postwar world, social rights.

   D. At the same time, labor unions were brought on board through the establishment of cooperative relationships with business that would reduce strikes and facilitate collective bargaining.

   E. Scholars argue about where the major impetus for the welfare state lies.

   F. There were significant differences between countries in terms of the degree of state involvement and the level of corporatist planning, with the Scandinavian countries on one end and West Germany on the other.

III. In the United States, it was not until the Democratic administrations of the 1960s and the War on Poverty that the basic foundations of the New Deal were expanded.

   A. Even then, the different American context created a weaker version of state responsibility for individual welfare.

   B. In the early 1960s, first Kennedy, then Johnson pursued ambitious programs to reduce poverty.

   C. However, the targeting of specific groups was different from the European idea of universal social citizenship.

IV. In Europe, and to a lesser degree in the United States, the resulting welfare consensus worked spectacularly in the late

1950s and 1960s, until economic restructuring and the 1973 oil crisis undermined the dramatic growth that had fueled generous state programs.

A. Since the 1970s, politicians and economists have been arguing about the welfare state and dismantling parts of it, but no new consensus has emerged about the exact relationship between social rights and democratic stability.

B. Today, the future of the welfare state is subject both to theoretical and practical challenges. At stake is the question of what serves as the best basis for individuals to participate in a democratic society.

Essential Reading:

Donald Sassoon, *One Hundred Years of Socialism*, chapter 6, "Building Social Capitalism."

George Reid Andrews and Herrick Chapman, eds., *The Social Construction of Democracy, 1870–1990*, part 4, "Democracy and the Welfare State, 1930–1990."

Supplementary Reading:

J. Donald Moon, ed., *Responsibility, Rights and Welfare: The Theory of the Welfare State*.

T. H. Marshall, *Citizenship and Social Class and Other Essays*.

Questions to Consider:

1. In the United States, the defenders of *welfare capitalism* have been considerably weaker than in Europe, especially in the last two decades, so much so that the word *welfare* is used differently on each side of the Atlantic. In the United States, *welfare* often refers to demeaning handouts, while in Europe, it refers to a broader system of social organization and rights. What are the implications of such different meanings?

2. What do you think about the debate between defenders and critics of social rights and their relationship to citizens' ability to participate in their society?

Lecture Thirty—Transcript
The Welfare State

While the Cold War may have undermined liberal democratic practice in certain ways, it also provided—at least indirectly—for a dramatic democratization of liberalism that came to be known as the *welfare state*, which will be the topic of today's lecture.

The postwar construction of the welfare state continued pre-World War II trends but further developed as an answer to the communist critique of capitalist inequality and as an attempt to better integrate the masses into a liberal democratic system. In other words, with the memory of the deep political fishers of the interwar period, the postwar leaders try to imagine a new consensual political order that could bring all social and economic groups together. At the center of what became known in Western Europe as the postwar consensus was, then, an expanded idea of the nature of democratic citizenship that required a new role for the state in economic affairs. This was the welfare state, or welfare capitalism as it was sometimes referred to, which was a new hybrid system of economic principles.

The welfare state accepted the basic principles of capitalism, private property, free enterprise, and so on while promising to cushion the impact of its crises on those less-fortunate individuals and at the same time to redistribute its benefits more widely. In simple terms, it sacrificed part of classic liberal philosophy to save the basic capitalist system; that is, it abandoned the idea of the perfectly free economic individual and replaced it with an economic individual who was protected by the state.

We talked earlier about the context in which this transformation happens, that is, how the Depression sparked a serious crisis of confidence in the liberal capitalist system, especially in the idea of a "self-regulating" market and a laissez-faire state. The specter of passive governments watching as millions lost everything they had, with nowhere to turn, left a deep impression on people, as did the apparent economic vitality of the non-liberal regimes of Nazi Germany and the Soviet Union during the war. Their use of massive state funds to propel the economy and create jobs created—at least the image of—a vigorous response to the Depression, which contrasted and seemed preferable to many to the classic hands-off liberal economic model that was pursued in the West.

The case for the state intervening to protect the welfare of the population was also made in Western Europe before the war by the Social Democratic parties, which had been pushing for social security measures to protect workers from the vagaries of the labor market, especially after 1929. The Social Democratic parties were advocating for social insurance, for unemployment benefits, for low-income support, pensions, housing support, and the like. So, these are the pieces that are later going to become part of the welfare state. In particular, you see in Scandinavia, the Social Democratic parties before the war were able to lead coalition governments that in many cases put together versions of the welfare state that will not be more widely spread until after 1945.

In more theoretical terms, before the war, the Depression had inspired a major rethinking of liberal economic thought by British economist John Maynard Keynes, who published his major work, *The General Theory of Employment, Interest and Money*, in 1936. Keynes argued that there was a middle ground between traditional laissez-faire liberalism and socialism that would save the capitalist economy; that is, in between hands-off liberalism and a planned economy there was a middle ground where both government and private enterprise could share power. Keynes thought that laissez-faire was a principle that had worked well in its time in what he called the abundant 19th century.

Keynes argued that laissez-faire no longer applied in the 20th century, which was a period of scarcity as he said, and that if capitalism wanted to survive the challenge of Bolshevism in the 20th century that it had to be more flexible. In other words, Keynes proposed sacrificing the series of economic policies known as liberalism to save the basic economic structure of capitalism. The key to this flexibility, in Keynes theory, was creating a greater role for government intervention, both to pursue development and economic growth and to soften the impact of crises on individual citizens in what will become known as a *safety net*. As he defined the aims of this new plan, we should "pursue the transition from economic anarchy to a regime which deliberately aims at controlling and directing economic forces in the interest of social justice and social stability."

So, the key to Keynes economics was government intervention in the economy both to stimulate a sluggish economy and protect citizens from the brutality of economic crises.

These two roles came together in Keynes's analysis of unemployment, which was the central problem of the 1930s when he was writing. Classical economics, that is liberal economics, viewed unemployment as a function of overproduction, so they advocated that in the face of unemployment, we should keep wages low. But Keynes argued that unemployment was rooted in insufficient demand, and so he argued that the way to increase demand was to stimulate production by public words and by making societies' distribution and wealth more equal. So, government intervention could both jumpstart the economy through stimulating demand and address the needs of the unemployed worker at the same time. In this way, Keynes borrowed some of the sense of social responsibility from socialism but at the same time argued that it could be adopted to strengthen capitalism by raising wages; by redistributing income, the capitalist system could be strengthened, and there comes the idea of the middle ground.

In the 1930s—somewhat ironically, I guess—the major liberal country that adopted Keynes ideas was the United States. As the crises of the Depression worsened and fear of possible social revolution and unrest pressured the government, the United States—under President Franklin Roosevelt, who was elected in 1933—decided to undertake what was essentially a Keynesian experiment. The government tried to help pull the country out of the Depression. This experiment is known as the New Deal, and it came to represent a major, early attempt to find that middle ground between socialism and laissez-faire capitalism. The New Deal consisted more of a panoply of programs than a coherent plan; in other words, it was not an overt attempt to put Keynes into practice but it added up to that.

All of these programs shard the similar idea that the government could help the economy and that government could—and should—help people who were suffering from a depressed economy. As a result of these ideas, the New Deal put forth two types of programs. The first type was a safety net to provide programs for the unemployed and the poor—that could help them survive the economic crisis. The second set of programs was designed to jumpstart the economy in what Roosevelt called "intelligent direction" for the government to intervene. In other words, the Roosevelt administration was tacitly accepting the Keynesian idea that the government was both responsible for individual well-being and that it could actively work to create the conditions for prosperity. If you look at the first category of programs, we have acts for housing loans; building low-income housing; and the Social Security Act, which was a crucial turning point, which provided a government pension fund and unemployment insurance for those who could not find jobs. These programs implied for the first time that Americans not only had political rights but economic rights. What we get, at least on the implied level, is an expansion of the scope of democratic citizenship; that is, democratic citizenship includes something more than just the right to vote or the right to free speech.

In the second group of programs, we have the National Recovery Administration, which set industrial prices and limits on production; there was also a similar organization for limiting agricultural productions and introducing the provision for subsidies for farmers not to grow too much food. These programs implied that the economy was not self-regulating and that some sort of planning would produce better results than the anarchy of the market.

Also in this group of programs was a Works Project Administration (WPA) whose mission was to create jobs for unemployed people through big public works programs. They set artists to painting murals on public buildings, construction workers to build public housing, other workers to build roads and national parks, and so on. In other words, the government spent massive amounts of money in order to put people back to work. The idea behind this was that if you put people back to work, unemployment will be lowered while raising consumer demand and increasing demand for products. This is classic Keynesian economics, which advocated government deficit spending in a depression in order to raise the level of consumption and stimulate demand, which would then stimulate production.

Scholars still argue about the success of New Deal programs, that is, whether these programs stimulated the economy and recovery, or if it was really the Second World War and the rearmament that was the key factor in restarting the economy. Both Keynesians and neo-conservatives look back to the New Deal, either supporting it or attacking it in terms of backing up their own ideas about the welfare state.

Either way, whether you accept or reject the New Deal as an effective approach to the Depression, either way it marked a dramatic new path that postwar Western states continue to follow. Even though there is wide disagreement about its impact, no one can argue that there was a fundamental shift with the New Deal. There has never been a return to the idea of a purist model of laissez-faire economy. Even today, within the debates about the welfare state, few people seriously question completely dismantling the safety net and dismantling programs such as Social Security. So, that is not on the table; we have not gone back to a purist idea of laissez-faire capitalism.

While the New Deal marked a significant departure, after 1945, it was Western Europe that was the major testing ground for these new ideas. In the context of moral, physical, and economic destruction of Europe that we talked about last time, the key word of reconstruction was *cooperation,* between European countries and between formerly warring classes, as well as between business and labor. The sobering reality of where past antagonisms had led created a new climate of openness, broad coalitions, and a sensitivity to some of the limitations of prewar liberal regimes. So, it was a completely new political culture in this postwar period.

The problem of class warfare, which had led to both communist revolution and fascist reaction, was to be diffused through a generous social welfare system that provided health care, unemployment insurance, pensions, subsidized housing, and education. In most Western countries, it was precisely the Social Democratic parties who had been pushing these programs before the war and that now took the lead in forming broad coalition governments and in putting forth cooperative programs that explicitly dropped their former revolutionary rhetoric. The Social Democratic parties, after the war explicitly, dropped the idea that they were trying to overthrow capitalism eventually and accepted the idea that their role was not to overthrow it, but to manage the worse inequalities of the capitalist system. In this, they entered into a cooperative relationship with other parties rather than an antagonistic one. Moreover, the viability of their ambitious plans to redistribute income and to protect individuals depended on a flourishing capitalism because there had to be enough growth produced to be redistributed. These were completely different Social Democratic parties.

While the Social Democratic parties led the way, even conservative parties realized that the mood had shifted. As the German Christian Democratic Party Program of 1947 declared, "The new structure of the German economy must start from the realization that the period of uncontained rule by private capitalism is over." So, there is a new mood across the political spectrum. Out of this new mood came the basic idea that the state had a responsibility for the economic welfare of its population. The flip side of that responsibility was that individuals had new rights. What was implicit in the prewar New Deal becomes explicit in the postwar welfare state—the idea that individuals have certain economic rights to certain benefits regardless of their income.

The most famous postwar theorist of citizenship, the British sociologist
T. H. Marshall defined what he called the three levels of citizenship. The first level was civil rights, which he said Europe had achieved in the 19th century—the rights to free speech, free association, and so on. The second level of citizenship was political rights, which had been achieved, he said, in the early 20th century—essentially the right to vote. But now, Marshall said, was a third level of citizenship, which he called social rights, which were going to be achieved in the postwar period. As social rights to welfare, health, security, and education developed, he argued, class distinctions would be eliminated and the universal promise of democratic citizenship that had been raised with the French Revolution would finally be realized. Without these social rights, he argued, individuals could not fully utilize their political and civil rights. The three levels of citizenship were interconnected. In order to participate politically as citizens, people needed the kind of economic and social stability to do that. So, the implicit extension of democratic rights that we see in the New Deal gets explicitly articulated.

At the same time, as new social rights were being articulated, formerly antagonistic labor movements were brought into the process of making democratic citizens through the establishment of a series of cooperative relationships with business, following a model that had been set in Scandinavia before the war—models in which collective bargaining arrangements were institutionalized so that business and labor could cooperate in a system that would reduce labor strikes and facilitate negotiations—and in fact, it worked very well. Unionized workers won unprecedented security on the job with fixed seniority rules, fringe benefits, job protection, and the recognition of union bargaining rights. As the economy recovered and wages rose, this led to one of the least contentious periods of industrial relationships in the modern European economy.

While labor won tangible benefits, capitalist employers also gained a more stable workforce, and as wages were rising this anchored a new consumer-driven economy in which production could rise as well; again, this is classic Keynesian economics.

What held this cooperative relationship together? Partly, it was commitment of the government and the parties to make this work, but also it was partly the dramatic growth of a postwar economy that helped anchor this new system.

Scholars still argue about what the major impetus of the welfare state was, what was the factor that really pushed the development of this new idea of the relationship between the state and the economy. Some scholars emphasize the role of social democracy, that it was the left who was pushing these programs from below; it was an achievement of the working class, an achievement of the left—that they had to win the recognition of social rights.

On the other hand, some scholars argue that it was simply timing; that is, the antipathy to prewar economic policies was so great, the Depression had such a great impact on people across the political spectrum, that the postwar governments would have implemented some kind of welfare system regardless of whether the Social Democratic parties were pushing it or not.

Finally, another position argues that the political decisions were much less important than the growth, the level of economic prosperity, which made welfare capitalism a win-win situation for everyone.

Whichever factor carried the most weight, the transformation in political culture across Europe—which created the space for this new consensus—was remarkable, even though there were significant differences between European countries, especially in terms of the degree of state intervention and involvement in corporatist planning, with the Scandinavian countries on one end of the spectrum and West Germany on the other end. In Sweden, for example, there is the strong position of the Social Democratic Party, remember they had been in power already in the 1930s and they were at the head of government coalitions from the 1930s through the 1970s. They took the lead in forming a more socialist version of the welfare state. As the prime minister from the Social Democratic Party said in 1932: "The role of the welfare state should be to break down all the social and economic barriers that now divide citizens into privilege and disfavored, into rulers and dependents, into rich and poor, the glutted and the destitute, the plundered and the plunderers."

So, building on prewar rhetoric and reforms, Sweden established national health insurance in 1956, a national pension plan in 1959, and followed an active full-employment strategy. Sweden marks one end of the spectrum, and Britain followed a reduced version of the Scandinavian model, under a postwar labor government that established a whole set of programs including the National Health Service, established in 1948, which was used by 95 percent of the population by 1950. The Education Act of 1944 guaranteed secondary education for all students and a dramatic increase in progressive income taxes to redistribute income.

In contrast, West Germany pursued a more market-centered approach using incentives to establish what one German politician called "the free enterprise economy with a conscience." Germany was the most physically devastated country in Europe, and the emphasis there was on simply growth and recovery, getting business back on its feet rather than the focus in other Western European countries on protection of citizens. Nevertheless, even the West German state implemented widespread social security measures, including a state insurance plan for all workers regardless of employment.

In general terms, if we look across Europe, the institutional frameworks of the welfare state were in place by the mid-1950s across Europe.

The United States was somewhat different. Despite the early experiment of the New Deal, the United States was actually further behind Western Europe in terms of putting some of these programs into practice. It was not really until the 1960s and the democratic administrations of that period that the basic foundations of the New Deal are really implemented and expanded. Even then, the American context is different; that is, the political culture of postwar America is not the same. You have a weaker history of class struggle and of social democracy. So, you don't have that impetus to push for these programs; the country is focusing more on Cold War anti-communism so there is that different focus. Finally, in the United States, there is a greater skepticism about the state and the state's role in society and in the economy. All of these things created a weaker version of state responsibility for individual welfare in the United States and in Western Europe.

But the impetus for revisiting the New Deal principles came in the early 1960s, as evidence of endemic poverty in the United States began to undermine confidence in the classic liberal assumptions that economic growth was the path to prosperity for all. I think the key turning point was the publication of a book in 1962 by the American socialist Michael Harrington called *The Other America*. It was a very influential book when it came out at the time, and it was an exploration of poverty in the United States in which he argued that some 25 percent of the United States population lived in poverty, and that the government needed to take an active role in reducing that, thus becoming a turning point.

Before his death, President John Kennedy—as a result of the response to this book—initiated a discussion about expanding the government security programs, but he died before he could pursue that, and this becomes eventually Lyndon Johnson's War on Poverty, which he initiates at the beginning of his administration.

The poverty legislation, which comes out of Johnson's War on Poverty, begins with the Economic Opportunity Act, which funded a number of programs, from Head Start Preschool Education to the Job Corp for inner-city youth. The centerpiece of the package was a community action program, which was supposed to combine government funding with local participation in community welfare programs, especially in inner-city poor areas of the country.

The evaluation of the effectiveness of these programs is controversial. Many of those programs were too under-funded to really evaluate their impact. Perhaps the most wide reaching of the programs that are most accepted today were Medicare and Medicaid (which were established under the Johnson administration), which provided medical insurance to the elderly and to the poor.

If we put Johnson's War on Poverty in the context of a larger evolution of the welfare state in this period, we still have to make a distinction between Western Europe and the United States. In other words, there was something that was very different about the War on Poverty, which was targeting specific groups and targeting specific core sectors of the population in trying to pull them out of poverty. That idea of pulling a disadvantaged group out of poverty was quite different from the idea in Western Europe of universal social rights.

So, even the broader security net in the United States, which remained in place, things such as Social Security that theoretically applied to everybody, even Social Security is linked to specific responsibilities, meaning Social Security comes from the monies that workers put into the fund. It still does not embrace the idea that people have basic rights to free higher education, health insurance, and job security—all of the basic cornerstones of the European welfare state.

In Europe, and to a lesser degree in the United States, the welfare consensus worked well into the 1970s, until the oil crisis of 1973, along with the basic restructuring of the global economy, began to undermine that predictable growth that had fueled these generous state programs.

Since the 1970s, economists and politicians have been arguing about the welfare state and dismantling parts of it, but no new consensus has emerged about the exact relationship between social rights and democracy. At stake in this rethinking of the welfare state (since the 1970s) is the question of what provides the best social and economic foundation for individuals to participate as equal citizens in a democratic society.

Lecture Thirty-One
The Process of Decolonization

Scope:

For the next eight lectures, we shift back to the non-Western world, which underwent a dramatic political transformation—that is, decolonization—in the first decades after the Second World War. This lecture introduces the phenomenon of decolonization and its symbolic importance in creating what became known as the *Third World*. It focuses on the mechanics of decolonization in Asia and Africa and tries to explain the diverse nature of the process, especially in terms of how early it happened and how peaceful the transition was. We compare the different policies of the major imperial powers, Britain and France, as well as those of the Netherlands, Belgium, and Portugal, and look at the difference between settler and non-settler colonies. Finally, we summarize the factors that explain the overall speed of the decolonization process, most of it concentrated in the 15 years following the Second World War.

Outline

I. Although the Cold War and the welfare state were crucial to defining the postwar world order, for the non-Western world, the fundamental transformation was the process of decolonization. Within 15 years after the Second World War, the majority of colonies had become independent nations, an extraordinarily rapid process that changed the face of what came to be known as the *Third World*, in contrast to the Western *First World* and the Soviet *Second World*.

   A. What did decolonization mean for the new world order?
      1. On the one hand, it confirmed the decline of European power, while on the other hand, it signaled the demand of the non-Western world for more power.
      2. The big question was whether the non-Western countries could chart their own political and economic futures and become players in a new world order defined by opposing superpowers.

3. In the 1950s and 1960s, when many of the new nations were created, there was a great deal of optimism that they could take a place as equals in a new global order defined by national independence.
4. But for all but a few ex-colonial nations, the hopes of independence have not been realized. Over the next several lectures, we will look at the problems faced by decolonized nations, the ways they tried to overcome those problems, and the successes and failures that resulted.

B. To begin with, we need to understand how and why centuries of colonization were suddenly reversed.
1. For decolonization to occur, two things had to happen.
2. First, European countries had to relinquish control, and second, the colonies had to demand independence.
3. Scholars argue about the balance of each force, but the overall interaction between "push" and "pull" was similar.

C. The degree to which the European countries were willing to give up their colonies varied widely.
1. In 1945, there were five remaining colonial powers, two major (Britain and France) and three minor (Belgium, Portugal, and the Netherlands).
2. Britain and France had extensive holdings in Asia and Africa.
3. The other three had one or two important colonies, also in Asia or Africa.
4. The British were the first and most accepting of decolonization, partly because of a plan to integrate ex-colonies into a federation called the *Commonwealth* and partly because the independence movement in India had been forcing them to face the issue for a longer time.
5. The French took a longer time to accept independence as opposed to self-government, especially in such colonies as Algeria, which were considered part of France.
6. Belgium, Portugal, and the Netherlands were the most uncompromising. As minor European powers, the stakes of remaining an "imperial" nation were greater for each of these countries.

7. Where colonial power resisted, the level of violence was higher and the influence of communism tended to be greater.

D. Despite these differing levels of acceptance, all the countries eventually gave in. Why?

   1. Partly this result was due to the external pressure of the United States and the USSR, both of which were against formal empires and criticized them as evil and exploitative.

   2. Perhaps as important as these pressures were the financial reasons; in the 19th century, formal colonies anchored European power, but in the 20th century, they only weighed down the weaker European nations.

   3. Simply the example of the two new superpowers, which maintained economic dominance without formal empires, set the pace for the future.

II. All the imperial powers finally acquiesced to decolonization, but the "push" from below was crucial in setting the process in motion, especially in Asia, where the combination of prewar movements and Japanese occupation created a strong momentum.

   A. Some argue that the process should be described as *national liberation* to emphasize the active role of the colonized.

   B. The independence of India and Pakistan in 1947 was the major turning point and is the best example of what became the *British model* of negotiated independence, propelled by a powerful nationalist movement. Following the same model, Britain gave up its other Asian colonies, Ceylon and Burma.

   C. But a powerful nationalist movement could also lead to bloody conflict when the European power refused to negotiate, as occurred in Indonesia. When the Japanese left in 1945, Indonesian nationalists under Sukarno took power, but the Dutch fought for four years to retake their old colony before finally granting independence in 1949.

   D. A similar but more protracted struggle occurred in French Indochina, where a strong nationalist movement declared independence in 1945 and fought France's attempt to recover its colony until the French left in 1954.

E. What made Vietnam different than Indonesia or India was the division of the nationalist movement between communists and liberals, with the former, under Ho Chi Minh, in the strongest position in 1945. While the French began by resisting independence, they ended by fighting on the side of the liberals against the communists.

F. Thus, the struggle in Vietnam, later picked up by the United States, moved from the terrain of decolonization to that of the Cold War.

III. As decolonization in Asia was winding down, it was heating up in Africa. Between the mid-1950s and the mid-1960s, virtually the entire continent decolonized, with a few holdouts.

A. How do we explain the rapidity of the process in Africa, given the general lack of strong independence movements?

B. At this point, the issue was largely timing. A new generation of African leaders, politicized during the Second World War, was inspired by the decolonization in Asia. At the same time, the European countries were starting to accept the inevitability of the process.

C. Still, however, there were different paths to independence, largely depending on whether the colonies were settler or non-settler.

D. In most non-settler colonies, the process was peaceful and rapid, carried out through negotiations with African elites.

    1. Perhaps the best example of this path was the independence of the Gold Coast, which became Ghana in 1957.

    2. Kwame Nkrumah's Convention People's Party, inspired by Gandhi, organized a nationalist movement that negotiated a decade-long transfer of power.

    3. There were exceptions to this rule of peaceful transfer, especially if no nationalist movement was able to accept power. In the Belgian Congo (Zaire), the combination of the lack of any educated elite and the Belgian decision to abruptly leave in 1960 opened a brutal civil war.

E. In settler colonies, it was the resistance of the local European settlers that made the process of independence more contentious, in most cases taking the form of guerrilla war.

1. In Kenya, 200,000 rebels joined the Land Freedom Army in the early 1950s, but it was not until 1963 that independence was achieved.
2. In Algeria, one million French settlers turned a guerrilla rebellion that began in the mid-1950s into a civil war, which finally ended with independence in 1962.
3. Similar revolutions ousted settler colonies in Angola and Mozambique (1975) and Rhodesia (1980).
4. The most intractable settler colony was South Africa, with more than four million white settlers. It was the only case where power was transferred to a white-controlled government in 1962, until a guerrilla war by the African National Congress achieved a democratic transition in 1994.

F. With the exception of the last settler colonies, by the mid-1960s, the imperial world order of the 19th century had virtually vanished overnight as the result of a remarkable confluence of changing political, economic, and ideological realities.

Essential Reading:

Leslie Derfler and Patricia Kollander, eds., *An Age of Conflict: Readings in 20th Century European History*, chapter 10, "The End of European Empire."

Ho Chi Minh, "Declaration of Independence," in Mark Kishlansky, ed., *Sources of World History*, vol. 2, pp. 349–350.

Supplementary Reading:

M. E. Chamberlain, *Decolonization: The Fall of the European Powers.*

Questions to Consider:

1. It is difficult to absorb the magnitude of transformation that occurred in such a short time, especially given that it involved so many different actors in so many different regions at the same time. Can we really comprehend such a dramatic shift in the prevailing culture?
2. Ironically, after decolonization, the main region that experienced rapid economic growth was Europe, which seemed to

demonstrate that colonies were economic liabilities more than assets. What implications can be drawn from this fact?

Lecture Thirty-One—Transcript
The Process of Decolonization

While the Cold War and the welfare state were crucial to defining the postwar world order, for the non-Western world, the fundamental transformation was the process of decolonization.

Within years after the Second World War, the majority of colonies had become independent nations, an extraordinarily rapid process that changed the face of what came to be known as the *Third World*, in contrast to the spheres defined by the United States and the Soviet Union.

So, what did decolonization mean for the new world order in the postwar period? On the one hand, the process of decolonization confirmed the decline of European power; it signaled the end of Europe's claim to rule the rest of the world. But, of course, from the Third World, it signaled the demand of these new countries for more power in the new world order. In other words, decolonization symbolizes the emergence of the Third World as a potentially independent entity for the first time in world politics. In fact, Third World nations usually define the process not as decolonization, but as *national liberation*—a more activist term.

We have talked about the two new superpowers as the major players in the new era, but now we need to talk about the introduction of dozens of new independent countries in Asia, Africa, and the Middle East. The big question was whether the non-Western countries could chart their own political and economic futures and become players in this new world order defined by the opposing superpowers.

In the 1950s and 1960s, there was a great deal of optimism among these new countries. They could finally come into their own and emerge from the shadow of submission that had been defined by the colonial world and take their rightful place as equals in the new global order that was defined by national self-determination for all and not just for the privileged few. Obviously, for all but a few ex-colonial nations, the hopes of independence had not been fully realized. Over the next several lectures, we are going to be looking at the problems faced by these new ex-colonial nations, the ways they tried to overcome these problems, and some of the failures and successes along the way.

In this lecture, we are going to try to answer the first question of why the whole process happened to begin with. Why do we get a sudden reversal of this century-long process of empire building when the primary political reality of 1900, which was empire, suddenly vanishes from the face of the world in a space of about 15 years?

In simple terms, the process of decolonization required two things. First, the European countries had to relinquish control, and second, of course, the colonies had to demand that they relinquish it. Scholars and nationalists still argue about which was the primary impulse, the "pulling" or the "pushing." Was this process decolonization or was it national liberation? Was it something that was demanded, or something that was given? The balance between these forces was different in each case, but, in general, we can say both contributed to the end of empire.

By the end of World War Two, the European empire was still largely intact, so it is really a postwar process entirely. There were five main colonial powers remaining if we don't include the United States, which gave the Philippines independence in 1946, directly after the war. Those five colonial powers were Britain and France—the two major powers—and three smaller powers—Belgium, the Netherlands, and Portugal. Britain and France had extensive holdings in both Asia and Africa, while the other three had one or two important colonies. Portugal had Mozambique and Angola in Southern Africa. Belgium had the Belgium Congo in Central Africa, and the Netherlands had Indonesia.

Thus, the primary focus of colonial empires was Asia and Africa. Latin America had achieved its independence earlier in the 19th century, and Middle Eastern countries were given independence either during the war or directly after the war.

If we look at the attitudes of the "imperial" powers in the postwar period, they differ greatly as to how accepting they would be of decolonization, and this affected the process of decolonization in each of their colonial empires.

The British policy was generally the most accepting of decolonization, with the hope that the newly decolonized countries would join the *British Commonwealth* and thus, retain certain ties to the former colonial power. The British Commonwealth was a federation of British colonies and ex-colonies that was established to keep economic and cultural ties with the mother country. It had been established in 1931 with the Statute of West Minster, which included Australia, New Zealand, Ireland, and South Africa. It recognized full political independence for all of the federated countries, but established common ties through common loyalty to the British Crown and a common sense of history. The Commonwealth, in other words, helped the British Empire undergo that painful transition from being an imperial power to being simply another country; at least, it gave the British a sense of continued international prestige and presence.

Another important factor in changing British attitudes and making the British more accepting was its experience with the long independence struggle in India. Britain had really been faced with this issue for decades because of the "push" for the Indian nationalist movement. Even though the British had no direct plan in 1945 for independence in India, it had already given India a great deal of government in the years before the war, especially with the Government of India Act in 1935. The Government of India Act had been trying to hold off independence through reforms. So, it was not that they were undergoing a gradual process towards independence. What happens is that the turning over of increasing powers to the Indians establishes a president and momentum that is then hard to reverse in the postwar period. When Britain finally agrees to Indian independence after the war, then this sets the pace for the rest of the British Empire.

France, in contrast to Britain, had a much more difficult time in coming to terms with independence of its colonies. This is partly because there is absolutely no discussion of this in the French Empire in the prewar period. There is not, as for Britain, the Indian model pushing the envelope. For example, in a meeting of French colonial civil servants in 1944, which was to draw up proposals for imperial reorganization after the war, there was not even a consideration that independence would be an option. As the preamble to this document declared categorically, "The ends of the civilization work accomplished by France and the colonies exclude any idea of autonomy, all possibility of evolution outside the French block of the empire. The eventual constitution even in the future of self-government in the colonies is denied." So, there is categorical refusal to even consider the possibility. What France tries to do after the war is to end discontent by giving the colonies more representation within the French Empire in what becomes known as "French Union." After the war, they allowed the colonies to elect representatives directly to the government in Paris. In initial negotiations with nationalists in Algeria and Indochina, the French refused to talk about any reforms that did not reinforce the French Empire. It took the French a long time to accept that these conceptions of representation, of self-rule, were not enough any longer because the French simply could not admit that the empire was not a part of France. As Charles DeGaulle at one point in these early years said, "Giving Algeria independence would be like cutting off the right arm of France." As a result of this attitude, the first French colonies to go—which were Algeria and Vietnam—were violent and protracted struggles. After these initial colonies, the French began to realize what was happening; they realized the inevitability of decolonization, and then they adopted an attitude that was more like the British, an attitude of acceptance and negotiation.

If we look at the attitudes of the other three minor imperial powers, these held the most uncompromising attitudes, the most resistance to the process of decolonization. If Britain was willing to give independence early on, and the French were willing to give representation or some type of self-rule, the other three were committed to giving as few concessions as possible and holding onto their colonies at all costs for as long as possible. None of these three countries were major powers any longer; they were minor powers in the world, and in some sense, their stake in the remaining colonial powers was greater because of this.

In one classic study on the Dutch struggle to maintain its last colony of West New Guinea for more than 12 years, a tiny colony even after Indonesian independence, the author emphasized the psychological motives more than economic advantages. At the root of the refusal of the Dutch to let go of West New Guinea, he argued, there was a frustrated nationalism, an insecurity and inferiority complex that were nursed over several centuries of declining Dutch power. West New Guinea had become a symbol of the last presence of the Dutch in the world, the last symbol of national grandeur, we might say. Similar arguments would be made about Belgium and Portugal. Portugal had once been a great world empire and its African colonies are the last remnant of that period of national greatness.

What was the impact of these contrasting attitudes on the decolonization process? In very general terms, the level of violence was higher in the cases where the European countries resisted more. In those cases of greater resistance—whether Algeria, or Indochina, or Indonesia—the violence of the process tended to be greater.

Second, in the influence of communism, national liberation movements tended to be greater in the cases where the European countries resisted more, that is, general differences depending upon the contrasting attitudes of the European powers.

However, despite these dramatic differences in attitude, eventually everyone gave independence to their colonies; the process happened, and it still happened fairly rapidly. Why did this happen? Partly because the European countries were pressured by the United States and the Soviet Union. The two superpowers were against imperialism, at least against formal imperialism, which they criticized as evil and exploitative. The two major powers of the postwar period were pressuring against it. Perhaps as important as these moral or political pressures were the financial reasons; in the 19th century, formal colonial empires had anchored European power, but in the 20th century, they were like economic weights. Simply the example of the United States as the major economic power of the period and not being a colonial empire showed the way towards a different kind of economic relationship with the world. At some point, most of the European colonial powers realized that their economic recovery was actually hindered by having colonies, and this point was only reinforced by the fact that European economic recovery after 1955 was actually paralleled by the decline in their colonies. It seemed that the more they were willing to let go of their colonies, the quicker they recovered.

While all the imperial powers finally acquiesced to decolonization, the "push" from below is crucial in setting the process in motion. Some have argued that *decolonization* is too passive a word to describe the process, that *national liberation* captures the active nature of this process. In this reading, the process of decolonization should be tracked, not in European Parliaments but in Third World movements. The return of Gandhi to India in 1915, the emergence of nationalism during the First World War, the Japanese conquest of European empires, the victory of Mao in the Communist Party in China in 1949, and Kwame Nkrumah's return to the Gold Coast in

1947—all of these would be decisive moments in a process that was defined as *national liberation* as opposed to *decolonization*.

The best evidence that supports this perspective, that independence was something seized from the West, was precisely that decolonization begins in those countries that have the strongest nationalist movements. For this reason, the process of decolonization begins in Asia, where the combination of prewar movements and Japanese occupation created a fertile locale for getting the ball rolling. In this process, the earliest major event (as I mentioned earlier) was the severing of India and Pakistan from the British Empire in 1947. This, more than any other event, really turns the tide in making people both in Europe and the Third World realize that it was the beginning of the end. It made sense that India should go first, given that it had the strongest and most solid nationalist tradition. India provided a model, not only for nationalist agitation—that is, that many people look to the Indian national movement as a model—but it also becomes a model for the British mode of independence in giving increasing power to the nationalist movement in a negotiated, prolonged transition. In the wake of Indian and Pakistanian independence, Britain gave up its other South Asian colonies in Ceylon, which becomes Sri Lanka and Burma, also in 1947; so, the entire Asian-British Empire goes in one fell swoop.

However, a powerful nationalist movement did not mean a peaceful transition when the European power resisted, and this is the case in Indonesia when a European power refused to negotiate independence. The Japanese had overthrown the Dutch administration during the war, so that by the time the Dutch tried to return in 1945, local nationalists under the charismatic leader named Sukarno had already established themselves in power. Instead of accepting the inevitable, the Dutch decided to fight, to reestablish the colonial empire. So, they fought a brutal war for more than four years until they finally realized they lacked the military means to both defeat the nationalists and run a hostile country. Eventually, Indonesia won independence in 1949, not long after India but through a very different process defined by the distinction between British and Dutch attitudes.

A similar but even more protracted struggle occurred in French Indochina, where the Japanese occupation (similar to Indonesia) had ousted the French Empire during the war and left the space for a nationalist movement to come in and declare independence in 1945. The Vietnamese Declaration of Independence, which was issued in 1945, says, "We have wrested our independence from the Japanese not the French." In their mind, the French were already gone, and now 1945 symbolized their own independence from the Japanese. What happens in Indochina is that after seven years of an increasingly unpopular and seemingly un-winnable war, the French finally give up trying to recover their colony in 1954. But—and this is one reason that the war drags on for seven years—what makes Vietnam so different from Indonesia or India was the strong communist influence in the nationalist movement. In a sense, Vietnam looks much more like China than it does these other models. In both Vietnam and China, there was a split in the nationalist movement back from the 1920s, between a communist-dominated and a non-communist Western-oriented movement. The communist movement was called the *Viet Minh* under the leadership of Ho Chi Minh. Also, as in China, the communist movement in the north had gained support in the 1930s and 1940s through carrying out local land reform, land redistribution movements, and community-building programs in its strongholds in the north of Vietnam. By 1945, the Viet Minh were the strongest nationalist force in Vietnam. What happens, then, when the French come back in 1945 is that, at first, they try to reestablish colonial power, much as the Dutch did in Indonesia. But by the end of the war, the French have turned from trying to reestablish their colonial power to fighting a war with the non-communist south against the communist north. The colonial struggle in Vietnam turned from being one about decolonization to being one about preventing the spread of communism, and it turns into a Cold War issue.

By 1954, the French had finally been defeated by a combination of the Chinese who had come in to help Ho Chi Minh's forces in the north, and the French agreed to leave. The only concession they were able to win was a divided Vietnam, a southern non-communist sphere in the northern communist sphere, much like occurred in Korea. In the south, the United States helped find and install a new leader, Ngo Dinh Diem, and after that Vietnam becomes simply part of the Cold War struggle to define the spread or the containment of communism.

Just about the time that decolonization winds down in Asia in the mid-1950s, it revs up in Africa. In fact, between the mid-1950s and the mid-1960s, almost the entire African continent—with a handful of exceptions—went from being colonies to independent nations, again, a remarkably rapid transition. By 1975, there were 46 ex-colonies that had become new nations.

How do we explain the rapidity of the process in Africa, given the fact that you don't have the strong nationalist movement that existed in Asia? Partly, I think, the issue here is timing. A new generation of nationalist leaders had been politicized by the Second World War, in which they were drafted to fight for the colonial powers and then returned home to being subjugated colonial subjects again. This generation of leaders who had become the nationalist leaders was politicized by the war. In this state, they watched and were inspired by the process of Asian independence; in particular, the Indian movement was looked at and followed by many of the African leaders. At the same time, of course, Asian independence had begun to convince the European powers of the inevitability of the process, so their letting go in Africa was easier and quicker than most cases.

Still, despite this general trend, you have two different models in Africa, essentially based on the distinction between settler and non-settler colonies. In most non-settler colonies, the model was peaceful transition carried out through negotiations with African elites and colonial powers. The most successful of these peaceful transitions was the first colony to achieve independence in this way, the Gold Coast, which had been the most prosperous of the British African colonies, and which becomes Ghana in 1957. It was successful largely because it followed, in a sense, the Indian model it had developed by the late 1950s—a fairly popular and well-organized nationalist movement under the leadership of Kwame Nkrumah. He was typical of the Western-educated elite. He had gone to the United States to get his Ph.D. and returned to the Gold Coast in 1948. He formed a new political organization called the Convention People's Party, and he began to organize a mass movement modeled on Gandhi's nationalist movement in India. They organized mass rallies, boycotts, strikes, and so on. What happens, then, is that the British eventually give more power to Nkrumah's party in a gradual transition that transpires over the course of the decade until they achieve actual independence in 1957. However, this method of peaceful transfer of power did not always work well either, in particular, where there was no nationalist infrastructure to take power. That happens, in particular, in the Belgium Congo, where the Belgians leave dramatically and very quickly in 1960, but there is no infrastructure in place to establish even the beginning of a stable government.

So, the combination in the Belgium Congo of the lack of any indigenous, educated elite and the Belgian decision to simply leave abruptly without this prolonged transition, as in the *British model*, meant that their exodus in 1960 opened a period of brutal civil war that is not ended until the seizure of power in the mid-1960s by the self-serving dictator, Mobutu, who remains in power until he is overthrown in 1997. Clearly, the nature of Belgium's colonial rule, which had made no effort to create a local administration or to educate the population, left this ex-colony woefully unprepared for the basic requirements of self-government.

The second model of African independence was in the settler colonies, where the problem was the local resistance of European settlers rather than the colonial powers that slowed down the process. The main settler colonies were Algeria, Rhodesia, Kenya, and South Africa. Because of resistance in these colonies, the struggle for independence turned violent, with African nationalists turning to revolutionary guerrilla tactics to try and attain independence. The guerilla war began in Kenya in the early 1950s, with the formation of the Land Freedom Army, which began a campaign of terror.

At its height in 1954, some 200,000 rebels were involved in the Kenyan struggle. The British first crushed this movement in 1956, but then it finally forced the British into negotiations with the non-violent nationalists under Jomo Kenyatta, and in 1963, Kenya achieves independence.

Algeria was the second case of a settler colony achieving independence, and here the struggle is even more violent, I think, largely because there were 1 million French settlers in Algeria compared to thousands in Kenya. Not only did 2 percent of the French population live in Algeria, the capital was only 500 miles south of Marseilles, so there is a sense of Algeria being much closer to France. Algerian nationalists organized a guerrilla organization, the National Liberation Front, in the mid-1950s. At first, the French repressed this organization, but they finally grant independence in 1962.

Similar revolutions ousted settler colonies in Portuguese Angola and Mozambique in 1975, as well as British Rhodesia in 1980. The most intractable settler colony was South Africa, which was the only case in which the colonial power actually gave independence to the white settler colony. Here again, the number of settlers is important; 4 million European settlers created an intractable problem for the British government. In that case, black nationalists continued a revolutionary guerrilla war under the African National Congress until both sides finally agreed to a negotiated solution in 1990.

If we sum up the whole picture, then, the majority of the decolonization process occurred during the 15 years after the Second World War. In those 15 years, dozens of new countries were formed, solidifying their identity by entering into the new international body of the United Nations. If we ask the question of why it happened so fast, it was clearly the result of a remarkable confluence of changing political, economic, and ideological realities. No colonial power gave up without being pushed, whether through violent or non-violent means, and each colonial power had to come to the realization that it was more trouble to hold onto their empires than to give them up.

By the mid-1950s, it was also becoming apparent to Europe that colonies could be as much of an economic drag as a benefit. Europe began its economic recovery in the 1950s, which seemed to support the idea that Europe did not need colonies.

After decolonization, Europe continued to recover and flourish economically, seemingly unscathed by the end of an empire domination. Thus, only a few decades after the war, the idea of colonial empires vanished from the world's consciousness in one of the most astounding transformations in world history.

Lecture Thirty-Two
Challenges for Post-Colonial Societies

Scope:

Decolonization raised tremendous economic and political hopes for dozens of new countries, but moving from formal independence to political stability and economic prosperity proved a daunting task that few achieved. This lecture examines, in general terms, the serious problems faced by these new post-colonial nations. It focuses on such issues as economic dependency and poverty and the debates over neo-colonialism, the conflicts provoked by ethnic and religious diversity, the lack of an experienced political elite, and the influence of Cold War politics.

Outline

I. The process of forming a politically and economically stable and independent state after decolonization was a daunting task, and there were a number of issues that were difficult for democratic governments to resolve.

   A. The combination of optimism and sobriety expressed by new leaders was well articulated by Indonesian President Sukarno at the 1955 conference organized for ex-colonial nations at Bandung.

   B. But most of the new states from this period did not gain self-reliance and prosperity.

II. The first general problem was the Cold War itself, which distracted the superpowers from real development needs and turned countries into pawns in larger global power games.

   A. In particular, as Ghana's Nkrumah complained, the superpowers focused a great deal of aid on military equipment and weapons to wage their proxy wars, instead of on economic assistance.

   B. The militarization of Third World regimes helped fuel protracted civil wars that further devastated these states, physically, economically, and politically.

C. The impact of the Cold War in Africa provides a good example of proxy wars in Somalia and Ethiopia, as well as Angola.

III. More endemic than the Cold War were the staggering economic problems faced by virtually all the new countries, partly as a result of colonialism and partly as a result of preexisting poverty, although scholars have argued about the weight of these two factors.

A. As we discussed earlier in regard to China, colonial economic development focused on the export of raw materials and the import of European industrial goods. Thus, most new countries were left with little industrial base.

B. Some scholars have argued that these countries were better off than before colonialism, which at least constructed the boundaries of a market economy.

C. Critics of this proposition argue that simply citing statistics of increased import-export activity does not prove that the country was better off economically. The problem, these critics argue, is that these countries were pulled into a global market economy in which they could not compete.

D. One of the most widely read critics of colonialism was Frantz Fanon, a French-trained psychiatrist and nationalist from colonial Martinique, who became involved in the Algerian struggle for independence. His book *The Wretched of the Earth* became a veritable handbook for Third World national liberation movements.

IV. The debates about economic dependence continued after political independence, and critics argued that the transition from economic dependence to independence was made more difficult by forms of neo-colonialist control.

A. Ghana's Nkrumah laid out this critique in a 1965 book.

B. He argued that the methods of dependence could take different shapes.

C. In extreme cases, direct military intervention could be used.

D. The most endemic military control was established by the French government over their former African colonies.

E. Most often, more subtle limits on economic policy were placed by the terms of loans and the mounting debt racked up through loans made for essential capital investments in infrastructure.

F. Thus, the European economic community set up special trade relationships with African nations that reinforced dependency.

G. Alternatively, loan centers, such as the World Bank or the International Monetary Fund, imposed unpopular domestic austerity programs as a condition of continued aid.

H. The necessity or efficacy of these economic limits is still hotly debated today by economists, politicians, and Third World leaders. Whether we see them as a cause or a result of economic dependence, they certainly demonstrate its existence.

V. Getting out of the cycle of dependency has been daunting, partly because of poverty and neo-colonialist strictures, but also because of the inherent difficulty in catching up in a race that had started centuries before.

A. As Nkrumah said, these nations must do in a generation what it took developed countries 300 years to accomplish.

B. The problem is that the jet-propelled modernization that these countries wanted seemed easier to achieve by the Soviet strong-state model than by the Western democratic model. Democracy and rapid modernization did not always go hand-in-hand.

C. The "catch-up" challenge was reflected in the broader problem of trying to establish nation-states in places where the *nation* had little historical or political meaning.

D. Beyond basic economic problems were other equally serious challenges, including the ethnic and religious diversity of many of the new nations.

1. Scholars argue about whether ethnic diversity itself or simply the way diversity is deployed by political groups undermines democratic stabilization. Either way, it certainly has. Around the world in the 1990s, there were more than three dozen ongoing ethnic conflicts destabilizing nations, most of them in the form of civil wars.

2. The problem of diversity has taken different forms. In India, the conflict has been between a majority religion and a number of minority religions, especially Muslims but also Sikhs, who have been at virtual war with the Indian government over the issue of Kashmir for the last two decades.

3. Despite the endemic nature of religious conflict in India, it has not destabilized democratic government too badly, because the majority ethnic group is able to control the democratic institutions of government.

4. In many African nations, on the other hand, the lack of a majority ethnic or religious group has helped prevent democratic stabilization.

E. A final obstacle to political stability and economic prosperity was the lack of political experience, education, and skills among the local population.

1. There was a huge variation between such countries as India, with a large educated elite, and the Belgian Congo, which had 16 university graduates in 1960.

2. In general, this was a greater issue in Africa, where illiteracy rates were as high as 98 percent.

3. Even where the new political elites had good intentions to educate their populations, often, lack of resources convinced them to fall back on more authoritarian colonial forms of rule.

VI. Not surprisingly, the combination of all these serious problems turned what began as an optimistic quest for Third World political and economic stability into a quagmire from which few countries have successfully emerged. Over the next few lectures, we will examine some case studies of at least partial successes, as well as failures, before evaluating the prognosis for general democratic stabilization in the future.

Essential Reading:

Theodore von Laue, *The World Revolution of Westernization*, part 6, "The Third World: Decolonization, Independence and Development."

Supplementary Reading:

Tony Smith, ed., *The End of European Empire: Decolonization after World War II*, part 5, "The Question of Neo-Colonialism."

Roger Stone, *The Nature of Development.*

Questions to Consider:

1. Do you think decolonization could have had other, more positive, outcomes than the replacement of one form of dependency for another?

2. The debate over whether democratic government can successfully manage ethnic and religious diversity is one of the most pressing issues in the world today, not only in the Third World, but in post-communist Eastern Europe, Ireland, Spain (the Basque problem), and Israel, to name some of the prominent examples. Where do you stand on this question?

Lecture Thirty-Two—Transcript
Challenges for Post-Colonial Societies

The process of decolonization that we talked about in the last lecture raised tremendous economic and political hopes for dozens of new countries, but moving from formal independence to political stability and economic prosperity required overcoming of number serious obstacles that decolonization had not addressed. In other words, the achievement of formal political independence was only one of the many challenges that these new countries had to face. As the Algerian nationalist Frantz Fanon put it, "The apotheosis of independence is transformed into the curse of independence." Moreover, many of the obstacles were particularly difficult for democratic governments to resolve. As a result, the upshot is that democracy and Third World development have had a troubled relationship.

In this lecture, we will talk in general terms about what those obstacles have been and why it has been so difficult to address them before we move on in future lectures to particular case studies.

While there was a great deal of optimism in the 1950s and 1960s, the new leaders were not naïve; they realized that they had tremendous challenges to overcome, but they also thought that political independence would finally give them the impetus they needed to carve out their space in the world. This combination of sobriety and hope was nicely expressed in a speech given by the new Indonesian President Sukarno in 1955 at a conference that had called for 29 ex-colonial nations at Bandung. The purpose of the conference was to announce the presence of these new nations on the world stage. The challenge, he said, was that "we have been unregarded, the people for whom decisions were made by others whose interests were paramount, the people who live in poverty and humiliation. Then, our nations demanded—they fought for—independence and achieved independence, and with that independence came responsibility." To move from being the unregarded, the helpless, and the poor to being acknowledged, self-reliant, and wealthy were enormous challenges for these new countries. However, at the same time, you can see in that quote the sense of optimism that taking responsibility now was enough to move these countries forward, that the Third World could create for itself what the First World had, which was that they could modernize and become real players in the world. As the new president of India, Nehru, said at an earlier conference of non-Western nations in 1947, "We live in a tremendous age of transition, and already the next stage takes shape when Asia takes her rightful place with other continents." If you look at these early conferences, they symbolize the readiness of the Third World to take off, that sense of sobriety but enthusiasm at the same time; obviously, this did not happen except in a few cases. Most of the new states from this period are still poor; they are still unregarded and not self-reliant. While each of the countries had their own particular obstacles, there are some general problems that we can articulate, and that is what I want to do in this lecture.

The first general problem was the Cold War itself, which distracted the two superpowers from the real issues of development and turned countries into pawns of larger power games, as we talked about in an earlier lecture on Korea. As Ghana's Nkrumah complained, "A great deal of the energy and resources funneled into the Third World was directed to military aide and arms instead of development assistance." The militarization of the Third World then helped fuel protracted civil wars and regional conflicts that further devastated them physically, economically, and politically. The most well known example is Vietnam, which we know about in the United States, but there were African countries like Somalia, Ethiopia, and Angola crippled by military conflict, which were exacerbated by the Cold War.

While the Cold War affected some regions more than others, a more endemic challenge for all the new nations was economic development. The obstacles to economic development were partly a result of preexisting poverty and partly a result of colonialism. Although scholars continue to argue about the weight of each side, some put more weight on the preexisting poverty and others on the legacy of colonialism. If you look at all of the colonial regions before they were empires, most of these economies—or all of them—were poor to begin with. Many of them were based on subsistent agricultural production and very limited market structure—although not in every case, if you remember the Indian example, which had a developed textile industry in a fairly developed market. Under the colonial empires, economic development did occur but it tended to be focused on creating an export market for raw materials from the colonies—whether minerals or food products—and creating an import market for Western industrial goods. While colonialism, then, helped make the transition from the subsistent to a market economy, it did not create indigenous industrial development.

Now, scholars who emphasize the positive impact of colonialism in economic terms argue that these countries were already poor; they were not made poor by colonialism. Furthermore, they argue that if one examines the statistics of economic growth of the period of colonialism, that these countries were better off at the end of the colonial period than they were in the beginning. To give one example, in Ghana, formerly the Gold Coast, per capita income quadrupled between 1890 and 1960; likewise, whereas in 1890 there were virtually no exports from Ghana—it was virtually a subsistence agrarian economy. By 1960, Ghana was exporting 400,000 tons of cocoa annually, all of it produced on farms established and owned by Africans. During this period, the overall value of imports and exports rose from 1 million pounds in 1890 to 100 million pounds in 1960; the development of a market really occurs during this period.

Finally, in 1890, the only communications networks consisted of a few dirt roads, and by 1950, the colonial power had built paved roads and a railway system. So, citing these kinds of statistics, those who emphasize the positive impact of colonialism in economic terms argue that these countries were left in a better, not worse, position.

On the other hand, critics on the economic impact of colonialism argued that the main legacy was not development but dependence. In other words, the development that was promoted by colonial powers was designed to fuel their own modern industrial economies by expanding markets for their goods. Thus, market economies in these regions were established to benefit the colonial powers—not the colonies, which were no more than cogs in a huge global economy biased towards Western interests. One illustration of this kind of dependent relationship is the promotion of opium production in India for the global trade among Europe, India, and China. The critics would argue, then, that simply citing statistics of increased export/import activity does not prove that the country was better off economically. What is more important, in their minds, was the structure of those imports and exports—not simply that there is more economic activity that the market has established, but what is the structure of what is being imported and exported, the way in which this structure left the new post-colonial nations positioned dependently in the world market. Colonialism dragged its colonies into a modern capitalist world economy, and then left them unfit to compete on equal terms in it. Furthermore, they would argue, that exposure to the West through colonialism gave countries the ambition to get rich and modernize but left them without the resources to do so. They could never go back to the isolation of a subsistent economy, but they did not have the tools to compete in a world they did not create.

One of the most widely read critics of colonialism and its economic as well as psychological impact in the 1950s and 1960s was Frantz Fanon, a French-trained psychiatrist from colonial Martinique, who became involved in the Algerian struggle for independence when he was stationed in a hospital in Algeria during the conflict. From a psychological as well as an economic perspective, Fanon argued that colonialism established a level of dependence and subservience that required a complete and violent break before colonial peoples could find the path to self-reliance. In his most famous book called *The Wretched of the Earth*, which was published in 1961 just before his death from cancer, Fanon railed against the colonial powers for leaving their colonies in a state of poverty and underdevelopment— in his words: "The wealth of the imperial countries is our wealth too. Europe is literally the creation of the Third World, the wealth which smothers her is that which was stolen from the underdeveloped peoples." Fanon's passionate and angry attack on the legacy of colonialism became a virtual handbook for Third World national liberation. The debates about colonialism and economic dependence continued even after colonialism ended, when critics argued that the transition from a colonial economy to economic independence was being made more difficult by what were to become known as neo-colonial forms of control. The debate continues in terms of the relationship between developed and undeveloped economies, even in the post-colonial world.

In a book written by Nkrumah—president of Ghana in 1965—called *Neo-colonialism: The Last Stage of Imperialism*, he defined neo-colonialism as this: "Its essence is that the fate, which is subject to it, is in theory independent and has all the outward trappings of international sovereignty, but in realty its economic system and, thus, its political stability, is directed from outside." So, neo-colonialism is a condition of formal independence but through various indirect means; their economic and political policies are not autonomously produced. As may be obvious from the title which is a play on Lenin's book *Imperialism: The Highest Stage of Capitalism*, Nkrumah was picking up on Lenin's argument and Fanon's argument, as well, that imperialism functioned to raise living standards at home in the developed world at the cost of colonial impoverishment. What Nkrumah was arguing here is that this exploitive relationship could continue after the end of formal colonialism. The methods and forms of economic dependence, he says, can take various shapes. In extreme cases, troops can be sent in to directly control the policies of the government; that would be the most extreme form of neo-colonialist control. Examples of such direct intervention occurred especially in cases where Western countries sought to prevent new ex-colonial nations from nationalizing the companies that controlled their raw materials. That occurs, for example, in the American-sponsored invasion of Guatemala in the 1950s, which was partly due to the Guatemalan government decision to expropriate parts of the United Fruit Company's holdings in Guatemala. Likewise, in 1953, the CIA-induced coup in Iran was partly due to that government's decision to nationalize the Anglo-Iranian Oil Company. Those were rare cases when troops were formally sent in to change indigenous economic policies.

A more extensive and endemic form of military control was established by, for example, the French government over its former colonies in Africa. Through a series of military alliances signed with former colonies, the French established the right to set up bases in half a dozen African countries, and to intervene in regional disputes if security interests were threatened, or if any of the African nation's security interests were threatened. The French had 10,000 troops stationed in West Africa, and those troops helped to defend French clients' regimes in Chad, Niger, and Gabon and the Cameroons between the 1960s and the 1980s. It was not really until the 1990s that the French begin to withdraw from their position as West Africa's gendarme, or police force.

Most often, to return to the categories of Nkrumah essay, neo-colonial control was exercised through economic or monetary terms, as opposed to the military, based on the countries' desperate need for capital to develop economically; in other words, none of these countries had internal sources of capital so they were dependent on getting capital from outside. If that capital came from national governments, argued Nkrumah, it was generally used for the exploitation of national resources rather than for internal industrial development. For example, in the 1960s, beginning with the 1963 Yaoundé Convention, the new European economic community established a set of preferential trade agreements with African nations, which funneled millions into an African development fund. However, the vast bulk of these millions were earmarked for the purchase of manufactured goods from Europe and even obligated the African nations to purchase these goods at rates above those on the world market, while African products that competed with European goods were slapped with high tariffs so they could not be bought in Europe.

Other than these kinds of special dependent relationships, the major source of foreign capital came from the World Bank and the International Monetary Fund, which created the more subtle dependence of massive debt. Thus, Africa's total foreign debt rose from 14 billion dollars in 1973 to 150 billion in 1984—from 20 percent of the gross national product in 1973 to 40 percent of the gross national product in 1984.

This indebtedness allowed wealthy donor countries that controlled these institutions to dictate local, economic, and sometimes even political policies including the imposition of what became very unpopular austerity programs, which forced Third World countries to slash domestic spending as a condition for receiving new loans. That meant that they had to slash educational programs, social welfare programs, things that helped the poorest sectors of the population; that is what made them very unpopular. However, the World Bank and the International Monetary Fund insisted they were necessary as a way of stabilizing their economies in financial terms.

Economists still argue today about whether these programs are effective and necessary, and I would say that the debates and arguments are increasing rather than decreasing. Whether we see them as a cause or a result of economic dependence, they demonstrate its existence.

Nkrumah, himself, was partly, at least, a victim of this dynamic of dependence. He began his presidency with big plans for industrial development, that is, indigenous industrial development that, of course, required foreign capital to do so. But, his populist, socialist rhetoric sent off alarm bells in the international financial community and caused Western lending agencies to boycott his projects, which partly led to the coup that overthrew him in 1966, a year after his book was published. Getting out of this cycle of dependency has proved daunting, partly, then, because of existing poverty and partly because of neo-colonial structures, but also partly because of the inherent difficulty of catching up in a race that had been started several hundred years before in the most developed countries. Nkrumah acknowledged this problem in his autobiography, as he said: "All dependent territories are backward in education, agriculture, and industry. The economic independence that should follow and maintain political independence demands a total mobilization of brain and manpower resources. What other countries have taken 300 years or more to achieve, a once dependent territory must try to accomplish in a generation if it is to survive. Unless it is as if it were jet-propelled, it will lag behind and, thus, risk everything for which it has fought." The problem is that this need for jet propulsion or total mobilization in order to catch up was easier to achieve in a non-democratic than in a democratic setting—a government that could impose what Nkrumah called "emergency measures of a totalitarian kind." So, many of these countries trying to catch up were looking not to the United States or England as their model, but looking to the non-democratic late industrializers like Japan or the Soviet Union for their model. The "catch-up" challenge was also reflected in the broader problem of trying to establish nation-states in these regions where the *nation* had no historical meaning from any people. We talked in an earlier lecture about the problem that Latin American nations had in the 19th century, trying to establish a coherent identity in societies that were deeply divided between Spanish emigrants and indigenous populations. Now, with Asian and African decolonization, we have societies with no preexisting common identity faced with trying to form a coherent political identity at the same time they are trying to pull themselves out of poverty. In other words, the problems of political stability and economic prosperity have to be pursued at the same time.

In a world that is defined by nation-states in economic terms but also in political terms, when membership in the United Nations is based on nation-states in this world, it is impossible to imagine going back to some sort of pre-national tribal organization. This meant adapting themselves to a form of political organization that was designed by the European world to solve their particular problems in the early modern period. This lack of coherent political identity was reflected in, and the result of, both the cause and the effect of the tremendous religious, linguistic, and ethnic diversity of many of these new nations.

Scholars argue about whether ethnic diversity itself causes political instability, or whether it is simply the way that ethnic diversity is mobilized or manipulated by political groups to separate and divide people. So, scholars argue is it the existence of diversity or its deployment that is really the cause. Either way, it certainly has destabilized these new political regimes. Ethnic conflict does seem to have flared up precisely after the initial euphoria of independence, after the initial euphoria died down and people were looking for ways to vent their frustrations over continued poverty and lack of development.

Around the world in the 1990s, there were more than three dozen ongoing ethnic conflicts, most of them civil wars. The collapse of the USSR in the late 1980s, early 1990s, opened a whole new wave of ethnic conflicts in that region of the world.

If we look at all of these ethnic conflicts, the least destabilizing form of ethnic religious conflicts has been in cases like India, where conflicts occurred between a majority group and a number of minority groups. In India, the conflict has been between the majority Hindu population and the minority Muslims, Sikhs, and others. Because the Hindus are a majority of the population, they have been able to maintain control of democratic institutions and keep those in place when there is a majority group in control. Thus, endemic strife has not destabilized the Indian democracy.

On the other hand, in many African countries, there was no majority religious or ethnic group around that could stabilize the regime. In the continent, as a whole, there were some 5,000 languages and numerous ethnic groups. Moreover, the borders between the new nations often had little relationship between linguistic and ethnic divisions.

Virtually none of the nationalist movements that won independence were unified, and this is in contrast to the Indian case, when you have a unified nationalist movement that is able to hold the national liberation movement together; whereas, in Africa, virtually none of them were unified, and many of them were divided along ethnic or religious lines. The most dramatic ethnic conflict has been that between the Tutsis and the Hutus in Rwanda, which began in the 1960s and has claimed more than a million lives.

A final obstacle to political stability and economic prosperity was the lack of political experience, education, and political and technical skills on the part of the local elite. There was a huge variation between such countries as India. If you remember, in India, the British education system in the 19th century had established a fairly large elite who not only spoke English, but who were well-educated and also held certain posts in a local administration. You have a large Indian middle class to pass the reins to; whereas, if we take the other extreme of the Belgian Congo, at independence, there were 16 people in the Belgian Congo who had college educations. The variety was tremendous.

In general, this was a greater issue in Africa than in Asia. The illiteracy rates in Africa were as high as 98 percent, and the leadership was left in the hands of a small cadre of Western-educated elites, like Nkrumah who had a United States Ph.D. in theology and education.

Even where these Western-educated elites had the good intentions of trying to educate their populations and instill democratic practices, it was often difficult to do that since they did not have the economic resources, and even well-intentioned leaders often fell back on more authoritarian measures and authoritarian methods that were easier to use than democratic methods in a population that did not have the educational base to participate as full citizens.

The tragic irony was that in these cases, local elites actually ended up simply inheriting and using the colonial system, rather than dismantling it. They simply took over colonial systems of rule by local elites, rather than taking them apart.

If we look at all of these various obstacles to development and political stabilization, it is not surprising that what began as an optimistic quest turned into a quagmire from which few countries have emerged successfully.

Over the next few lectures, we will examine some case studies of at least partial successes, as well as what we might call failures, before evaluating the prognosis for general democratic stabilization in the 21st century.

Lecture Thirty-Three
Competing Nationalisms—The Middle East

Scope:

The issue of ethnic and religious diversity and the competing nationalisms inspired by it are nowhere more tragically apparent than in the Arab-Israeli conflict and the ongoing political tensions in the Middle East. This lecture charts the evolution of the conflict, focusing on the origins of the competing nationalist claims in the late 19th century and the escalating tensions that culminated in the creation of the state of Israel in 1948. It also examines the impact of imperialism and the Cold War in exacerbating existing tensions, instead of helping to resolve them. The lecture concludes by considering the broader issues of competing nationalist claims and the problematic intersection of nationalism, ethnic and religious diversity, and democracy.

Outline

I. The conflict generated by the competing Arab and Jewish nationalisms in the Middle East is one of the most tragic case studies of the challenge of managing ethnic and religious diversity in the framework of democratic nation-states. In addition, the conflict demonstrates how first imperialism, then the Cold War exacerbated rather than soothed existing tensions.

    A. How, as scholars, do we approach a case of competing nationalisms over the same territory?

    B. One expert has argued that we must accept the validity of each claim within that group's cultural and historical context, without making judgments about the broader justice of those claims. This approach will help us to understand without taking sides.

    C. What was the origin of these competing nationalisms?

        1. For nationalists on both sides, the origins lay in antiquity, in the historical presence of the Jewish or Palestinian Arabs in the region.

2. Both peoples entered the region in about the 12th century B.C., but political dominance shifted among Jewish, Christian, and Islamic forces until the 20th century.

3. For scholars of modern nationalism, the origins of claims of nationalism have more modern roots, in the late 19th-century popularization of "nationalism" in European society.

4. In the late 19th and early 20th centuries, the nationalist claim that every "people" should have its own political territory, that is, a nation-state, came to be a standard rallying cry.

II. Both Jewish and Arab nationalism had their roots in this late-19th-century European culture; before that time, these identities were not linked to political units.

    A. Jewish nationalism, or *Zionism*, is most closely linked to Theodor Herzl, an assimilated European Jew.

        1. In 1896, Herzl wrote a book called the *State of the Jews* that called for the creation of a Jewish state, although not necessarily in Palestine.

        2. He organized the First Zionist Congress in 1897, which laid out the Zionist program, and helped form and lead the Jewish National Fund and the World Zionist Organization to promote this goal.

        3. His strategy was to gain international recognition for the idea of a Jewish state through diplomacy.

        4. Herzl's major audience was among non-assimilated Eastern European Jews, who brought a different perspective to the movement.

        5. After Herzl's death in 1904, their greater religious commitment to Palestine and their strategy of de facto settlement became the dominant position in Zionist organizations.

        6. This group used international Zionist organizations to raise money to buy land in Palestine and to recruit immigrants who would settle there in farming communities.

        7. By 1914, they had founded 14 agricultural settlements in Palestine, with another 30 populated by the small historical Jewish community and the trickle of individual immigrants, who came mostly from Russia after the start of the pogroms in the 1880s.

8. The total number of Jews in Palestine by 1914 was about 60,000, or 1/10 of the population.

9. The first outside recognition of Zionist claims came in 1917, when the British foreign secretary, Arthur Balfour, issued the Balfour Declaration, which made vague promises about supporting the aspirations for a Jewish homeland.

B. Like Zionism, Arab nationalism is a recent phenomenon.

1. Throughout most of the Ottoman Empire, there was no demand for an independent Arab nation-state, but only for religious self-government within the empire.

2. The first Arab nationalist tract was published in Europe, as was Herzl's book, by a Maronite Christian Arab living in Paris in 1905. The author, Naguib Azoury, also formed the League of the Arab Fatherland.

III. It was the First World War and its aftermath that really propelled the expansion of Arab nationalist sentiment.

A. The Arab countries of the Middle East experienced a similar sense of disillusionment as other regions, including India and China, which heard the proclamation of "national self-determination" in the Paris peace treaties and watched as they were treated differently.

1. As in China, colonies taken from the defeated power (in this case, the Ottoman Empire) were transferred to the victorious colonial powers, rather than given independence.

2. In the Middle East, this transfer was in the form of protectorates, which were supposed to be preparing for independence.

3. This outcome was all the more humiliating because the British had encouraged Arab nationalism during the war as a way of getting Arabs to fight the Turks.

B. As the British were supporting Arab nationalism publicly, secretly, they signed the Picot-Sykes Agreement in 1916, which carved up the Middle East into British and French spheres of influence.

1. The anger created by the secret deal; the lack of progress toward independence, especially in French-controlled Lebanon and Syria; and the heavy-handed repression of Arab nationalism by both French and British fueled nationalist sentiment in the region before World War II.

2. For Arab nationalists, Zionism was simply another form of European imperialism.

IV. Tensions between Jewish and Arab nationalism grew dramatically in the interwar period in British-controlled Palestine.

A. Between 1914 and 1945, the immigration of European Jews to Palestine increased dramatically, jumping from 1/10 of the population in 1914 to 1/3 in 1939.

B. More than simply numbers, the immigrants were constructing an entire economic and administrative infrastructure, as well as a thriving cultural and intellectual life in Hebrew.

C. Moreover, following the socialist utopian principles of the Zionists, it was a society built on egalitarian relations but in an exclusively Jewish community.

D. By the 1930s, conflicts between Jews and Palestinian Arabs over settlement expansion, Arab exclusion policies, and other issues had reached almost civil war proportions.

E. The creation of the Israeli state in 1948 did nothing to resolve the tension.

1. The creation of the state of Israel by the UN recognized both Arab and Jewish nationalist claims, but only the Zionists accepted the UN mandate.

2. When the British rapidly withdrew in 1948, the first Arab-Israeli war over the contested territory followed.

3. The UN finally brokered an armistice in 1949, but the two sides could not agree on terms to repatriate the 750,000 Palestinian refugees who had fled during the war.

4. A series of wars in 1956, 1967, and 1973 were fought between Arab and Israeli forces over the Arabs' refusal to recognize Zionist nationalist claims.

V. For both Israelis and Arabs, the constant pressure of competing nationalist claims has also exacerbated internal identity struggles.

   A. Particularly in recent years, the Arab-Israeli conflict has reached such a level of bitter contention that it is virtually impossible to predict when, if, and how it will be resolved.

   B. By looking back at the origins of the opposing nationalist claims, however, we could, perhaps, ask how and if they could have worked out in a way more conducive to democratic development in the region.

Essential Reading:

Charles Smith, *Palestine and the Arab-Israeli Conflict*, Naguib Azoury from "The Awakening of the Arab Nation"; Theodor Herzl, "The Jewish State."

Supplementary Reading:

Anita Shapira, *Land and Power: The Zionist Resort to Force, 1881–1948*.

Zeev Sternhell, *The Founding Myths of Israel: Nationalism, Socialism and the Making of the Jewish State*.

Questions to Consider:

1. When examining a historical subject so emotionally laden as this one, how would you frame the best scholarly approach?

2. The "two-state" solution would resolve some of the tension between ethnic nationalism and democracy by maintaining majority Jewish and Palestinian populations in their respective states. Are there other problems that the two-state solution does not resolve?

Lecture Thirty-Three—Transcript
Competing Nationalisms—The Middle East

In the last lecture, we talked about some of the general problems facing new nation-states in the post-colonial period, including the problematic relationship between ethnic and national identities.

In this lecture, we'll look at the origins of the conflict generated by the competing Arab and Jewish ethnic religious nationalisms in the Middle East, up to the formation of the state of Israel in 1948. Rather than examining the recent history of the conflict, our task will be to understand how two groups came to have nationalist claims on the same territory.

In a case such as this one, which raises powerful emotional responses from many people both inside and outside the Middle East, how can we define a scholarly approach? Charles Smith, the author of one of the best scholarly syntheses of the conflict has argued that, "we must accept the validity of each claim within the context of that group's cultural and historical context, without making judgments about the broader justice of these claims." This means, as he says, "opinions and claims abhorrent to observers may become entirely comprehensible when viewed as part of a people's history and interaction with others." The job of the historian is not to decide who is right, but to understand their claims and even be sympathetic with the competing claims for which there may be no real solution. This approach will help us understand these competing claims without taking sides.

In the effort to understand the origins of the conflict, we must begin with the roots of these competing nationalist claims to the region of Palestine. For nationalists on both sides, the origins lay in antiquity, in the historical presence of Jews or Palestinian Arabs in the region. In fact, both sides can point to a long history; the names Israel and Palestine derive from two peoples who entered the region at approximately the same time, that is, the 12th century B.C. The Jews called themselves the people of the tribe of Israel, the Israelites, and believed God gave the land to them. Palestine refers to the Philistines, a people of Greek origin who settled in the coastal plain areas at around the same time as the Israelites settled in the hills. The first written reference to the region as Palestine is found in the writings of the Greek historian, Herodotus, in the 5th century B.C.

The Philistines and the Israelites co-inhabited the territory for about 200 years before the Israelites, under King David, united to defeat and subjugate the Philistines and establish the Kingdom of Israel in 1000 B.C. It was during this short-lived kingdom that David conquered Jerusalem and his son, King Solomon, built the first temple, making Jerusalem the sacred center of their monotheistic religion. After King Solomon's death, the kingdom split in two; the northern kingdom survived until its defeat by the Assyrians in 722 B.C., while the southern kingdom lasted until its defeat in 586 B.C. by the Babylonian Empire. There was one other brief period of Jewish independence between 140 B.C. and 63 B.C., when the revolt of the Maccabees restored much of Solomon's former kingdom for 80 years before it was finally absorbed by the Roman Empire.

After the end of formal independence of the formal Israelite kingdom, most of the Jews who remained in the region were concentrated in the Galilee. By 300 A.D., half the population of this valley was Jewish. Under the Roman Empire, and later the Byzantine Empire, the Jews had varying levels of religious and administrative independence, although the Christian rulers increasingly saw Jews as rivals in Palestine—especially in terms of Jerusalem, which was seen as a sacred spot for both religions.

The entry of a third major religion into Palestine came in the early 7th century when Muhammad unified the Arab tribes around Mecca, where he was born with a message that he had been sent to preach God's word. By his death in 632, he was accepted in much of central and south Arabia as the prophet of Allah, and his followers used the new religion as a rallying cry for expanding their dominion. Jerusalem fell to the Muslim armies in 638 A.D., and by 730, the boundaries of Islam had extended from India to the Pyrenees in Europe. Now, the Islamic world was not united either politically or religiously as conflicts over the legitimate successor of Muhammad created opposing Sunni and Shiite sects, which tended to be concentrated in different caliphate dynasties. Nevertheless, both sects of Islam invested Jerusalem with sacred authority. Again, all three religions have a sacred investment in Jerusalem.

In this case, it was because Islam was considered to be the culmination of Judaism and Christianity, but also because Muhammad was said to have stopped in Jerusalem on his way to heaven. The place where he set foot is a rock where the Jewish temple—which had been destroyed by the Romans in 70 A.D.—had stood, and in 691, an Islamic caliph built a shrine called the "Dome of the Rock" to commemorate the step of Muhammad.

As Palestine moved from Christian to Islamic rule, the status of the Jewish community remained fairly stable; it did not change that much, being subservient to one religious rule or the other. Under the Christian Byzantines, they had been discriminated against but not generally persecuted, and that is how it remained under Islamic rule. Except for the brief period when Christians recaptured Jerusalem during the Crusades of the 12th century, and during this period of Christian rule, neither Jews nor Muslims were permitted to practice their religion; other than that, Palestine remained under Islamic rule until the early 20th century. From the early 16th century until World War I, the rulers were the Ottoman Empire, which continued the pattern set by the earlier empires of religious pluralism in their huge multiethnic, multi-religious empire.

While Arab and Israeli nationalists look back to these historical roots for their nationalist claims, for most scholars, the origins of nationalism have more modern roots in the late 19th-century popularization of "nationalism" within European society. The existence of historical communities of people in and of themselves does not create national identities. It is only in the 19th century that there is a new claim that every "people" should have its own nation-state; it is only in that context that nationalism comes to be a rallying cry. It is at this point, argue scholars, that nationalist groups then look to the past historical communities to legitimate their claims for a nation-state in the present, and they base their claims to certain territories on this past history. It is in this context that the Israelite kingdom of 1000 B.C., or the Islamic conquest of the 7th century A.D., took on nationalist as opposed to historical significance.

After the First World War, this nationalist world view becomes codified in the Paris peace process, which declares as one of its goals to establish that relationship of self-determination, that every people needs and deserves to have its own state, and that becomes one of the guides to sort out the territorial chaos left by the collapse of the empires.

If we look, then, at the specific origins of Jewish and Arab nationalism, both movements have their roots in this late 19th-century European culture. It was at this point that the older religious and cultural identities were reformulated to link them to claims for political identity. At this point, political identity becomes the only acceptable goal of a people's development.

Jewish nationalism, or *Zionism*, is most closely linked to Theodor Herzl. Herzl was an assimilated European Jew from the multiethnic Austro-Hungarian Empire. He was a beneficiary of the civil equality that had been gained by Jews in most of Western Europe, and in particular, after the French Revolution. He was trained as a lawyer and moved to Vienna in 1878 and became a journalist. Herzl's political relationship to Judaism began with his response to the Dreyfus Affair in 1894, which Herzl covered as a reporter. The Dreyfus Affair was a complicated event in French history. It involved a military trial of a French army officer, Alfred Dreyfus, who was accused of treason. What happens with the Dreyfus Affair is that it brought to the surface a number of brewing tensions within French society and politics of the period. Because Dreyfus was Jewish, one of those brewing tensions was anti-Semitism. What this revealed was that even in a society like France, in which the Jews appeared to be so well assimilated, anti-Semitism was still a powerful force. Herzl, on the basis of this experience, came to the conclusion that full assimilation into European society would never be possible for the Jewish people because of the intense prejudice against them. In 1896, he wrote his most famous work, *The State of the Jews*, in which he called for the recreation of a Jewish state—in other words, going back and legitimizing his claim based on the historical existence of a Jewish state in the pre-Christian era. In calling for this state, Herzl makes the leap from considering anti-Semitism a religious and social question to making it a national question. He says: "We are a people – one people." Where would this Jewish state be, according to Herzl? While Palestine was in his words, "our unforgettable historical homeland," he also said they would take whatever territory was given to them and whatever Jewish public opinion desired. He wasn't fixed necessarily on Palestine.

To promote his cause, Herzl organized the First Zionist Congress in 1897, which produced the movement's basic program. In the words of the preamble, "The aim of Zionism is to create for the Jewish people a homeland secured by public law."

In the years until his death in 1904, Herzl also founded the Jewish National Fund and the World Zionist Organization to promote, in the words of the 1897 program, "the strengthening of Jewish national feeling and national consciousness."

In addition to trying to recruit Jews to his cause, Herzl's major strategy was to gain international recognition for a Jewish state through diplomacy through diplomatic negotiations with major political figures in Western Europe. The British colonial secretary, Chamberlain, actually did offer Uganda as a potential location for the Jewish state, but the 6th Zionist Congress rejected this in 1903.

While Herzl himself was an assimilated Western European Jew, his ideas found their main audience not among other assimilated Western Jews, but among Eastern European Jews who were still actively marginalized and persecuted in their own societies. Many of the Western European Jews were hostile to Zionism because they thought it would threaten their assimilated status. In contrast, it was in Russia where Jews were still confined to live in certain areas, and they were prevented from full participation in Russian society. It was there that the Jews were most receptive to Herzl's ideas.

In Russia, formal discrimination was reinforced after 1881 by government tolerance of anti-Jewish riots or pogroms on the part of Russian peasants; they beat up Jews, destroyed property, raped, and sometimes killed Jews. The pogroms proved to many Jews in Russia that they would never be emancipated there, leading to the immigration of almost 3 million Russian Jews between 1882 and 1914—most of them went to the United States, but a handful went to Israel, to what would be in the future, Israel.

It was these Russian Jews who responded to Herzl's call and who, after his death in 1904, took majority control of the World Zionist Organization, which in turn came to reflect their perspective on how to build a Jewish nation. For these religions Jews, the biblical significance of Palestine was determinative. They were not open to just any Jewish homeland; they wanted Palestine. It was after this that Zionism becomes fully identified with Palestine. Likewise, they favored a different strategy of building a Jewish state. Herzl worked for international recognition, and what they advocated was a more bottom-up approach of actually settling the territory and establishing a de facto presence, and then later gaining international recognition.

Thus, the international Zionist organizations raised money to buy land in Palestine and to recruit immigrants who would settle there in farming communities.

Before this period, there had been a few thousand Jews living in Palestine, and that number is—historically—reinforced by about 30,000 Russian Jews, who came as part of the exodus from the pogroms, although these Russian Jews did not come for Zionist motives, in particular.

The first Zionist agricultural settlements were established after 1904. By 1914, they had founded 14 agricultural settlements in Palestine, with another 30 populated by the small historical Jewish community. All together, the total number of Jews in Palestine by 1914 was about 60,000 or 1/10 of the population. Included in this first wave of Zionist settlers was David Ben-Gurion, who later became Israel's first prime minister.

While the Jewish organizations pursued this de facto strategy of immigration, the first formal recognition, or a goal, of a Jewish homeland came in 1917 when the British foreign secretary, Arthur Balfour, issued what became known as the Balfour Declaration, which made vague promises about supporting the aspirations for a Jewish homeland. In its words, "the establishment in Palestine of a national home for the Jewish people" avoiding the word *state*, and that is what made it vague; it talked about a home but not specifically a state.

Where did this promise come from? It came out of a complex set of motives. Remember, this is during World War I that this promise was made, and partly it included sympathy for the plight of the Jews, but also it was out of a hope to mobilize Russian Jews in the war against the Bolsheviks in Russia, and partly it was out of a hope to mobilize American Jews to pressure the United States to enter the war on the side of the Allies. There was a complex set of motives out of which this declaration arises. Despite the complex set of motives, the Balfour Declaration becomes an important symbolic rallying point after the war, much like the British government's declaration that it would institute responsible government in India. That was made during the war with the hopes of keeping the population united.

However, at the same time the British were encouraging Zionism, they were also encouraging Arab nationalism as a way of mobilizing the Arabs against their enemy, the Ottoman Empire. Before we talk about the conflicts that this engendered in the postwar period, we need to go back and understand the origins of Arab nationalism, which, like Zionism, was a recent phenomenon.

If we look at the history of the Ottoman Empire up until the very late 19th century, there was never a demand for an independent Arab nation-state; that is, there was no historical political identification between Arabs and the nation-state.

The only demands that came within the Ottoman Empire were demands for religious self-government within the empire. Within Palestine, in particular, there were about 550,000 Arabs living there at the outset of the First World War, about 85 percent Sunni Muslims and the rest Christian. Scholars generally agree that there was no national consciousness of this population in the 19th century; although, sources from the 17th century indicate there was identification with a geographical region called Palestine, which is not the same as nationalism, and the idea that they know that they lived in Palestine; you get that already from the 17th century. There was some form of identification with the territory but nothing that could be called nationalism.

As with Zionism, the first Arab nationalist tract was published in Europe by a Maronite Christian Arab living in Paris in 1905, and the tract was called *The Awakening of the Arab Nation*. The author, Naguib Azoury, a former Ottoman Empire bureaucrat also formed the League of the Arab Fatherland, to promote complete separation of Arab lands from Ottoman rule. In his book, Azoury calls for the formation of a broad Arab nation—stretching from the Tigress and Euphrates Rivers to the Suez Isthmus, as well as from the Mediterranean to the Arabian Sea.

While this tract was partly a response to frustration at the Ottoman Empire, the new Zionist movement was also one of the motives here, and Azoury mentions specifically the Zionist movement as a direct threat to Arabs in the region. As he says, "Both Zionism and Arab nationalism are destined to fight each other continually until one of them wins. The fate of the entire world will depend on the final result of this struggle between these two peoples representing two contrary principles."

While Arab nationalism was born in the prewar period, it was really the First World War and its aftermath that turned it into a popular movement. In particular, the Arabic peoples of the Middle East experienced a similar sense of disillusionment as was experienced in the other colonial regions, such as India or China, which heard the proclamation of "national self-determination" in the Paris peace treaties, and then were disappointed at the treatment they received from the imperial powers.

As in China, colonies were taken from the defeated power (in this case, the Ottoman Empire) and divided up among the British and French colonial victors. In the Middle East, this transfer was in the form of protectorates, not direct colonies.

The outcome of being divided up into French and British spheres of influence was all the more humiliating because the British had encouraged Arab nationalism during the war; so, this felt like a betrayal of the promise. It was a way of getting them to fight the Turks during the war, which they did as all of you who have seen the movie *Lawrence of Arabia* know. At the end of the war, Arab nationalists believed they had won their independence on the battlefield through fighting against the Ottoman armies.

While the British were supporting Arab nationalism publicly, secretly, they signed the Picot-Sykes Agreement in 1916, which carved up the Middle East into British and French spheres of influence. The anger created by this secret deal; the lack of progress towards independence after the war, especially in French-controlled Lebanon and Syria; and the heavy-handed repression of Arab nationalism by both the French and the British fueled nationalist sentiment in the post-World War I period.

For Arab nationalists, Zionism was simply another form of European imperialism, and it is important to understand the roots of that. In Azoury's 1905 book he mentions specifically the threat of imperialist Zionism. Reinforcing this view, Theodor Herzl, the Zionist, used the colonial framework to make this project comprehensible to Europeans. He portrayed the establishment of a Jewish state in Palestine as a form of a settler colony. He says, for example, "Many nations are endeavoring to found overseas colonies to deal with the problem of overpopulation," and the Jewish state would be another version of that. What happens after this early period is that the link between Western imperialism and Zionism becomes a standard trope for Arab nationalists. This trope is reinforced by the fact that Jewish immigrants are coming from Europe.

From these origins, then, tensions between Jewish and Arab nationalism grew dramatically in the interwar period in British-controlled Palestine. Between 1914 and 1945, the immigration of European Jews to Palestine increased dramatically, rising from 1/10 of the population in 1914 to 1/3 of the population in 1939.

More than simply numbers of Jews coming in, the immigrants were constructing an entire economic and administrative apparatus, an infrastructure, as well as a thriving cultural and intellectual life in Hebrew under the leadership of the semi-autonomous Zionist Commission, which had been established in 1918.

Moreover, following the socialist utopian principles of the Zionists, it was a society built on egalitarian relationships but in an exclusively Jewish community. It was supposed to have been isolated from the surrounding Arab community. They lived on land that had been legally bought from Arabs, but which also displaced thousands of Arab tenants who were supposed to be protected in land transfers but were not necessarily.

By the 1930s, conflicts between Jews and Palestinian Arabs over settlement expansion, Arab exclusion policies, and other issues had reached almost civil war proportions. In a conflict over the control of the Wailing Wall in 1928, for example, 133 Jews and 116 Arabs were killed in weeklong riots. During this civil strife, as the tension between Jews and Arabs is rising, the British never really clarify the status of these competing claims, and they seem to shift ground over time.

In 1939, in response to Arab complaints about the Jewish presence in Palestine, the British government issued a White Paper that essentially repudiated the Balfour Declaration and set limits on Jewish immigration. The White Paper of 1939 mandated a cap on the population, which was not to go above 1/3 of where it was already in 1939. When the Second World War began and there was a flood of Jewish refugees leaving Europe, the attempt to contain Jewish immigration only increases conflict and causes more strife.

After the war, the creation of the Israeli state in 1948 did nothing to resolve this tension. The final decision to create a Jewish state emerged out of the shame and horror of the Second World War. Even so, the creation of the state of Israel by the United Nations recognized both Arab and Jewish nationalist claims in the region, but only the Zionists accepted the UN mandate. Independence was followed by a series of wars contesting Zionist authority—wars in 1948, 1956, 1967, and 1973. Thus, when the British rapidly withdrew in 1948, the first Arab-Israeli war over the contested territory followed. The UN finally brokered an armistice in 1949, but the two sides could not agree on terms to repatriate the 750,000 Palestinian Arab refugees who had fled during the war. These refugees became the focus of Palestinian national demands, and the refugee camps in which they were housed became the best breeding grounds for the next generation of Palestinian Arab nationalists.

Since the Palestinian uprising in the occupied territories, relations between Arabs and Jews in the region have become so embittered that it is difficult to imagine when, if, and how a peaceful resolution will be achieved.

Beyond the blame that we might lay on one side or the other for escalating the conflict, we can see the problem of two competing ethnic nationalist claims, in which the rhetoric of the self-determination of each people makes it impossible to imagine a shared nation.

Lecture Thirty-Four
Development Models—Communist China

Scope:

One of the fundamental challenges faced by all the Third World nations was economic development. In this lecture, we begin to look at different roads to development, using case studies to compare and contrast their successes and failures. First, we examine the evolution of the Chinese Peoples' Republic, from 1949 through the 1970s, as an example of the communist development model that was adopted by a number of post-colonial nations. We examine the basic elements of this model, which included a strong state-directed economic policy, a plan to equalize income and wealth, and authoritarian limits on political expression. We conclude with an evaluation of the results of this model in terms of economic growth, the reduction of poverty, and political freedom.

Outline

I. Before evaluating the successes and failures of economic development in Third World nations, we need to define what success meant for newly emerging nations.

   A. Most important for poor countries was to achieve economic modernization that would lead to self-sustaining growth.

      1. Essential to managing this modernization was a stable state.

      2. Finally, new countries wanted to raise the standard of living for their populations, providing literacy, education, health care, and other basic benefits.

   B. While most nations agreed on these goals, they followed different political paths to pursue them.

      1. In general terms, the paths can be grouped into three categories: the communist, the democratic, and the authoritarian roads.

      2. In practice, the paths overlapped in certain areas, but we will look at each path, in turn, through specific case studies that achieved at least partial successes: China as the communist model, India as the democratic model, and Japan as the authoritarian model.

3. Through the case studies, we will evaluate the strengths and weaknesses of the different paths to development for Third World nations.

C. For comparing the socialist and democratic models, China and India are excellent case studies, because they shared many of the same problems when first established in the late 1940s. (Japan is quite a different case, neither a new nation nor poor.)

1. Both were largely rural, poor societies, with high rates of illiteracy among the majority peasant populations.

2. Both also had huge, diverse populations and land masses.

3. Both had high rates of poverty and low rates of economic growth.

4. On the other hand, they both had the advantage of new ruling elites with several decades of experience as an opposition movement before taking power.

5. Finally, they both are relative success stories in the Third World, having made significant advances in economic development.

II. In the Chinese socialist model of development up to the 1980s, democracy and political freedoms were sacrificed in pursuit of economic equality. The tradeoff was that, before the changing economic policies of the 1980s, serious poverty had been virtually eliminated, but at the cost of a repressive society.

A. The question of why the pursuit of economic equality entailed repression lies at the heart of liberal criticisms of communism.

1. To eliminate poverty, communists argued, private property had to be abolished and managed and distributed collectively.

2. Furthermore, as a revolutionary movement, this process was to be rapid, not gradual.

3. This process requires expropriation of individual property and, thus, sets up the parameters of a coercive state.

4. The coercive state was justified by the goal of "democratizing the life of the country," as Deng Xiaping put it in 1980, which referred not to political rights but to spreading education and material benefits.

B. With the coercive state as the arm of development and egalitarian prosperity as the goal, the Chinese government pursued a two-pronged policy of rapid growth and redistribution of resources.

    1. In promoting growth, China followed the Soviet *command economy* model, in which the state established and implemented a plan for industrialization and the collectivization of agriculture.

    2. Because the vast majority of the population was made up of peasants, it was in the agricultural communities that the egalitarian ideal was put into practice and that came to represent the heart of the Chinese communist society.

C. What were the results of the Chinese socialist development model up to the 1980s?

    1. China had some impressive growth statistics, but the success of a command economy in generating growth is more uneven than a market economy.

    2. As China has pursued more market-oriented policies in the 1980s and 1990s, growth rates have increased.

    3. On the other hand, earlier growth was achieved without major foreign loans, because the capitalist world ostracized China and capital had to be generated internally, largely from agricultural surplus.

D. The strengths and weaknesses of a command economy can be demonstrated by example.

    1. In the late 1950s, the Chinese government embarked on an agrarian experiment, the so-called Great Leap Forward, which moved peasants into large communes. The experiment disrupted production so severely that 30 to 50 million people died in a massive famine in 1960–1961.

    2. The problem with a centralized economic policy defined by bureaucrats in the capital is that it takes no account of local conditions, has no flexibility, and leaves no other options if it fails.

    3. On the other hand, when the government has a good idea, centralized planning can distribute its effects widely and rapidly.

4. Thus, when the government broke up the communes in the 1960s and replaced them with smaller work brigades, it used this structure to disseminate the benefits of the "green revolution" and dramatically increase agricultural production.

5. Overall, it seems clear that capitalism has proved the better model for growth.

E. If both China and India achieved impressive (but, for China, more uneven) economic growth, what about the reduction of poverty and rising living standards?

1. It is in this area that the communist model in China was most successful.

2. Rates of literacy, child mortality, malnutrition, and life expectancy were all significantly better than in India.

3. Interestingly, since market reforms of the 1980s, the gap between rich and poor has been growing.

F. But the price to pay for a better fed and healthier population was a repressive enforced equality.

1. The radical commitment to equality and its consequences culminated in the late 1960s and early 1970s with the Cultural Revolution's attempt to impose absolute social and economic uniformity through various coercive methods.

2. Millions of those accused of being "above" the masses were purged from their jobs and forced to do manual labor and learn "peasant values."

3. Mao's fanatical Red Guard troops imposed this equalization policy through mass terror.

4. When Mao died in 1976, a new leadership rejected this path and began to chart a more pragmatic course.

G. From the 1950s through the 1970s, though, the Chinese communist model demonstrates the dangers of enforcing equality through a tyrannical state; at the same time, it illustrates how a state committed to raising the living standard of its population can achieve dramatic results. The question raised by this unattractive tradeoff is about the balance between equality and freedom: What is the ideal balance, and what is the best path to achieve it in societies with large populations of the poor?

Essential Reading:

Jonathan Spence, *The Search for Modern China*, chapters 19–22.

Supplementary Reading:

Anita Chan, Richard Madsen, and Jonathan Unger, *Chen Village: The Recent History of a Peasant Community in Mao's China.*

Elizabeth Perry and Li Xun, *Proletarian Power: Shanghai in the Cultural Revolution.*

Questions to Consider:

1. The tradeoff between "freedom" and "equality" is a complex one, depending on how one defines those terms, but it clearly has different implications, depending on the social and economic structure of a society. Discuss the factors involved.

2. Whatever the merits of the command economy in generating economic growth in the short term, in the long term, the model appears to be unsustainable, as witnessed by the collapse of the USSR and the economic reforms of China in recent decades. Would you agree?

Lecture Thirty-Four—Transcript
Development Models—Communist China

In the last lecture, we looked at the challenge posed by competing ethnic or religious nationalism in post-colonial countries. Using the same sort of case study approach, in the next several lectures, we are going to look at the general problems of economic development, which was perhaps the most fundamental of the challenges faced by all these Third World nations.

Before we can compare and contrast, we have to begin by defining what success and failure meant in terms of economic development for these emerging nations. The one thing that everyone agreed on was the importance of poor countries to achieve economic modernization that would lead to some self-sustaining growth. In virtually all the cases, the model they had in mind was the Western model of industrialization; that is, virtually none of these new countries imagined a modernization model that was based on the production of raw materials, that to them symbolized the dependence model. All of them imagined some sort of industrialization modernization model.

Second, modernization also meant a centralized nation-state that could unify the citizens and provide the kind of stability for economic development to maintain independence and autonomy.

Finally, modernization also meant raising the standard of living for largely poor populations, which included everything for economic maintenance to literacy, education, health care, and so on. All of those things were part of the modernization model, and this is how we can judge failures and successes.

While most nations agreed on these goals, they disagreed on the kind of political social order that would produce this modernization. There were a variety of answers to this question, and you could break it down into numerous sub-models. It can be grouped, I think, into three main categories: the communist road to modernization, the democratic road, and some form of authoritarian developmental model.

While in practice, these roads overlap in different respects, and we are going to focus on each one, in turn, using a specific country to talk about each model. We are going to focus on countries in which at least partial successes were achieved, so that we can compare and contrast the strengths and weaknesses of each model. We are going to use China to talk about the communist road, India for the democratic road, and Japan as the authoritarian developmental model. Then, we are going to evaluate the strengths and weaknesses of each approach as a way of talking about solutions to the problems of Third World nations.

For comparing the communist and democratic models, China and India make a good comparison in many ways. They both began the process at the same time. They achieved independence, or their new nation-states really took off, in the late 1940s, and, unlike Japan, in the 1940s, they were both largely rural poor societies with a minority of Western-educated elites and a majority of illiterate peasants. Finally, of course, unlike Japan, both countries had to deal with a huge population and landmass. China has 1.2 billion people and India about 900 million people. As a result of these similarities, China and India had similar fundamental problems—nations that were poor in overall economic growth and also nations that had low standards of living. They have high levels of poverty and low levels of growth.

At the same time, both countries had the similar advantage of a new ruling class with several decades of leadership preparation as an opposition movement; in that, there was a significant advantage that some other countries did not have. They really make a perfect point of comparison; they share many of the general problems of the Third World; they share some specific advantages, but then they each use a different model of development to pursue modernization, and both of them achieve relative success in the Third World.

In the Chinese communist model of development that we are going to discuss in this lecture, political freedoms were sacrificed in the pursuit of economic equality. The tradeoff was that, before the changing economic policies of the 1980s (and we will discuss that in a future lecture), before this period, China achieved significant economic growth and had virtually eliminated serious poverty, but at the cost of a highly repressive society. That is the Chinese tradeoff.

The question of why the pursuit of economic equality sacrificed political freedoms really goes to the heart of the liberal critique of communism. To eliminate poverty, communists argued, you had to abolish private property; that, of course, was the communist ideology—that private property was the cornerstone of inequality. However, to accomplish this, property and wealth had to be taken away from the rich and redistributed to the poor majority. Since people are unlikely to give up their riches voluntarily, that means either you had to have a long period in which people are persuaded to do so through education—that would be one way—or you have to have a violent revolution where people are expropriated. Since the landless peasants are not going to wait a whole generation for this process of education and persuasion, it was the second option that the communists pursued, that is, violent revolution. So, reaching their goal required not a gradual consensus politics in which everyone engaged in some sort of give and take, but coercive politics that would force the old wealthy class to give up their land and power, and make sure that no new privilege class replaced them.

Thus, we get the model of a coercive state that forcibly implements the interests of the poor against the rich. In fact, what happens soon after 1949, the new Chinese government undertook and forced land redistribution programs in which 80 percent of the land, which had been owned by 10 percent of the population, was redistributed and given to 300 million landless laborers.

At the same time, Mao later admitted that at least 800,000 so-called "class enemies" had been killed in the first five years of the new regime. For the communists, it was the equalization of wealth that constituted real democracy—not the rights of a minority of property holders. As Chairman Deng Xiaping said later in 1980, the goal was "democratizing the life of the country and raising people's standard of living." —not the other sort of political democracy that would "plunge the country, once again, into anarchy and make it harder to truly democratize." They are using that word in a very different way. In other words, this view of democracy was incompatible with the Western idea of political democracy.

With the coercive state as the arm of the development, the communist version of modernization was to pursue rapid growth, in order to raise the general level of wealth in a society, and also to redistribute it more or less equally among the population. In promoting this growth and equality, China pursued essentially the same *command economy* model of the Soviet Union that we talked about earlier—more specifically, a rapid state-directed industrialization program and the collectivization of agriculture;

these were the same two fundamental programs that were pursued by the Soviet Union under Stalin.

There was a difference, I think, in the brutality of the collectivization process in the Soviet Union versus China; that is, in the Soviet case, what you had was an urban Communist Party, which was attempting to terrorize rural society into submission. In the Chinese case, the Chinese Communist Party had much greater knowledge of peasant society and practices gained through its years of guerrilla organization in the hinterlands. It put a great deal more thought and energy into how to achieve collectivization of agriculture, so it was a less brutal transition.

What were the results of the communist economic revolution? If we use the standard of overall economic growth, China has some impressive statistics during this period on overall growth. The impact of the command economy is more uneven. In the 1950s, China managed to double its industrial output and establish a solid heavy industrial base. During that period, the economy grew an astounding 18 percent a year. The decades of the 1960s and 1970s were more uncertain, but then early in the 1980s the growth rate goes back up to about 9 percent. After the early 1980s, China's pursuit of more market-oriented economic policies really changes the model. When we speak of the communist road to development, we are really referring to the 1950s through the early 1980s. Even if we focus only on the overall growth during this earlier period, it is even more impressive if we consider that up until the 1980s, China had to come up with all her individual capital, all the capital within the country; they did not have access to the World Bank or the International Monetary Fund and all of the capitalist sources of capital.

This isolation was exacerbated during the Korean War when the United States sponsored a trade embargo against China. Moreover, the isolation was even more exacerbated when China broke with the USSR in 1960; so, it did not even have Soviet help after that. China really had to follow a complete self-reliance strategy to finance her own development. As a result, China avoided the huge indebtedness that many Third World countries fell into.

Where did the capital come from then? It was largely extracted from agriculture. What Mao managed to do was to modernize agriculture and increase output sufficiently that the population could be fed, but the surplus could then be funneled into industrial investments. China used, somewhat, a modified version of the West's original industrialization model, which had begun with an agricultural revolution whose surplus was then used to industrialize. Of course, in the West, this agricultural and then industrial revolution was accomplished by millions of independent entrepreneurs—whereas, in the Chinese case, it was a state-directed process. The other difference from the Western model is that both the agricultural and industrial products that were produced were produced for internal consumption, and not for an export market.

If we examine the actual evolution of this state-directed agricultural revolution, we can see clearly the strengths and weaknesses of a command economy in producing overall growth. After an initial phase of expropriation of the large landowners that we discussed earlier, where the land was redistributed to 300 million landless laborers in farming cooperatives, in the late 1950s, Mao embarked on a more intense reorganization of rural society that he called the Great Leap Forward. With the claim that China was going to soon overtake Britain in industrial development, the Communist Party organized all the peasants into large rural communes of about 25,000 each, which were to collectively manage all production. Villages became production teams; several teams made up a production brigade, and each team or brigade was given quotas of goods they had to produce, whether agricultural or industrial. Then, they would go back and turn out this number of goods. However, the Great Leap Forward was a dismal failure; not only did it fail to reach the quota set by the government, but it disrupted production so much that it resulted in a massive famine between 1960 and 1961. As in the Soviet Union during the collectivization process of the early 1930s, the dismal results were hushed up but later the figures started leaking out. Estimates range from 30 million to 50 million people died of starvation or malnutrition in one of the worst famines in modern history.

There are similarities with the Soviet famine of the 1930s in terms of disruption in agricultural production that comes with this rural transformation. However, in the Soviet case, there was more a direct war that was waged against the peasants by Stalin and the Communist Party; whereas, in the Chinese case, the famine was really much more the consequence of bureaucratic ineptitude and bad planning. Here, I think, is where we get the downside of the command economy; that is, in the Chinese case, what you have are bureaucrats in the center dictating specific policies for peasants in the field—on the ground that made no sense in their local setting. You have a policy that is directed from the center that leaves no flexibility or room for local conditions. Fields were over-planted to meet unrealistic goals. Crops failed because they were over-planted. Labor was arbitrarily shifted between tasks, and resources were misallocated to fit grand schemes that were designed by central planners. So, the problem with a centralized economic policy is that it takes no account of local conditions; it has no flexibility, and if it is not working, it leaves no other alternative. Everything is funneled into one plan, and if that plan does not work, everything collapses.

On the other hand, there is sometimes an upside of a command economy; that is, when the government has a good idea it works well. For example, when the government realized that the Great Leap Forward had been a disaster, it changed policies again, and broke up the huge rural communes into smaller work brigades. The government gave those work brigades incentives to produce more without the same kinds of very specific quotas that they had before, and they were rewarded not just for quantity but for quality.

It, then, used this new structure to disseminate the techniques of the "green revolution" in the 1960s and 1970s. The green revolution was dramatically increasing agricultural yields around the world in the 1960s and 1970s. What it consisted of was newer high-yield seeds, chemical fertilizers that were used to increase yields, and increased irrigation. There is a whole set of techniques that are grouped under the roof of the green revolution and that really revolutionized agricultural production in the Third World.

The results in China were dramatic increases in agricultural production in the 1960s and 1970s. The green revolution spread even more rapidly than in India, partly because once the government has an idea and wants all the brigades to do it, they are going to adopt it; whereas, in other parts of the world, sometimes peasants put up more resistance, did not want to take on these new techniques. Also, it was spread more widely because the government could actually provide these expensive techniques to poor communes who would not ordinarily be able to purchase them.

This, we might say, is the positive side of the command economy; when the government had a good economic plan, it could achieve dramatic results. In terms of overall growth and modernization then, China did achieve impressive growth since the 1940s, but it is clear that the capitalist model of development produced more consistent overall growth; it was more flexible, and it did not have the kind of ups and downs that this command economy approach had. In fact, the clear superiority of the capitalist model in introducing overall wealth made the Chinese government turn in the 1980s from the command economy to more market-oriented policies because they had reached stagnation. Of course, when they turned in the 1980s to these more market-oriented policies, growth rates went up again dramatically. Over the 1980s, growth rates were about 10 percent, which was quite high, and in the 1990s, growth rates were as high as 12 percent.

While the creation of wealth is clearly a strength of the capitalist versus communist system, how about the impact of that growth in raising the standard of living? That is the other real indicator of success or failure, raising the standard of living of the majority poor sector of the population. Clearly, it is in this area that the Chinese communist model shines; this is where its strength was, in eradicating poverty. Because of the forced expropriation of land and wealth, China reduced the drastic division between rich and poor, and was able to guarantee everyone food and a job. As a result, even the impact of the green revolution was different in China than in a place like India. Without private property, it was not the rich farmers who were able to use the green revolution techniques, but, again, all of the peasant brigades that were given these new techniques, and new seeds, and so on, by the government. The government also tried to provide universal health care by sending rural doctors and medical assistants to the smallest villages in the hinterlands, and by teaching peasants to use modern medicine instead of folk healing techniques.

Also, in terms of education, the Chinese achieved basic literacy and schooling, while in India, a third of the children still don't attend school even in the 1990s, and almost half the population is illiterate.

If we pursue more statistical differences, you can see that this difference in living standard is quantifiable. China did not have that endemic hunger and malnutrition that India had, and consequently, the basic health indicators in China are higher. We look at the indicators of infant mortality and life expectancy, and the Chinese figures are quite impressive compared to India. So, infant mortality had fallen to 35 deaths out of 1,000 as compared to India's 89 deaths out of 1,000; so, that is more than twice the developed world's 10 infant deaths out of 1,000 by the 1980s. Likewise, life expectancy in the 1990s was 70 years, whereas, in India, that number was 61. So, because of the Communist Party's commitment to social and economic equality, then, growth did get translated into an improved standard of living for the majority of the population for the average Chinese peasant.

Interestingly, these conclusions have been reinforced by the fact that the gap between the rich and the poor has been growing since the 1980s, that is, growing since the introduction of more market-oriented capitalist growth policies.

Before the 1980s, in the period we are discussing, the price for a better-fed and healthier population was a repressive enforced equality. Life in the rural cooperatives was closely monitored, with the government officials trying to enforce rigid social and economic equality and an absolute commitment to the principles of communism. In one classic local study of a place called Chen Village, the best symbol of the government's presence in people's lives was the loudspeakers that were outside, in the center of the village square, which were on two hours in the morning and two hours in the afternoon—making announcements and giving pep talks, and criticizing slackers and praising hard workers, very much like the image of the Big Brother in Orwell's book *1984*. You could hear the loudspeakers whether you were inside or outside your house—the symbol of the government presence in individual lives.

The repressiveness of this radical pursuit of equality became even greater during the Cultural Revolution of the late 1960s, when Mao became convinced that true equality had not yet been achieved. To renovate the revolution that he felt had fallen into bureaucratic stagnation, he launched a major purge of members of the elite professions: teachers, party leaders, intellectuals—anyone who was judged to be tainted by bourgeois influence, by upper class influence, or who considered themselves somehow better than the masses. Millions of people lost their jobs, their livelihoods; many of them were sent to camps to be re-educated in proletarian values. As one of the slogans of the Cultural Revolution put it, it is "better to be red, than expert." Opera singers were sent to clean bathrooms.

Intellectuals were sent to work on farms, in order to learn simple "peasant values." Some 17 million high school graduates were assigned to work as manual laborers on farms, again, in order to teach them simple values, and this program went from the late 1960s until the late 1970s, when it was discontinued.

In general, all white-collar workers were required to spend at least two months a year doing manual labor. In contrast, peasants were put in administrative posts, and janitors became plant managers in this radical attempt to impose some sort of equality. To publicly signal the equalization of status, everyone was supposed to wear the same overalls and the same hat to eliminate all class distinctions. There is a poignant scene in one of the great cinematic treatments of this period—the Chinese film, *To Live*—in which we see the chaos of a hospital in which the doctors have been purged, and the young students who have taken over finally realize what it means to be red instead of expert, when they are helpless to stop a pregnant woman from hemorrhaging to death on the operating table.

As in the earlier purges in the Soviet Union, many people were terrorized into implicating friends and relatives and neighbors, and those accused could be sentenced without any direct evidence. Mao called on young people to be the shock troops of this new revolution, and he gave these fanatical, young Red Guard troops broad powers to root out inequality and root out the remnants of capitalism mentality and traditional hierarchy.

The goal, then, was an absolutely equal society but the price was terror, oppression, and persecution of an estimated 100 million people who were thought to be intellectuals or bourgeois-influenced in some way; the burning of libraries; the closing of universities; and so on.

So, the Cultural Revolution declared that the regime would impose a cultural, economic, and social homogeneity that it defined as equality through a process of mass terror. Once again, the Cultural Revolution seemed to realize the worst fears of the mass society critics that we discussed earlier, creating a society in which uniformity had replaced all individual distinctions on virtually every level.

When Mao died in 1976, his widow tried to lead a movement to continue this radical policy of equalization, but a new leadership rejected this path, and in fact, Mao's widow and her cronies were arrested. The so-called Gang of Four were arrested and put in jail, and the new leadership tried to chart a more pragmatic course that accepted greater interaction with the West, more integration into the market economy, and less emphasis on radical equality; that is why we get a new mixed model that comes in the later 1980s. However, from the 1950s through the 1970s, the Chinese communist model demonstrates the dangers of enforcing equality through a tyrannical state; at the same time, it illustrates how a state committed to equality, committed to raising the standard of living of its population, can produce dramatic results in basic health indicators. The question raised by this unattractive tradeoff is about the balance between equality and freedom.

To further explore this balance, in the next lecture, we are going to focus on India, where a different equation produced a different set of tradeoffs.

Lecture Thirty-Five
Development Models—Democratic India

Scope:

Turning to a different development case study, this lecture uses India as an example of the successes and limits of the capitalist democratic model in the Third World. Because China and India began the process of development with similar problems, they provide ideal points of comparison between the two development models. We begin by outlining the elements of India's pluralist political system and its economic policy based on private property and a general adherence to the free market. The conclusion weighs the results of India's development model, evaluating its accomplishments in the area of economic growth and political liberties and its limits in reducing levels of poverty.

Outline

I. The capitalist democratic model in the Third World, that is, in societies with serious economic inequalities, endemic poverty, and traditional economies, had its successes and limits.

  A. India provides an excellent case study for evaluating democratic development, because it is one of the first (and few) new post-colonial nations to establish a stable, functioning democratic system.

    1. In the 1950s constitution, India established a British-style parliamentary system along a federalist design modeled after the United States.

    2. Beyond formal structure, India generally functions as a democracy, with significant political pluralism.

    3. Despite the uninterrupted rule of a single party for 47 years, elections have been vigorously contested and generally honest.

    4. Furthermore, because of decentralization, there has been a good deal of independent political activity at the local and regional levels, where other parties have held power.

    5. Democratic practice is also clear in India's vigorous pursuit of civil rights.

6. In addition to the basic liberal freedoms of speech and association, India has pursued an active policy of legal anti-discrimination to counter the hierarchies of Hindu caste society.

7. At the same time, India has pursued development through the democratic principle of gradual and consensual change, which is supported by the majority of the population.

8. There have been exceptions to democratic rule, especially in the disputed province of Kashmir, which has been under military rule since 1989.

B. In economic policy, India has tried to promote growth and prosperity in the framework of a capitalist model, that is, respecting private property and free enterprise.

1. Within a basic free market system, India has followed what has become the "catch-up" version of development, which allows a larger role for the state than in classic laissez-faire models.

2. Thus, the government set out national economic plans, created some state-owned businesses, and tried to coordinate private businesses behind a national development plan.

3. Since 1991, India has moved away from this planning model toward a more American-style liberalization.

4. In the 1950s, plans focused on improving agricultural yields and feeding the population.

5. In the 1960s, industrialization was added.

6. In the 1970s and 1980s, India entered the high-tech field.

II. What have been the successes of India's democratic capitalist model of development?

A. The most impressive results have been in the rates of growth.

B. Propelling this growth was a virtual agricultural revolution, in which India tripled food production between 1947 and 1985.

C. In terms of industrialization, India has managed to find a competitive niche for its manufactured and high-tech goods in Third World markets.

D. Finally, in terms of social gains, India has one of the largest middle classes in the Third World and has improved health indicators, such as life expectancy and infant mortality.

III. On the other hand, there have been limits to the Indian model, as the Nobel prize-winning economist Amartya Sen has pointed out.

    A. The key problem, he says, is that there has been no significant reduction in poverty, and in fact, the gap between rich and poor has widened.

        1. High rates of poverty have kept the life expectancy rate low compared to China, and endemic malnutrition is still a serious problem.

        2. How is it possible that India is technically self-sufficient in agriculture but suffers endemic malnutrition?

        3. In contrast to China, where the green revolution was made available to all farming communities, in India, the expensive fertilizers were accessible only to wealthy farmers.

        4. Further, as Sen has pointed out, *self-sufficiency* in a capitalist economy does not mean that everyone is adequately fed; it simply means that the market demand for food has been met.

        5. The gap between high growth and quality of life for the masses has been compounded by a limited program of welfare and social services, which has not made a major effort to redistribute wealth through entitlement programs.

        6. The assumption that growth would take care of poverty was further reflected in the liberalization plan of 1991, which focused on encouraging more foreign trade and investment to stimulate growth.

    B. Why hasn't India been able to reduce poverty more effectively?

        1. Sen uses a comparison with Sri Lanka to demonstrate that it is not simply a problem of more growth.

        2. Sen argues that this inability is the result of the elitist nature of Indian politics, controlled by the educated upper-caste minority.

3. In other words, the roots of the problem go back to India's socially conservative path to independence.

4. One could also pose the broader question about the limits of a democratic capitalist model in reducing poverty in such a place as India.

5. The capitalist system leaves in place the existing property structure, no matter how unequal, while a democratic polity makes it difficult to carry out serious voluntary reforms.

C. As in the Chinese case, we are left with a series of tradeoffs. India has created dramatic growth and a stable democratic government, but these achievements have been at the cost of reducing poverty. Given the contrasting tradeoffs of the Chinese and Indian models, the question is whether it is possible for democratic governments to address serious problems of economic inequality, or whether economic justice requires the sacrifice of political freedoms.

Essential Reading:

Amartya Sen, "How Is India Doing?" *New York Review*, December 16, 1982, and "How Has India Fared?" *Frontline*, August 22, 1997.

Supplementary Reading:

Stanley Wolpert, *A New History of India*, chapters 23–26.

Questions to Consider:

1. In Amartya Sen's evaluation of "how India is doing," he thinks the negatives outweigh the positives: What should the criteria for "successful" development be?

2. Is there a way to imagine combining the benefits of the Indian and Chinese models, or would that involve too many contradictions?

Lecture Thirty-Five—Transcript
Development Models—Democratic India

Turning to a different development case study, this lecture analyzes the development in India as an example of the successes and limits of the capitalist democratic model in the Third World, that is, in societies with serious economic inequalities, high levels of poverty, and traditional economy.

India provides an excellent case study for evaluating democratic development, because it is one of the first (and one of the few) new post-colonial nations to establish a stable, functioning democratic system that has survived throughout the entire second half of the 20th century.

As we talked about in an earlier lecture, the liberal democratic model was one of the legacies of British imperialism and its extensive school system, which really trained a generation of Indian elites in democratic ideas and ideals. India's commitment to this democratic tradition was nicely expressed in the words of the first President of India, President Nehru, in his first speech in 1946 to the constituent assembly, whose job it was to write India's first democratic constitution. As he said, "I think of the various constituent assemblies I have gone before and of what took place at the making of the great American nation when the fathers of that nation met and fashioned a consititution which has stood the test for so many years." Nehru saw India as following in that tradition, and now he hoped that they were ready to take up the mantle of democracy. In fact, India did adopt a model democratic constitution, which her ex-masters—the British—helped develop. The constitution that was promulgated in 1950 was essentially a Western document that established a parliamentary system like Britain but a federal system like the United States, in which significant powers were given to state and local governments.

The purpose of the idea behind the federal system was to give significant voice to the diversity of Indian society. In practice, there have been some limitations with India's democratic process, but in essence, India has really—truly—been a function of democracy, not just of democracy on paper. Moreover, it has managed to hold the nation-state together through the democratic process, which has been one of the most difficult things for a Third World nation to do—to be a function of democracy and to hold the nation-state together.

If we look at some of the indicators of India's functioning democracy, the first one is the degree of political pluralism that has to be explained. If you look on the surface, a single party—the Congress Party—was actually in power, almost uninterrupted for about 47 years. Despite the fact that at the national level a single party is in power uninterrupted for 47 years, elections have been vigorous and honestly contested. As one Indian commentator put it, "India has democracy in the sense that every five years, the rulers feel shaky; they need to come to the people literally with folded hands." Of course, in May 1996, the Congress Party was finally defeated at the national level for the second time since 1947, leaving other parties to form the national government since then—most recently, the BJP, a Hindu nationalist party, which has been in power since 1998.

Even though the Congress Party ruled for so long at the national level, because of the decentralized organization of the state, there was a lot of political pluralism at the regional and local level. This decentralization was even more marked after the regionalist revolt in the mid-1950s, when India's provinces were redrawn along ethnic and linguistic lines. The 16 regional states that were drawn out of this reorganization were established around the borders of linguistic communities and what were considered the 16 major languages of the subcontinent. Each of these 16 major languages had its own history and culture and was spoken by more people than many of the European languages. Hindi, the language spoken by 30 percent of the population (particularly around the New Delhi area and the upper Ganges Valley) was declared as the national language, so everyone had to learn Hindi but regional states could declare their own regional language.

After this reorganization, after 1956, many of the states had their own official language and tried to assert their own cultural and political identities. In fact, other parties have held power at the local and regional level at different points. Before the 1996 election when the Congress Party was defeated at the national level, at the regional level only about 20 percent of regional governments' regionalist parties held those elections. There is a great deal of political pluralism below the surface of national politics.

In contrast to many African countries—where ethnic and linguistic divisions seem to undermine democratic government—in India, they were at least partially channeled into this active local politics that seem to invigorate rather than undermine democracy. Perhaps it was precisely the strength of the Congress Party at the national level that provided the space for this more pluralistic local politics. In any case, then, one-party rule in India has not meant the same thing that it meant in China, which had a more centralized and monolithic state.

More evidence of a functioning democratic regime can be found in India's pursuit of civil rights. In China, the regime concentrated on providing a legal framework for equality of citizens across ethnic linguistic boundaries (and religious also). The principle of equality across the boundaries is one of the fundamental characteristics of a democratic regime. So, it established freedom of the press, free speech and assembly, the tolerance of diverse opinions—all of the things that the Indian economist Amartya Sen calls "freedom of the mind." India truly has freedom of the mind.

In addition to the basic liberal freedoms, India pursued an active policy of legal anti-discrimination to counter the hierarchies of the Hindu caste society. Women were given equal legal rights; they were allowed to vote, and certain practices like *Sati*—in which the widow throws herself on the funeral pyre of her dead husband—were outlawed. For untouchables, the lowest caste in Hindu culture, the government set up perhaps the first affirmative action program; quotas were set in bureaucracy, government posts, Parliament, and so on that had to be filled by untouchables, which were those individuals who constituted the bottom 15 percent of the population. These scheduled castes had to fill certain numbers of seats in government positions.

In other words, the Indian government used some of the same strategies as has been used in the United States to create political equality of opportunity for all its citizens.

At the same time, it has pursued a quality of opportunity through the gradual consensual method of majoritarian democracy, rather than through the model of forced change that we saw in the communist case.

If you recall from an earlier lecture, this follows clearly form the pre-independence movement in India and the distinction between that movement and the Communist Party in China. The pre-independence nationalist movement was not based on a social revolutionary philosophy and was socially conservative, so it did not come in with a plan of having to turn society upside down. When the Congress Party and Nehru got in power, they continued to embrace this principle of gradual change in which all sectors of the population could work together in a commitment for the democratic process. They embraced the idea of democracy as a consensus-building system in which every group gets some of what it wants but not everything, so a give and take idea of democracy. The depth of commitment to these values was demonstrated in a 1997 poll in which 59 percent of the population believes that their vote made a difference, and only 30 percent said the country would be better off without elections and competing political parties. This demonstrates a high commitment to the whole notion of the democratic process. If we consider all of these factors, India clearly serves as one of the best examples of a functioning democracy in a non-Western world. There have been some exceptions to democratic rule within India, especially in the disputed region of Kashmir, in which a majority Muslim province has been subjected to military rule since the 1989 separatist rebellion. Kashmir lays between Pakistan and India, and in 1948, it theoretically had the choice to join either India or Pakistan. Although the country had a majority Muslim population—and for this reason one might think it would have joined Pakistan—Kashmir had a Hindu leader who basically held off declaring which country he would join until local Muslim forces from Pakistan invaded Kashmir. Only then, did the Hindu leader of Kashmir turn to India asking for help in driving out its invaders, and in return joined with India. It was a deal made between the leader and the Indian government; whereas, the Kashmir people never had a chance to democratically decide their fate.

The eventual cease-fire divided Kashmir into a Pakistani section and Indian section, but the tensions over Kashmir's status were not resolved. The brutal repression by India of the successionist movement since 1989 demonstrates how ethnic tensions can threaten but not destabilize a democratic government when you have a majority ethnic religious group.

If we move from political structure to economic policies, the government clearly has followed a capitalist model of development, but more specifically, what we have identified as the "catch-up" capitalist model of development set by Japan in the late 19th century. It tried to promote economic development and modernization within the existing structure of private property, but with a greater role for government encouragement and structuring of the economy than was the case in classic laissez-faire Western models. It respected private enterprise, but the government also created some state-owned businesses, especially large enterprises. Likewise, it allowed the market to function but also set out national economic goals—a series of five-year plans in which it asked private businessmen to contribute to these national goals, but did not coerce them or force them to do so. The government tried to coordinate private businesses behind a national economic policy, and since 1991, the Indian government has tried to move away even from this partial planning model towards a more laissez-faire liberal Western model. Since then, India has looked even more like a classic liberal democratic capitalist system.

What do the economic plans of the early years focus on? In the 1950s, economic policy focused on encouraging rural development, improving agricultural yields, and feeding the population. In the 1960s, the plans added industrial development. In the 1970s and 1980s, India began to enter high-technology industries—building electronic equipment, computers, and nuclear power. In the 1990s, with liberalism, they have sought to let Indian industry compete openly on the world markets without subsidiaries and protection.

What have been the successes of India's gradualist democratic path to modernization? As India's Nobel prize-winning economist Amartya Sen pointed out in an article that he wrote in 1982 (called "How Is India Doing?"), there have been some impressive victories; the biggest victory has been economic growth. From 1947 on, India's GNP has been growing faster than its population, which tripled in 50 years. To complement the continued economic growth, the government has helped slow down population growth with a massive family planning campaign that reduced the birth rate to about 2.2 percent, the third lowest birth rate among four nations. Thus, in the 1980s, India's population was growing at a rate of 2.2 percent while its economy was growing at a rate of 4 percent to 5 percent—so it was keeping ahead of population growth. Since 1991 and the liberalism policies, the economy has been growing faster; in the 1990s, it was about 6 percent. At the center of this economic growth was a virtual agricultural revolution. From 1947 to 1985, India managed to triple food production, and this agricultural victory was largely due to the "green revolution" of the 1960s. New strains of rice were introduced that could be planted three times a year, and thus increase productivity. As a result of this agricultural revolution, India became self-sufficient in food production for the first time. In doing so, it basically eliminated the possibility of major famine—so the last major famine in India took place in 1943, just before independence. Since then, food crisis situations never escalated into famine.

In addition to the gains in agricultural, there had been clear gains in industrialization as well. India has become the tenth largest industrial economy in the world. India's technical and scientific research is much more developed than most countries in the Third World category and in its GNP bracket as well. India has made inroads into export markets in high-technology goods, and especially services, including having become a member of the nuclear family. India created its niche in this high-technology goods market not in the West, but in other non-Western countries where they could sell computers and other high-technology goods at lower prices than those made in Japan or in the West. In the 1990s, India's niche market has been the outsourced information technology of Western companies who are taking advantage of a large, well-trained class of engineers and computer programmers.

Finally, if we look in terms of social gains, India has one of the largest middle classes in the Third World and one of the highest percentages of the population in higher education, about six times that of China. India has succeeded in advancing some members of the untouchable class into prominent positions. Its anti-discrimination or affirmative action campaigns have had some impact. It has also considerably improved health indicators, like life expectancy and infant mortality. In 1947, the expected life-expectancy age was only 33; that went up to 52 years old in 1982, and up to 61 years old in the 1990s—and, infant mortality went down from a very high 151 deaths per 1,000 to the moderately high 89. However, as Amartya Sen points out, there have been limits to the Indian model. Significantly, Sen came to the same conclusion in a follow-up article that he wrote in 1997. The key problem is that despite good indicators of overall growth, there has been no decisive reduction in poverty. Thus, growth has ended up expanding the wealthy and middle classes dramatically, but it has widened the gap between the poor and the middle and upper classes. While India has a large number of middle-class college students, up to 48 percent of the population is still illiterate.

In terms of income, in the late 1990s, about 1/3 of the population fell below the government's poverty level of an annual income of $100 a year. That was down somewhat from 50 percent of the population at independence, but still much higher than the world average of 26 percent. Even though there have been no more famines since 1943, there remains an endemic hunger and malnutrition that especially touches rural India. Endemic malnutrition means that people don't die in spectacular numbers during short famine periods, but that their bodies are slowly starved for nutrients over a long period of time. The results of that are higher rates of disease and lower life expectancies, and higher infant mortality when compared to China's.

Another impact has been the continuation of female infanticide, where families in poor rural areas continue to kill their baby daughters, so they don't have to support them—a practice that has been outlawed but is still practiced. How is this continued poverty and malnutrition possible given the dramatic yield increases of the green revolution? Ironically, the green revolution did little to address the problem of poverty, but simply increased yields. Why? For one thing, because farming with those new strains of rice was more intensive and more expensive, the only farmers who could afford to adapt to that were the wealthier farmers. Because the government never carried out a major land reform, poor farmers and landless laborers actually fell further behind once the green revolution technologies were introduced. In other words, because the green revolution was carried out through private investment, it had the consequence of increasing rural inequality rather than decreasing it.

Further, as Sen has pointed out, the fact that more rice was grown does not mean that everyone who was hungry was getting it. In a capitalist economy, what *self-sufficiency* meant, literally, is that everyone who can afford to buy food can buy it, not that everyone who needs it gets it. So, although the market demand for food has been met, that does not mean the caloric needs of the population have been met as well. The real improvement in people's quality of life is not as dramatic as the overall statistics or the overall claim that India reached self-sufficiency in agricultural production would indicate. This is compounded, as Sen points out, by a very limited program of social services in India, which does not make a major effort to redistribute some of the national wealth through entitlement programs, or to provide what he calls social opportunities, like health care and education. Here, Sen makes the comparison to neighboring Sri Lanka, which has the same per capita income as India but an extensive program of social services, including subsidized rice and medical supplies. The results in Sri Lanka are lower mortality rates and less endemic hunger. In reality, although India began in 1947 proclaiming the double goals of poverty reduction and growth, in fact, it concentrated more on growth than on eradicating poverty; or, to put it another way, India assumed that growth would take care of poverty. This assumption is still evident in the 1991 economic reforms, which concentrated on getting more foreign investment and foreign trade through a free market, with the hope of a trickle-down effect. However, at least in the short term, the results were mostly increased consumer prices and population discontent, which was reflected in the 1996 defeat of the Congress Party at the national level, because the Congress Party was blamed. As one critic put it, the 1991 policy seemed to be intended to open up the country for business so the top 25 percent could benefit. Whether India's dramatic entrance into the high-technology market in the 1990s will have a long-term impact on poverty is still unclear.

Why hasn't India been able to deal more effectively with the poverty problem? As Sen demonstrates with his case study of Sri Lanka, it is not simply a problem of more growth; it is a decision that the government makes as to whether feeding its people or redistributing income is a priority of the government.

So, why wasn't this a priority of the Indian government? Sen argues that it is due to the elitist nature of Indian politics, which is controlled by an educated, wealthy upper-caste urban elite that ignores the rest of India. As another critic said during the election campaign in the late 1990s, "I think the central government has said to hell with the 50 percent who live in the dark villages of the interior." What Sen argues implicitly, then, is that India's failure to reduce poverty is linked directly to the socially conservative nature of its independence movement, its path to independence. Beyond the specificities of Indian history, one could pose the question about whether the democratic capitalist model has certain limits in the Third World, in a place like India where you have dramatic gaps between rich and poor. In other words, the capitalist system leaves in place the existing structure of private property, no matter how unequal it is, while a democratic consensus model makes it difficult to carry out serious social reforms. For example, what the democratic system offered to untouchables was anti-discriminatory legislation included in Parliament, not land reform. What the government offered to baby girls were laws against killing them, rather than sufficient economic assistance to convince families that they could support them. It is this combination of factors that militated against ending poverty. The regime began as an elite-dominated country with huge gaps between rich and poor, and the model of democratic capitalism offered few channels to change this existing elite system.

So, what do we conclude about the India model of development? On the one hand, the results were impressive in encouraging growth and in building a democratic system; however, on the other hand, the Indian model falls short when it comes to the third criteria of reducing poverty. The positive side is that India is an open and pluralistic society with a great deal of freedom, but the downside is that it is still an economically and socially polarized society with a severe poverty problem. If we look at the two models, China and India, we see China with a better fed, healthier, and broadly more literate population—a more equitable distribution of wealth and privilege, but with massive political repression and with the powerful presence of a government forcing equality on the population. On the other hand, we have India, with the political liberties and economic growth, but over a third of the population living at—or below—a starvation level.

Sen asks the question of whether India's political liberties are worth it? Would it be better to feed the population healthier and give up those liberties? But he answers no, that the Chinese tradeoff, as he says, is not an attractive one either. To give a stark illustration of the tradeoff, while in India families kill baby girls because they cannot support them economically, in China, families kill baby girls because the government imposed a one-child policy. The lack of economic choice versus the lack of political choice is not a very attractive tradeoff; they both lead to equally grim results.

The Indian model demonstrates how easy it is for great social and economic inequalities to survive despite a democratic system. But, the Chinese model demonstrates the danger of enforcing equality through a tyrannical state. The big question, of course (and it is not a new one), is whether these two values—freedom and equality, or freedom and social economic justice—are mutually exclusive especially in countries with vast gaps between rich and poor. Or if not, how can we imagine a path to modernization that balances the freedoms of a few with the needs of the many.

Lecture Thirty-Six
The Authoritarian Development State—Japan

Scope:

As was the case before World War II, Japan's economic redevelopment was in a class of its own. This lecture examines the hybrid model used to achieve its spectacular prosperity, a model that has taken elements from both the classic liberal and the communist approaches to development. The components of what some scholars have called *soft authoritarianism* include a state economic policy but a capitalist market, a democratic constitution but an effectively one-party regime, and a collective mobilization of different sectors of the population behind development goals.

Outline

I. Although Japan was, in many ways, already a "developed" country in 1945, it was faced with the considerable challenge of rebuilding a shattered economy and reconstructing a political framework that had been discredited.

   A. Furthermore, the Japanese model of (re)development served as a guide for other poor Third World countries in Southeast Asia that were developing for the first time; thus, it has some applicability in the non-Western world.

   1. What made Japan different from most of the Third World nations was that it retained many advantages despite economic devastation, such as an educated homogenous population, skills, technology, and so on.

   2. Nevertheless, it was faced with the common problem of quickly building a competitive industrial economy and a stable political system.

   3. It also still suffered from a lack of raw materials, energy sources, and farmland.

   B. The model followed by Japan until the early 1990s exemplified what some scholars have called the *authoritarian developmental* model.

   1. In some ways, it combines aspects of the democratic/capitalist and socialist models.

2. On the one hand, it relies on a strong state to push modernization from above and one-party rule to neutralize opposition and focus development.
3. On the other hand, it respects free enterprise and private property.

C. On the surface, Japan's American-designed constitutional system appears democratic, not authoritarian, especially compared to the regime it replaced.

1. Despite the democratic framework, however, the regime has operated as what some political scientists have called a *soft* authoritarian state.
2. Thus, despite the existence of several political parties, the Liberal Democratic Party held uninterrupted power until the 1990s, and even since then, it has been the dominant partner in many coalitions.
3. De facto one-party rule in Japan differs from that in India because of the greater centralization of Japanese politics and the authoritarianism of non-elected institutions, such as the bureaucracy and the police.

II. Why did large majorities continue to vote for the same party over so many years?

A. At first, the government used heavy repression to control trade unions and communists, but by the 1960s, prosperity provided legitimization for many.

B. In other words, if a mildly authoritarian state can achieve economic development and prosperity for its population, people may be willing to make the tradeoff between economic well-being and lack of political choices.

C. What's crucial here seems to be the minimum level of authoritarianism that guarantees stability and encourages economic growth without stifling it.

III. How did the soft authoritarian state encourage development?

A. The role of the state has been to help private business succeed in the free market, even more aggressively than in democratic "catch-up" states, such as India.

B. In political science lingo, the state has used *market-conforming* methods of intervention, as opposed to the socialist *market suppression* methods.

C. Thus, the government disseminates information to businessmen on market opportunities and provides incentives for certain kinds of economic activities.

D. Instead of leaving companies to figure out their own market niches (laissez-faire) or mandating what companies should produce (command economy), the government sets out collective goals and tries to convince people to follow them.

E. One of the main tasks of the government has been to mobilize people around these collective goals.

    1. One of the catchy phrases invented to express this collective ideal is "Japan, Inc.," the idea that the entire country is an integrated corporation in which all members are making decisions to improve the well-being of the whole.

    2. In contrast to the American emphasis on individual initiative and profit and the fear that collectivism and self-sacrifice undermine capitalism, in Japan, workers and businessmen are called on to cooperate and sacrifice for the overall growth of the "company."

    3. Workers are asked to work hard, and until the economic crisis of the late 1990s, many were rewarded with lifetime job security.

    4. The labor relations system set up by the government depends on *enterprise unions*, which negotiate with management for contracts but within a context of intense loyalty to the firm.

    5. Another ingredient to a self-sacrificing and hard-working workforce has been mobilizing Japanese women as housewives and mothers and valuing their contribution to caring for overworked husbands and children.

    6. A final group, mobilized behind national economic policy, has been consumers. To support the export-driven strategy, consumers are asked to limit consumption of luxury goods so as not to drive up the trade deficit.

F. The results of Japan's development model are, of course, in a class by themselves.

1. In the 1950s, Japan pursued a low-wage, labor-intensive strategy that undersold First World textiles and other light industry.
2. In the 1960s, it moved to a capital-intensive strategy that began investing in automobiles, televisions, and later, high-tech industries.
3. By 1968, Japan was the third largest industrial nation, and by the mid-1980s, it was the second.
4. Without massive inequalities of wealth or high levels of poverty, Japan has excellent education and better social services than exist in the United States.

Essential Reading:

Chalmers Johnson, *Japan: Who Governs?*, "Japan: Who Governs?" and "Social Values and the Theory of Late Economic Development in East Asia."

Supplementary Reading:

Ronald Dore, *Taking Japan Seriously*.

E. Reischauer, *The Japanese Today: Change and Continuity*.

Questions to Consider:

1. What do you think of the claim that authoritarian development is the model of the future, while democratic development is the model for the past? How would you support or contest this position?

2. Another possible scenario is that the authoritarian development model works for the initial stages of development, but that at some point, people are no longer willing to sacrifice political freedoms for economic comfort. What do you think is the most likely scenario?

Lecture Thirty-Six—Transcript
The Authoritarian Development State—Japan

In this lecture, we turn to a very different development case study than either China or India, and that is Japan. In most ways, of course, Japan was not in any way comparable to other Third World nations after 1945 since it was already a "developed" country at that period. Still, it was faced with a considerable challenge of rebuilding a shattered economy and of reconstructing a political framework that had been completely discredited. Like the non-developed countries, Japan had to quickly build a competitive industrial economy and a stable political system that would support it. Japan also still retained some of the problems it had during its first industrialization of the late 19th century; it still suffered from a lack of raw materials, energy sources, and farmland—so, it still had some of the same problems it had earlier. In the face of these challenges, Japan superseded all expectations to become the developmental success story of the postwar non-Western world—some might say of the post-world in general. Japan has been so successful in economic developments since World War II that she quickly regained her status as the economic equal of the most powerful nations in the world. Japan quickly joins the First World, if it ever was not part of that.

So, is the Japanese case, then, so special that we cannot use it as a model? Is it simply a unique case rather than a model for other countries? Certainly, Japan had many special advantages that other countries did not have. Even in 1945, when Japan was brought to her knees, Japan was not that average Third World country with the kind of problems that China and India had. Even though her economy was devastated, the country still had many advantages. It still had a highly educated and fairly homogenous population. It had technology, skills, experience, a compact territory, and so on. Furthermore, Japan's economy was given an extra boost in 1945 by the American development aide that was funneled into Japan; that is the Japanese version of the Marshall Plan—directed toward rebuilding a thriving capitalist economy. As with the Marshall Plan in Europe, I think, the reason this developmental aide was so successful in Japan was because the basic structure and knowledge were already there. It was building on certain advantages that existed; so, Japan had a lot going for it even at its lowest point in 1945.

Nevertheless, though, I think we can make the argument that the Japanese case is not unique but is actually a model that is followed by other countries. In fact, beginning in the 1960s, the Japanese model starts to become exportive, we could say, and taken up by a number of East and Southeast Asian countries: First, Korea, Taiwan, and Hong Kong; and later, Malaysia and Singapore; and finally, even poorer countries like Vietnam, Indonesia, and Thailand begin to follow the Japanese path. What emerges, then, is a kind of Southeast, East Asian model of development, of which Japan stands as the most dramatic example. The latest country to take this path, I would argue, at least in part, has been China since the mid-1980s.

The Japanese model is important not because Japan is unique, but because it has spawned other success stories, particularly in the region. Moreover, Japan serves not only as a model but it actually played a direct role in sparking economic modernization within the region. So, Japan has been a motor for development in neighboring countries. In a sense, then, ironically, Japan ended up helping to create that East Asian co-prosperity sphere that it had been talking about in a more opportunistic way during the early 1940s, during the war.

What is the Japanese model of modernization? Until 1993, when the system began to destabilize a bit, Japan exemplified what some political scientists have called the *authoritarian developmental* model of modernization. In some ways, this model constitutes a mixture of the communist and capitalist democratic models that we talked about earlier. From communism, this model takes the idea of a strong state that pushes through modernization and economic development from above. It also follows the streamline idea of communist politics—that the most efficient way for a strong state to pursue these policies is if it is united in purpose rather than divided into a pluralistic system. The first characteristic of the authoritarian developmental model is a strong one-party state that maintains stability and neutralizes opposition.

On the other hand, the Japanese model takes certain things from the democratic capitalist model, in particular: free enterprise, the market, private property, and the basic capitalist structure. So, the Japanese model consists of an authoritarian state that promotes the development of a capitalist economy. So, the result is capitalism with democracy and a one-party state without communism. Now, as in the case when we discussed India, where we had to explain what it really means that India had a democracy, I think in Japan, we have to explain what that means—that Japan had an authoritarian state—because, on the surface, it does not look like that. On the surface, it looks like a Western constitutional system, which, of course, the Americans helped Japan to install; compared to the regime it replaced, it looks very democratic. Remember the openly authoritarian centralized state that had been set up in the 19th century under the Meiji restoration with its powerful emperor that is replaced in the postwar system by an American-designed democratic constitution, with free elections and a multi-party political structure, and so on?

How can we define this as an authoritarian state? Despite the democratic framework on paper, in practice, the regime operated since the late 1940s as what some political scientists have called a *soft* authoritarian regime—soft because it has the trappings of democratic practice, but authoritarian because these have been more superficial than essential. Despite, for example, the existence of several major political parties, that is the trappings of political pluralism, the country was ruled exclusively until 1993 by a single political party, the conservative Liberal Democratic Party or the LDP. The major opposition party was the Socialist Party, which never gained more than 20 percent of the vote throughout the period. Since 1993, the picture has muddied somewhat, and that is why I say the model has destabilized because the LDP lost its domination—its one-party rule—and has been replaced by a series of coalition governments. Even since then, the LDP has been the dominant partner in most of these coalition governments.

So, with this political model, the Japanese state was able to maintain a high degree of political and social stability, which—in turn—favors development. What has made de facto one-party rule in Japan different from India (remember, in India, there is effectively one-party rule at the national level as well)? What makes it different in Japan is the greater political centralization. Thus, one-party rule meant one-party rule at all levels of government; there is not the pluralist local and regional government arena as in India; so, the LDP ruled at all levels of government. Furthermore, authoritarianism existed in the power of non-elected institutions in Japan, particularly the central bureaucracy and the national police force. Both bureaucracy and the police force are extremely centralized and largely unlimited by any parliamentary oversight process. The real power in Japan has been wielded by appointed ministers and their bureaucratic staff in what represented more continuity than was apparent with the major restoration system; that is, the bureaucracy really continues to wield a great deal of the power. In India, this was not possible because the prewar bureaucracy was British, and they created a whole new system; it does not provide that same source of state power.

On the other hand, one-party rule was different from the Chinese case because this one party continued to be elected in free elections, and that was very different from one party that imposed itself.

Why did people continue to vote for the same party over 50 years? In the early years, the government used more heavy-handed measures to repress opposition—particularly, the communists and the trade unions. But by the 1960s, the ruling party did not have to do that anymore; it effectively had seduced most people with economic success. In other words, the economic success convinced people that the tradeoff was worth it and that other things compensated for the lack of real democracy. Thus, if a mildly authoritarian regime can achieve the economic development it pursues, this success can legitimize the regime in the minds of the population, despite the lack of political freedom. This argument has been made for other regimes like Spain in the 1960s and early 1970s, under the dictatorship of the authoritarian development there. Evidence is that until 1993, the government did not have to force people at gunpoint to vote for them; 50 percent or more of the population freely voted for them. What is crucial here, I think, is the minimal level of authoritarianism, which is where you get the soft qualifier to the model. This is not a Chinese-style regime trying to control every aspect of political and economic life. In a sense, what you could argue is that the Japanese found the minimal amount of authoritarianism that would encourage stability and economic growth, without provoking resentments and without provoking the sense that people did not have freedom to move.

How, then, did this soft authoritarian state promote development? Basically, the main goal of Japan's authoritarian state was to encourage and promote capitalist economic development. In fact, because of Japan's unique constitution, which prevented Japan from having a military force, the government did not have to waste its energies on military development. It could put all of its energies into economic development. To do this, it followed the pattern that was set in Japan's first rise to economic power; that is, the state took an active role in directing growth but within the basic structure of private enterprise, as I said before. It followed the basic late capitalist development model even more aggressively than in India, than in the democratic capitalist version of that.

What was this role, and how did it differ both from the socialist economic policies and from the older laissez-faire capitalism? We have talked about how even in the West, the classic laissez-faire state had been somewhat modified in the postwar period with the introduction of Keynesian ideas. There was no pure laissez-faire Western system, even in the postwar period. However, especially in the United States, government intervention into the economy has been limited to a handful of things: regulating markets, setting up standards, tinkering with interest rates, and so on. Even when state intervention extends beyond these measures, as it does occasionally, the attitude is still that state involvement in the economy is somehow a necessary evil—something done only in extreme cases—not a positive part of economic or national development. This negative view of government economic planning only increased in the 1980s under the Reagan administration in the United States and the Thatcher administration in Britain.

In contrast to this model, Japan accepted the positive role of government in setting national economic goals. How is this different than socialist economic planning when you have the government setting out plans? In the first place, most of the businesses are privately owned in Japan. But, a most important distinction is that the development state in Japan operates within the free capitalist market instead of ignoring the market.

In China, the state set national economic plans with goals for the production of a certain amount of goods, which was set by the state. You produce so many millions of widgets, and the state-owned factories were ordered to produce them. In Japan, the government sees its role as helping business succeed in the free market. In political science lingo, the state has used *market-conforming* methods of intervention, rather than *market suppression* methods. Instead of quotas for production, which a Chinese communist policy would promote, the Japanese government studies world markets and disseminates information to business leaders based on this information. Further, the government sets incentives to go into certain kinds of fields or produce certain kinds of products that it considers to have great potential on the world market, and discourages other industries, lets them die out if they don't feel as though they will have a comparative advantage in the world market. Instead of each company figuring out its niche in the world market, which is the American model, the Japanese government tries to do that for the economy as a whole, to figure out what the Japanese niche market will be. So, the government sets out collective goals and then tries to convince people to participate in them. This means, of course, that one of the main tasks of the development state is to mobilize the population around those goals; again, it cannot dictate that policy, and it has to mobilize them.

As a result, the state in Japan has a different relationship to its population than in either the United States or China. The catchy phrase invented to express this collective ideal is "Japan, Inc," the idea that the entire country is an integrated corporation in which all members are making decisions to improve the well-being of the whole. Think about the implications of that metaphor. The first implication is that economic growth is the primary goal of the nation and "Japan, Inc." is a corporation. But, it also means that there is a strong sense of collective identity and agenda. The idea of one integrated corporation means everyone is working for the same goals in the same direction. This stands in dramatic contrast to the American emphasis on individual enterprise and individual initiative and profit, and in fact, the fear that collectivism somehow undermines capitalism—so, it is the opposite. In Japan, the idea is that everyone cooperates together and sacrifices for the overall growth of the "company." In this company model, the relationship between businessmen and the government is quite different than in the United States.

In Japan, the government sets out to mobilize businessmen to contribute to economic goals. The relationship is one of close collaboration—not in the sense that business influences government, but also that government is able to impose its sense of the collective good on private business.

In the United States, business does have an important impact on the government; it can lobby the government to do things that favor business interests. On the other hand, in the United States, the government has little collective impact on business. It does not go both ways; there is no national economic plan that businesses are asked to participate in. Instead, the American government assumes, in classic liberal fashion, that the sum of private interest equals the public interest.

In the communist system, on the other hand, the government simply dictates what the public interest is, without any notion of private interest at all. In Japan, there is a collaboration between private and public interests. In ideal terms, there would be some kind of harmonious relationship between the public and private interests.

In the same way as businesses are mobilized, the state has also tried to instill in its workers the same sense of national mission. The results of this national mobilization around economic goals have created a dedicated and hard-working workforce. Everyone—from manual laborers to managers and technologists—often work late hours and weekends. The average Japanese workweek is five and 1/2 days a week, often working well into the evening. The pattern starts early; school children go to school six days a week. In the 1990s, they started giving children one Saturday off a month, and there was a huge uproar from those who were concerned about sinking standards.

In turn, for working so hard, workers are treated as valuable members of a collective. This attitude was institutionalized after the war in a labor relations system that was set up by the government. Most of the companies and firms have what are known as *enterprise trade unions*, which include everyone—from managers down to the lowest workers. These unions then negotiate with management for contracts, but within a context of intense loyalty to the firm, especially in the large firms. It was expected that most employees would stay their whole working lives with a single firm, giving them a strong incentive not to demand benefits that would hurt the long-range health of the firm. At the same time, it is important to point out that this system depended on an underclass of temporary workers, many of them female who were left out of the benefits of this system.

Another often hidden ingredient to this dedicated and productive workforce is the mobilization of women in the national economic mission. If you think of the intense working environment that I just mentioned—long workdays, five-and-1/2-day workweeks—it is very hard to imagine this without most Japanese women being at home, taking care of their overworked husbands, and, in particular, raising the next generation of workers—that is, their children, whose training is taken very seriously. The majority of Japanese women have been in what Americans would call a traditional role of full-time housewife and mother. But, it is not simply that the Japanese have chosen this role; the point is that it is a publicly valued role in which the government expends a lot of energy talking about the value of the traditional family, the centrality of it as a bulwark of social and economic prosperity. Specifically, the educating and raising of children is represented as a full-time serious responsibility that is entrusted to the nation's mothers. The evidence that most women actively embrace this goal is found in what is now a somewhat dated poll from 1984, in which 80 percent of the women believed that women should not work after having children. Seventy-six percent of Japanese mothers polled said their major reason for living was their children. That provides evidence that they have been mobilized into this larger goal.

The flip side of mobilizing mothers is that female workers have been discriminated against, even since the passage of an equal employment opportunity law

In 1986, many firms simply refused to hire women in permanent positions, assigning them to temporary jobs, and women consistently are paid only 50 percent of male wages for the same jobs.

Whether or not we emphasize the discriminatory aspect of supporting motherhood or the positive side of it—that is, motherhood is valued in a way that it is not in other places—what is clear is that the Japanese government has been able to harness certain aspects of traditional Japanese culture around this national economic mobilization for growth.

One final group that has been mobilized behind national economic policy is consumers. Because Japan lacks so many of the basic raw materials, the economic growth plan depended on massive exports that would then generate the money that could buy the needed raw materials. Of course, to have an export-driven policy, consumers cannot buy many imports; consumers must limit their consumption of luxury consumer goods so as not to drive up the trade deficit.

The Japanese have both worked very hard and lived austerely, especially compared to the Americans—without that kind of massive consumerism of American society, where working hard is rewarded by consumption.

The result has been low imports and high exports; so, consumers have effectively been mobilized around these national goals. In 1949, the Japanese economy exported virtually nothing; however, by 1961, their exports constituted 3 percent of the total world exports, and this rose to 10 percent in 1986, which is very extraordinary if you think about the size of the country.

The mobilization of all these different groups has produced dramatic results. Everyone knows the general success story, but here are just a few details. By 1956, a decade after the end of the war, the economy had basically recovered to its prewar levels through the pursuit of a low-wage, labor-intensive strategy that undersold First World textiles and other light industrial goods. In this early period, the label "made in Japan" denoted cheap—especially low-quality—goods, which were made possible by the low wages. Again, maintaining this strategy required that the government could neutralize trade-union opposition to low wages, and that there was an excess supply of labor that was willing to work under these low-wage conditions.

In the 1960s, this low-wage strategy had produced enough capital to move to a capital-intensive strategy that shifted to new industries—especially televisions, radios, motorcycles, and then automobiles. After little more than a decade in this market, the Japanese had virtually transformed the world market in all of these products. In 1981, 90 percent of the world's VCRs were made in Japan. In 1983, 28 percent of the world's motor vehicles were made in Japan; and in the year 2000, about 1/4 of the cars sold in the United States were Japanese. At the same time, those textile goods that were made in the 1950s (when Japan started exporting) declined from 30 percent of their exports in the 1950s, to 3 percent in 1984. So, here you see the impact of the Japanese government channeling businesses into new industries. The textiles declined, and their share of the market in these other areas went up, that transition being smoothed by government incentives and financial assistance. In the 1970s, the

Japanese government, again, shifted its priorities from capital-intensive products to technology-intensive products—particularly computers and telecommunications equipment, software, and so.

By the 1980s, the label "made in Japan" had come to mean something different; it had come to mean sophisticated, well-designed high-tech products that competed with the United States. In the process, Japan had become the third largest industrial economy by 1968; by the 1980s, it had surpassed the Soviet Union to become the second largest economy. As a financial power, it also surpassed the American economy in the mid-1980s, when the United States turned from being a creditor to a debtor nation, and Japan replaced the United States as the premiere banker of the world. The rising trade imbalance between Japan and the United States was the most visible symptom of this transition. In 1980, the trade imbalance between the United States and Japan was 7 billion dollars, while in 1985, it was almost 40 billion dollars, and in 1992, it was more than 70 billion dollars, almost 75 billion dollars.

Moreover, Japan's economic strength was produced without the growth of massive inequalities of wealth or high levels of poverty, and with a system of education and social services that is more extensive than in the United States.

Since the mid-1990s, the Japanese model has been destabilized by political rebellion and economic crisis, and it is not yet clear whether the development model itself has reached its limits, or whether it will adapt and recover. To help answer this question, in the next lecture, we will look at the export of the Japanese model in Eastern and Southeastern Asia, and try to analyze its overall strengths and weaknesses for Third World development.

Maps

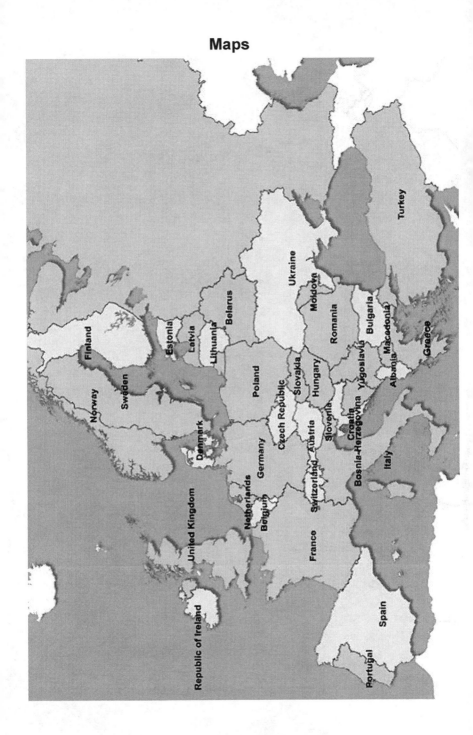

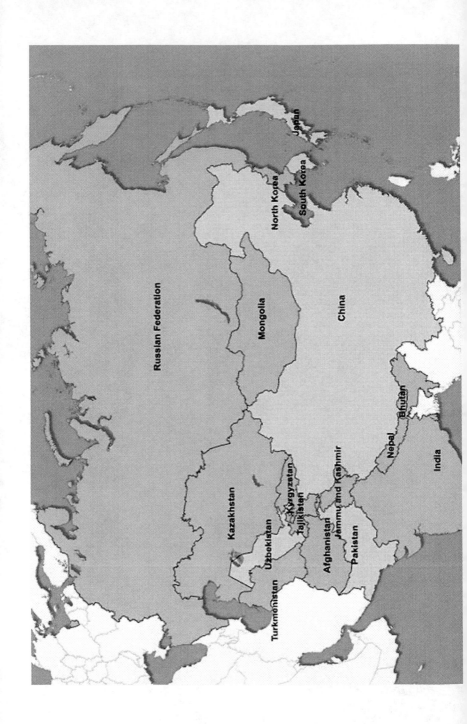

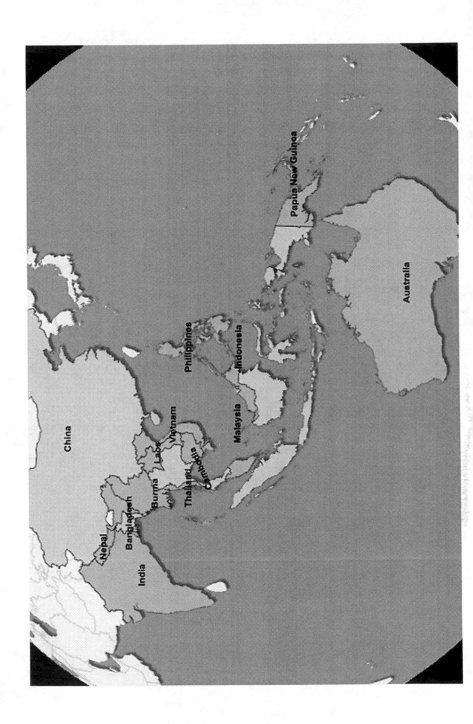

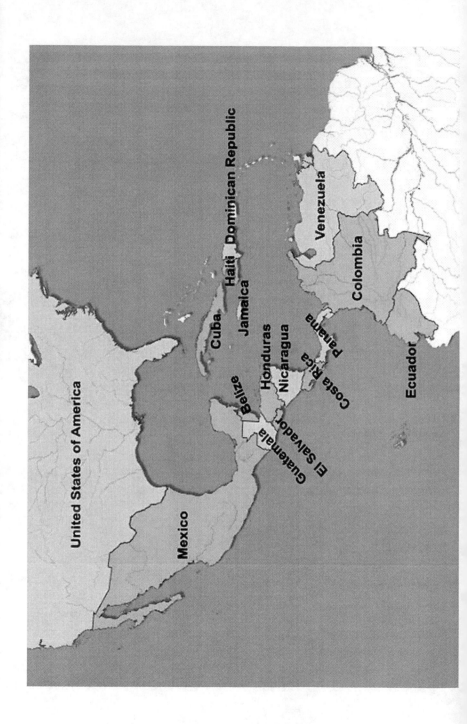

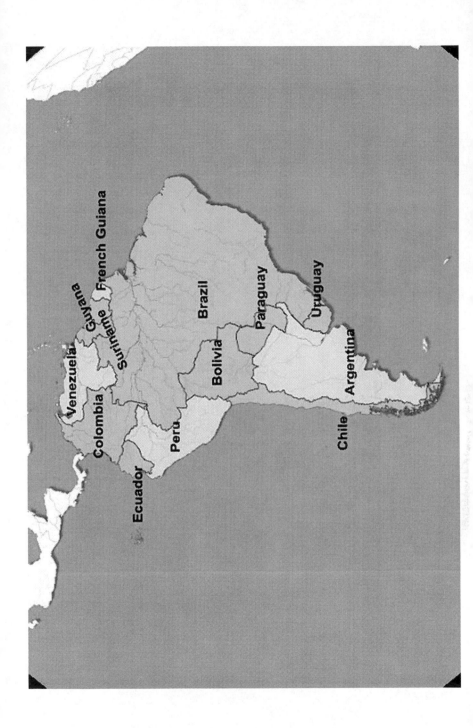

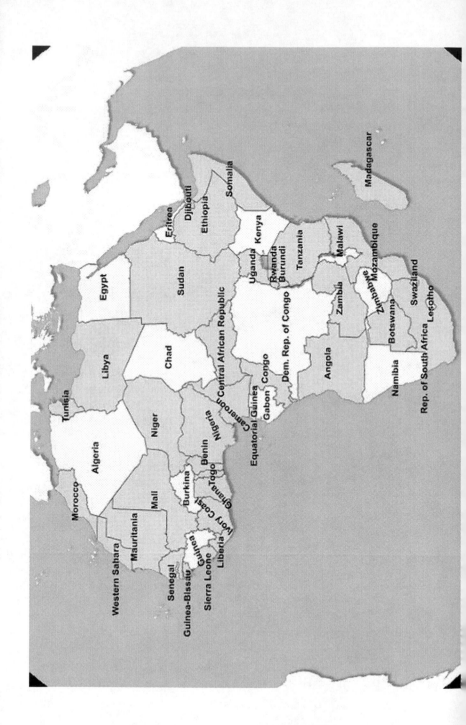

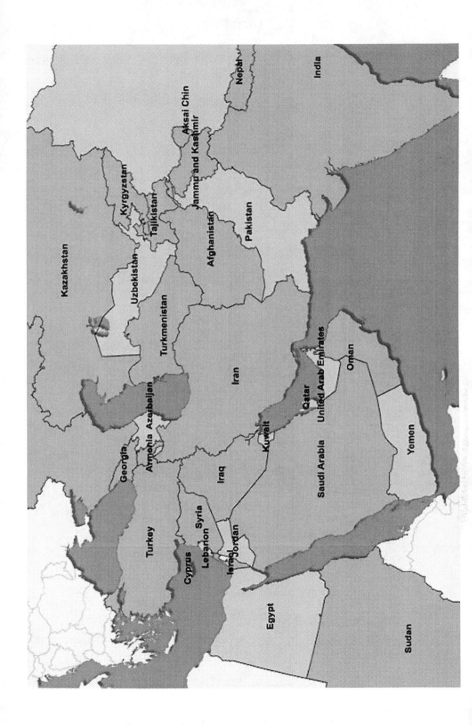

Timeline

1903	Establishment of the Ford Motor Company
February 1909	Futurist Manifesto published in Paris
November 1910	Mexican Revolution begins
1910	Japanese annexation of Korea
February 1912	Chinese emperor abdicates
June 28, 1914	Assassination of Archduke Ferdinand, heir to the Hungarian throne
August 4, 1914	World War I breaks out
September 1914	Battle of the Marne
February–September 1916	Ten-month Battle of Verdun, Germans against French
July 1916	Battle of the Somme, the British offensive, begins
February 1917	First Russian Revolution
October 1917	Bolshevik Revolution
November 1917	Balfour Declaration
1917	Mexican Constitution is signed
1918	Dada Manifesto is published in Zurich
March 1918	Treaty of Brest-Litovsk, which closed the eastern front when the Bolsheviks sign a separate peace
November 11, 1918	Armistice
March 1919	Mussolini's speech that launched the fascist movement
April 1919	Amritsar massacre

May 4, 1919 ....May 4th Movement, China

1919 ....Gandhi's first *satyagraha* campaign in Ahmedabad

June 28, 1919 ....Paris peace settlement signed after four months of labor

1921 ....Mao helps found the Chinese Communist Party

1924 ....Surrealist Manifesto published in Paris

1924 ....Hitler writes *Mein Kampf*

1927 ....First national radio networks are established in the United States

October 1929...............................Crash of the New York stock market

1929 ....Ortega y Gasset publishes *The Revolt of the Masses*

1929 ....Stalin consolidates his dictatorship of the USSR and launches the First Five-Year Plan

1930 ....Gandhi's Salt March (India)

1930 ....Freud publishes *Civilization and Its Discontents*

1931 ....Japan invades Manchuria

January 1933 ....Hitler is appointed chancellor in Germany

August 1934 ....Hitler inaugurates the Third Reich

October 1934...............................Long March begins

1934 ....Lazaro Cardenas is elected president of Mexico

March 1936 ....German troops march into the Rhineland

1937 ....Japanese occupation of Nanking, the official start of the Pacific war

September 1938	Munich Agreement, which gave Hitler parts of Czechoslovakia
September 1939	Hitler invades Poland, the start of the European war
1941	Japanese incursion into Southeast Asia
December 1941	Pearl Harbor, which leads to U.S. entry into the war
May 7, 1945	Germany surrenders, a week after Hitler's suicide on April 30
August 6 and 9, 1945	Atom bombs are dropped on Hiroshima and Nagasaki, ending the war in the Pacific
1947	Marshall Plan
1947	Indian and Pakistani Independence
May 14, 1948	State of Israel is declared and resisted in the first Arab-Israeli war
1949	Mao inaugurates the People's Republic of China
1949	Indonesia wins independence
February 1950	McCarthy's speech that unleashes the Red Scare
1954	*Brown v. Board of Education*, Supreme Court ruling on "separate but equal"
1954	CIA-backed force invades Guatemala
December 1955	Montgomery bus boycott, first major action of the civil rights movement
1955	The Bandung Conference of Ex-Colonial Nations

1956 ....Britain and France invade Egypt over the Suez Canal

1956 ....Khrushchev's speech to the Communist Party Congress admitting Stalin's mistakes

1957 ....Ghana becomes the first sub-Saharan African colony to win independence

1959 ....Cuban Revolution

1960 ....Nigerian independence

1962 ....Algerian independence

1963 ....Organization for African Unity is formed

1964 ....President Johnson announces the War on Poverty in the United States

1965 ....Military coup in Indonesia by General Suharto

1965 ....U.S. troops invade the Dominican Republic

1965 ....Civil Rights Act in the United States

January 1968 ....Tet offensive in Vietnam

1972 ....First International Conference on the Environment, Stockholm

1973 ....CIA-supported military coup in Chile

1973 ....Oil crisis

April 1976 ....Portugal receives a new democratic constitution

April 1977 ....Mothers of the Plaza de Mayo hold their first march in Argentina

December 1978 ....Spain adopts a democratic constitution

1979	Iranian Revolution
1979	China's first new "economic zones" are established
1979	Sandinista revolution in Nicaragua
1980	Zimbabwe becomes the last African colony to gain its independence
1983	Democratic elections in Argentina start a trend toward democratization in the region
April 1985	Gorbachev's speech to the Central Committee in which he declares a crisis in the USSR
1988	USSR withdraws its troops from Eastern Europe
November 11, 1989	Berlin Wall comes down, beginning the collapse of communist regimes in Eastern Europe over the next few months
1990	Civil war breaks out in Yugoslavia
1992	Second International Conference on the Environment, Rio de Janeiro
January 1993	Czechoslovakia splits into the Czech Republic and Slovakia
1994	NAFTA and Chiapas
1994	Multi-racial democratic elections in South Africa
1994	Half a million Tutsis are massacred in Rwanda
1999	Third democratic transition in Nigeria
1999	UN bombs Kosovo to try to end the latest phase of the Yugoslav civil war

Glossary

Civil society: This concept has been used in recent debates about the conditions that favor transitions to democracy. It defines the independent space between private family life and the state, where citizens interact with each other and form associations that can pressure the state to make changes in public policy.

Cold War: Situation of permanent tension between two superpowers, defined by the existence of nuclear weapons and the clash of opposing world missions.

Command economy: In the socialist states, the government dictated what products were made and how many were produced by setting quotas and fixing prices, rather than by allowing the market to determine these things.

Communism: Although this term was used in the 19th century to denote egalitarian communitarianism, in the 20th century, it was used to identify the political movement that emerged from the Russian Revolution and divided the European left into socialist and communist parties. The ideological distinction was not entirely clear at the outset, given that both parties pursued an eventual transformation to an egalitarian society, but by the post-World War II period, socialist parties had fully integrated into democratic parliamentary systems, while communist parties adhered to the Soviet model.

Dada: Nonsense word adopted to define an art movement; its basic principle was to tear down the false facade of rational order and expose the irrationality beneath. Its manifesto was written in 1917 by Tristan Tzara.

Democracy: On a basic level, democracy represents the "rule of all," but in practice, not everyone agrees as to what that means. Liberal democracy has tended to mean that all individuals in society have the same political rights, while social democracy includes social rights, as well.

Enlightenment project: Set of principles linked by the conviction that the social, political, and economic order should be organized around the rational individual.

Existentialism: Philosophy that emphasizes the responsibility of each individual to create meaning for his or her own life, often summed up as "existence precedes essence."

Fascism: New political movement that emerged after World War I; scholars disagree on how to define it. It was a revolutionary movement that sought to replace liberalism and prevent communism, and it adopted a number of new mass mobilizing techniques that helped transform mass politics. Between 1919 and 1945, it threatened the liberal democratic order in Europe.

Feminism: Movement aiming to empower women; it can be defined narrowly as the particular brand of equal-rights feminism that has fought for women's equal treatment in liberal democratic societies. Alternatively, it can be defined broadly as any movement, whatever it calls itself, that organizes women for the sake of improving their status and condition in life.

Futurism: One of the avant-garde artistic movements of the post-war period, although the manifesto was written in 1909 by F. T. Marinetti, who later became involved in the Italian fascist movement.

Gender crisis: This term describes the loss of certainty about the prescribed roles for men and women in society or its gender system.

Glasnost: The other key concept in Gorbachev's plan to reform socialism. Literally "openness," it signified the decentralization of power structures and the lifting of deadening bureaucratic controls.

Gleichshaltung: In German, this word means "coordination," and it describes the process by which all independent associations and groups were to be brought under the direct supervision of the Nazi regime.

Globalization: In simple terms, globalization describes the expanding nature and impact of interaction across national borders, whether through trade, cultural exchange, or other types of political and social relationships. Scholars disagree about whether this is a good or a bad thing in the form it is following, and some even reject the term itself.

Global village: Term coined to describe the consequences of global interdependence at the end of the 20th century, in which peoples' destinies are as intertwined as if they lived in the same village.

Green Revolution: In the 1960s, the development of new strains of wheat and fertilizers dramatically increased agricultural productivity and allowed, on a global level, the food supply to keep pace with population growth up to the 1990s.

Heisenberg's uncertainty principle: In scientific terms, Heisenberg argued that because it is impossible to measure the location of an object without distorting its speed and vice versa, it is impossible to know the exact location of a particle in motion. For postwar non-scientific culture, this idea reinforced a new skepticism about objective truth.

Imperialism: System of relationships of domination that is based on the establishment of formal colonial empires. Scholars have debated whether imperialism was primarily an economic phenomenon, a product of the desire to secure markets and raw materials, or whether it resulted from other types of motives. In either case, it was one of the key characteristics of the world order in 1900.

Keynsianism: Named after the British economist John Maynard Keynes, this theory challenged prewar laissez-faire economic assumptions and promoted an increased role for the government in both protecting citizens from economic downturns and in stimulating economic growth and employment through public spending. After World War II, it provided the ideological underpinnings of the welfare state.

Laissez-faire: Classical economic philosophy of Adam Smith, 19th-century liberals and now late-20th-century neo-conservatives, which argues that an "invisible hand" operates to make the economy function most efficiently and that government intervention in the economy only disturbs this self-regulatory process.

Liberalism: Philosophy that is the cornerstone of the Enlightenment project, based on a contract theory of government that recognizes the sovereign rights of individuals. In the economic sphere, it favors individual private property and an unfettered market and, in the political sphere, some sort of representative government.

Mass society: Concept that came into use in the 1920s and 1930s to express concerns over the reduction of individual differences between people and their submersion into an increasingly undifferentiated mass. In particular, the Frankfurt school of German philosophers theorized about its potentially dangerous links to totalitarianism.

McCarthyism: Named after Wisconsin Senator Joseph McCarthy, this phenomenon brought the Cold War home to American society by shifting the fear of communism abroad to the fear of communism at home. Specifically, it unleashed a "hunt" for communists in government positions in the mid-1950s.

Modernization: Concept used to define a series of transformations that have occurred at various speeds in different parts of the world, including the transition from agrarian to industrial economies, the growth of urbanization, and the establishment of a unified state that applies a uniform set of rules to its population.

Nationalism: Organization of a people around the claim for nationhood. It asserts the basic principle that the only way a "people" can fulfill its true destiny is through its own political unit, a nation-state. While scholars argue about whether *nations* are old or new, *nationalism* as a mobilizing concept is a product of the modern world, particularly the 19th and 20th centuries.

National self-determination: Principle embraced in the Paris peace treaties that recognizes the right of each people to have its own political unit through which it can guide its collective destiny.

Neo-colonialism: Concept invented to describe relationships of dependence, usually related to economic power, between First and Third World countries after the latter had achieved formal independence.

Perestroika: Concept, literally "restructuring," which was formulated by Soviet President Mikhail Gorbachev to define the need for less government control of the economy and more room for private initiative.

Religious fundamentalism: The call to return to religious values is not new, but in the 1970s, this concept was drawn on to describe the global rise in movements that criticize the process of secularization and advocate the application of sacred laws to society at large.

Satyagraha: Gandhi's concept of *satyagraha* was drawn from Hinduism and was adapted by him for the purpose of preparing and mobilizing the Indian people against British rule. Literally, the "search for truth," *satyagraha* was meant to purify the practitioner through the willingness to suffer for one's beliefs and, at the same time, to convince the enemy of the evil of his position.

Stalinization: This word describes the "second revolution" or the "revolution from above" that Stalin carried out after securing power in the late 1920s. What scholars have debated is the relationship between Stalinization and the first Bolshevik Revolution.

Surrealism: Post-World War I artistic movement influenced by Freud, which sought to explore the unconscious through artistic experimentation and discover a new reality behind the surface, a *sur-reality*. Its manifesto was written in 1924 by Andre Breton, a psychiatrist.

Totalitarianism: Concept coined by Mussolini to describe the Italian fascist regime, but it later became a term of scholarship defining a modern style of authoritarian rule that went beyond political control to pursue a "total" control of all social, economic, cultural, and even private functions.

Transvaluation of values: Nietzsche's term is a perfect illustration of the "crisis of meaning" opening up in Western civilization. By advocating that what was good should be considered evil and vice versa, this concept helped set the pace for a general questioning of accepted values.

Unconscious: Freud's life work was devoted to mapping this part of the brain, which was inaccessible to direct rational consciousness but was the repository for repressed memories. Instead, the unconscious had to be accessed indirectly, through dreams, free associations, and other techniques.

Welfare state: New conception of the state's responsibility for the welfare of the population, based on the expansion of citizenship rights into the social realm.

Woman question: Used to define the problem of women's exclusion from political citizenship in the late 19th and early 20th centuries.

World order: General rules and practices that guide the interaction between countries and that order their behavior in a particular time period. Rules can be informal or formal (the UN), and they are not necessarily consistently applied, but as the level of global interaction has increased, so has concern about the shape of the "world order."

Biographical Notes

Samuel Beckett (1906–1989). Arguably the most important dramatist of the 20th century, Beckett abandons traditional theatrical notions about language, plot, and characters in favor of creating a world that highlights the meaninglessness of existence. Before World War II, he was primarily a novelist and essayist, highly influenced by French surrealist authors and James Joyce. After the war (in which he served as a member of the French Resistance), he turned to drama. His masterwork *Waiting for Godot* was first produced in Paris in 1953 and was one of the first examples of *theatre of the absurd*. In *Godot*, nothing happens: Two tramps are waiting for Mr. Godot to save them from some unnamed situation or threat, but he never arrives. The work itself mixes together Nietzschean philosophy, allusions to Christianity, nihilistic violence, and music-hall humor to present a worldview that absolutely nothing is certain. Beckett further developed this theme (if one can speak of uncertainty as being a theme) in *Endgame* (1957) and *Happy Days* (1961). Although his work often baffled and infuriated conservative critics and audiences, his importance to world letters was formally recognized in 1969 when he was awarded the Nobel Prize for Literature.

Lázaro Cárdenas (1891–1970). Like Emiliano Zapata and many of the key players in the Mexican Revolution, Cárdenas came from a peasant family and spent most of the years between 1910 and 1920 serving in one or another of the various revolutionary armies. Cárdenas ultimately sided with Alvaro Obregón and was rewarded with high military posts, a provincial governorship, and various cabinet positions. This success, however, did not dim his leftist political views (as it did with many others), and he continued to support the need for land reform in Mexico. Cárdenas was elected president of Mexico in 1934 and instituted a series of reforms squarely based on revolutionary sentiments. He redistributed 45 million acres of land to the peasantry and instituted new communal holdings and doubled the number of schools throughout the country. He also nationalized the railways and the holdings of oil and gas companies in Mexico, most of which were owned and controlled by U.S. or British corporations. This move incensed the American government to the point that it withdrew all support from the

Mexican economy, and although Cárdenas agreed to compensate the corporations who lost their holdings, he also proceeded to expropriate land belonging to U.S. agricultural concerns. Cárdenas opened the country to leftist refugees from Europe, and by the time he left office in 1940, Leon Trotsky and numerous Republican exiles from Spain had settled in Mexico. Cárdenas remained a controversial figure even after he left office: He accepted the Stalin Prize for Peace in 1955 and supported Fidel Castro's regime in Cuba.

Frantz Fanon (1925–1961). Born in French Martinique, Fanon was, in many ways, the classic Western-educated nationalist intellectual. He studied medicine in France and served in the French Resistance during the Second World War. After the war, he became the chief psychiatrist at the state hospital in Algiers, Algeria, where he became drawn in to the nationalist movement, partly after witnessing the French repression of the Setif rebellion in 1945. He quit his post in 1956 to devote himself full time to the Algerian Liberation Front and died in exile in the United States in 1961. What made him more than a local nationalist activist were his extensive writings about the disastrous impact of colonialism on colonized peoples. *Black Skin, White Faces* looked at the problem of a dual-race society in Martinique; *Dying Colonialism* (1957) argued that colonialism caused pathologies; and his most famous book, *The Wretched of the Earth* (1961), is an impassioned call for socialist anti-colonial revolution.

Sigmund Freud (1856–1939). Freud began as a practicing neurologist in Vienna in the 1880s. While treating illnesses of the nervous system, he became interested in cases of mental illness that seemed to have no physiological basis. Through experimenting with different techniques, from hypnosis to free association to the interpretation of dreams, he discovered that patients would recall painful repressed memories and that this recall had a cathartic effect. His two major conclusions were that the painful memories were largely connected to sex, specifically childhood sexual development, and that the place where these memories were stored was the unconscious, where they festered, giving rise in extreme cases to mental illness. His most important work from this formative period was the *Interpretation of Dreams* (1900). Freud was a scientist who dedicated himself to understanding the process of repression and how the problems arising from it could be treated. In his later life, he turned these insights to analyzing society at large. In the last year of his life, he was driven from Vienna by Nazi persecution and died in London.

Mohandas Gandhi (1869–1948). Gandhi came from a wealthy merchant family and studied law in England. Finding no work as a lawyer in India, he traveled to South Africa in 1893, where his encounters with racial discrimination prompted a campaign to improve the rights of Indians throughout the British Empire. It was during these years that Gandhi developed his philosophy of nonviolent resistance and civil disobedience as a way of achieving his political goals; he was heavily influenced by the writings of Leo Tolstoy and named the farm he founded after the Russian author. Gandhi was accorded a hero's welcome when he returned to India in 1915. Following World War I—as it became clear that the British government was not only going to ignore the faithful service of Indians in the British Army but was going to try to increase its control over India—Gandhi turned his attentions toward independence. He espoused a policy of economic self-sufficiency and instituted a boycott of all British goods. In addition, he traveled around India denouncing the rigid Hindu caste system and promoting friendship and cooperation between Hindus and Moslems. Gandhi was imprisoned several times during the 1920s and 1930s; he also spent most of World War II in jail for refusing to lend his support to the war effort, in spite of British promises of independence. Gandhi actively campaigned against the increasing levels of violence that led up to Indian independence in 1947; he also campaigned against the partition that split the subcontinent into Moslem and Hindu states. He was assassinated by a Hindu extremist on January 13, 1948.

Mikhail Gorbachev (b. 1931). Born to a peasant family in southern Russia, Gorbachev spent most of his youth working on a collective farm. He moved to Moscow in 1952 to study law and there joined the Communist Party. Gorbachev spent the next 30 years moving upward through the Soviet hierarchy, working with the communist youth movement and as an organizer of collective farms, eventually becoming the party secretary in charge of agriculture. In 1980, he became a member of the Politburo (the group of officials that ran the party and, thus, the Soviet Union) and was elected general secretary of the Communist Party in 1985. In foreign policy, he worked with U.S. President Ronald Regan toward reducing the chemical and nuclear weapons stockpiles of both nations. His domestic policies centered on the ideas of *glasnost* ("openness") and *perestroika* (economic "restructuring"): Politically, he reduced state censorship and promoted toleration of dissenting political views and, economically, he introduced free-market reforms. However, Gorbachev's policies managed to alienate both conservative communists (who felt he was undermining the system) and radical reformers (who felt he was not moving fast enough). Although these policies helped to accelerate the collapse of communism in Eastern Europe, Gorbachev refused to countenance the breakup of the Soviet Union itself and cracked down on separatist movements in the Baltic states. He was elected president of the Soviet Union in 1990, but in August of 1991, he was arrested by a group of conservative communists attempting a coup against the government; the fact that the coup was defeated under the leadership of Russian President Boris Yeltsin—not Gorbachev—accelerated the disintegration of the USSR. Late that year, Gorbachev resigned his political offices and has since lived as a private citizen.

Theodor Herzl (1860–1904). Herzl came from the same milieu as his contemporary, Sigmund Freud: the assimilated Jewish middle class of the Austro-Hungarian Empire. Trained as a lawyer, Herzl moved to Vienna in 1878 and became a journalist with that city's leading newspapers; he also wrote several plays. His entry into the world of politics was caused by his reaction to the intense anti-Semitism aroused by the Dreyfus Affair in 1894 (which Herzl was covering as the Paris correspondent for the *Neue Freie Presse*). Herzl came to the conclusion that full assimilation into European society would never be possible for the Jewish people because of the intense prejudice against them; his solution was to be the foundation of a Jewish state where their security would not be in the hands of the Gentiles. His choice for the new state was Palestine, but the Ottoman sultan who ruled the region was cool toward the idea because it lacked financial backing. To promote his cause, Herzl organized the First Zionist Congress in 1897; however, its historical importance as the foundation of the modern Zionist movement was overshadowed by the lack of support for its aims by middle-class and wealthy Jews, who felt that Zionism had the power to destroy the progress made by assimilation. Herzl sought support for his movement from Kaiser Wilhelm II of Germany, Czar Nicholas II of Russia, Pope Pius X, and Joseph Chamberlain, the British colonial secretary. Because the critical support of the Jewish financial families, such as the

Rothschilds, was lacking, none of these men was willing to provide the political support needed to make the dream of Zionism a reality. (Chamberlain did offer Uganda as a potential location for the Jewish state, but this was rejected by the Sixth Zionist Congress in 1903.) Exhausted by his travels, Herzl died in July 1904. When the state of Israel was finally founded in 1949, his body was disinterred and his remains were reburied in Jerusalem.

Adolf Hitler (1889–1945). Few individuals have been subject to such intense scrutiny as Adolf Hitler. Born in an Austrian town across the border of southern Germany, he epitomizes the image of evil incarnate. Historians and biographers have struggled to find some theory to explain what happened to turn him from a failed artist living in Vienna before the war to a mass murderer and fanatical German nationalist, but there seems to be no "smoking gun." His marginal and alienated existence made him, in a sense, the prototypical fascist recruit. He joined the German army during the First World War, was profoundly disillusioned by Germany's surrender and humiliation, and like many disgruntled veterans, he joined one of the anti-democratic societies that proliferated, the German Workers' Party. His oratorical and organizational skills pushed him to the front of the party, and he turned it into a paramilitary fighting force, similar to Mussolini's *squadristi* in Italy. In contrast to Italy, however, the new Weimar democracy stabilized and Hitler was arrested in 1923 after his failed Beer Hall Putsch. He wrote *Mein Kampf* while in jail, but most agree that without the Depression and the crisis it opened up in German society, Hitler would have remained a footnote.

John Maynard Keynes (1883–1946). Born the son of a Cambridge don, this British economist discarded the classical economic theory of Adam Smith and developed the ideas that form the basis of the modern welfare state. Keynes began his career as a civil servant but rose to public notoriety in 1919 with the publication of *The Economic Consequences of the Peace*. He had attended the Versailles Peace Conference but disagreed with the harsh financial reparations the Allies imposed on Germany, which he felt were unjust and would ultimately make economic recovery from the devastation of the war virtually impossible—an argument that infuriated many people who were more concerned with punishing the defeated than helping them. Keynes spent the following years developing his economic theories, which were given their fullest and most lucid explanation in *General Theory of Employment, Interest and Money* (1936). At the core of his theory is the idea that the capitalist economic system does not have the potential to generate employment for everybody, as classical economists believed. Thus, states must incur deficit spending during economic downturns to stimulate employment and limit their spending during periods of prosperity to avoid inflation. Although these ideas caused intense debate, they were increasingly accepted by governments after World War II that sought to prevent a reoccurrence of the economic and social dislocations of the Great Depression. For his work and his public service during both world wars, Keynes was elevated to the British peerage in 1942.

Martin Luther King, Jr. (1929–1968). King came from a well-respected family in Atlanta's African American community—both his father and grandfather were Baptist ministers. He studied sociology and theology, eventually earning a doctorate in theology from Boston University in 1955. During this time, he developed views that were distinctly more liberal than those of traditional Baptist doctrine. That same year, King became pastor of a church in Montgomery, Alabama and became involved in the civil rights movement following the arrest of Rosa Parks for refusing to surrender her bus seat to a white man. It was during this time that King began to develop a philosophy of nonviolent resistance, influenced by Gandhi and traditional Christian principles. King was the founder of the Southern Christian Leadership Conference, which became one of the primary coordinators of the civil rights movement in the South. He was arrested in 1963 in Birmingham, and his "Letter from a Birmingham Jail" is the key document to understanding his philosophy. King's influence reached a peak later that year as he led a march of 200,000 people to Washington, D.C., where he gave his famous "I have a dream" speech. In 1964, he was awarded the Nobel Peace Prize. King's influence on the civil rights movement waned in later years as younger African Americans became more militant. King himself began to speak out on a wider range of issues, including the Vietnam War and poverty. He was assassinated in Memphis on April 4, 1969.

Aleksandra Kollontai (1872–1952). Although her father was a member of the officer corps of the Russian army, Kollontai received a liberal—almost radical—education that helped to shape her life.

She developed a strong independent streak that first manifested itself when she married against her parent's wishes; later, she left her husband in order to study at the University of Zurich, where she read deeply in Marxist theory and philosophy. Kollontai witnessed the Bloody Sunday massacre of 1905, and this seems to have influenced her radicalism: During the next few years, she forcibly argued that the only road to feminine equality was through Marxist revolution, which would eliminate the traditional family structure, and not through bourgeois tactics, such as emancipation. She traveled widely through Europe before World War I, lecturing on her philosophy; during the war, she returned to Russia and actively participated in the 1917 Revolution. By 1921, she headed the Women's Section of the Bolshevik Party, but her support for the idea of free love scandalized party leaders, who sent her abroad. Kollontai spent the years from 1922 to 1945 in the Soviet diplomatic corps, serving as ambassador to Norway, Mexico, and Finland. Her focus on feminist issues rather than party politics may have contributed to the fact that she survived Stalin's purges.

Vladimir Ilich Lenin (1870–1924). Lenin's early life is, in many ways, the prototypical story of the 19th-century Russian intelligentsia. He was the son of a provincial bureaucrat and trained as a lawyer but was inclined toward radical politics—a process accelerated by the execution of his brother in 1887 for involvement in an assassination plot against the czar. Lenin moved to St. Petersburg in 1893 and became a leading figure in revolutionary circles; he was arrested and exiled to Siberia as a result. After 1900, he lived in Western Europe and devoted his energies to promoting the revolutionary consciousness of the working classes. He concluded that a Marxist revolution could occur only if it was headed by a vanguard of intellectuals leading the proletariat. His stance that revolution must take precedence over all other forms of action split the Russian Marxists, and Lenin's faction adopted the name *Bolshevik* to distinguish itself. Lenin returned to Russia when the czar abdicated in 1917 and led the October Revolution, which overthrew the bourgeois provisional government. He used the resulting civil war to turn the Bolshevik Party into a dictatorship that ruled the country, but the chaos that resulted from the unrest forced him to allow a mixture of capitalist and socialist economic measures (known as the New Economic Policy) in order to regain political control. Lenin suffered a stroke in 1922 and was a virtual invalid until his death two years later. He was subsequently embalmed and put on public display at the Kremlin in Moscow, attesting to his enormous historical and political importance in the Soviet Union.

Nelson Mandela (b. 1918). Mandela was the child of a Xhosa tribal chieftain; he began his career studying law at Witwatersrand University and, subsequently, set up the first black law practice in South Africa. In 1944, he joined the African National Congress (ANC), a group dedicated to ending white-minority rule in South Africa. Although the ANC originally espoused a philosophy of nonviolence, Mandela and other younger members increasingly came to the conclusion that passive resistance only encouraged violence by the white population and that violent tactics would be necessary to achieve their aims. Mandela was charged with treason in 1956 but was acquitted. The ANC was banned in 1960, and Mandela turned to underground organization for the movement; in 1962, he was arrested for leaving South Africa illegally and sentenced to five years in prison—a sentence that was expanded to life in prison the following year, when he was found guilty of sabotage and conspiracy to commit guerrilla warfare. In the years that followed, Mandela increasingly became a symbol of the oppression of white rule in South Africa. In fact, he became an embarrassment to the government: He refused one chance for release because it would have meant cooperating with the regime, and his health grew increasingly fragile. He was released in 1990 and became president of the ANC the following year. Mandela now embraced an idea of cooperation with the white population, and he shared the 1993 Nobel Peace Prize with South African President F. W. de Klerk for his work. Mandela was elected president of South Africa in that country's first free elections in 1994, and he has since focused on healing the racial divide and rebuilding the economy of that nation.

Friedrich Nietzsche (1844–1900). The most important German philosopher of the late 19th century, Nietzsche erupted on the scene with a challenging series of books in the 1880s that expressed his contempt for traditional assumptions in a flashy language that quickly caught the attention of intellectual circles. He began his academic career at age 24, with a Ph.D. in classical philology, becoming a professor at the University of Basil. But his academic colleagues saw his work as too speculative and reckless, and he soon resigned from his post, writing books from his position as alienated intellectual. Although his ideas were not always well developed, their explosive nature gave them a wide-reaching impact. He was born in Prussia, the son of a Lutheran minister. Plagued by ill health his entire life, in 1889, Nietzsche had a mental breakdown from which he never recovered his mental faculties.

Kwame Nkrumah (1909–1972). Although he is arguably the most important and influential of the African nationalists that freed the continent from the European imperial powers, Nkrumah's important legacy has been clouded by his actions as the first president of Ghana. He was born to a humble family and first educated by Catholic missionaries; in 1935, he traveled to the United States, where he studied sociology, theology, and education, eventually earning a graduate degree in philosophy from the University of Pennsylvania. His political thinking was influenced primarily by Lenin, Gandhi, and Marcus Garvey, whose notion of pan-Africanism was crucial in shaping Nkrumah's political goals. Nkrumah moved to England to study law in 1945 and returned to Ghana two years later to take part in the nationalist movement seeking independence from Britain. He soon headed the most radical nationalist faction, actively agitating for independence; he became prime minister under the British governor in 1952, a post that he retained when Ghana gained its independence in 1957. Elections in 1960 turned the country into a republic, and Nkrumah became president. His political ambition now turned to uniting the African continent under the banner of pan-Africanism, a goal that became increasingly tenuous as each newly independent country tasted the fruits of its struggle for freedom. Meanwhile, Nkrumah's attempts to build a quasi-Marxist state in Ghana mired the country in corruption and economic decay; Nkrumah himself became increasingly repressive—instituting censorship, outlawing trade unions and opposition political parties, and building a Stalinistic cult of personality. He declared himself president-for-life in 1964 and was ousted in a military coup two years later, spending the rest of his life in exile.

Olusegun Obasanjo (b. 1937). It may be significant that Obasanjo entered the military as a last desperate means to finance his education when he failed to gain a scholarship to the University of Ibadan; his behavior has certainly been more enlightened than the stereotype of generals involved in African politics. He first came to prominence in 1975, when Nigeria's longtime military ruler reneged on his promise to return the country to civilian rule; Obasanjo became the chief of staff to the new military government, which promised a return to civilian rule within four years. The following year, the head of the government, General Murtala Muhammad, was assassinated and Obasanjo took his place. His government focused on creating economic stability for the region, mending the tribal and religious rifts that plagued the country, and opposing the white-controlled governments in South Africa and Rhodesia. Obasanjo kept his word and returned Nigeria to civilian rule in 1979, retiring to the country to live as a farmer. He continued to speak out against apartheid and the increasing problems in Nigeria's economic and political situation; in 1995, he was imprisoned by the military government of General Sani Abacha for his outspoken criticisms. Obasanjo was released in 1998 and was elected president of Nigeria for a second time the following year.

Josef Stalin (1879–1953). As in the case of Hitler, Stalin's enormous personal influence on larger historical events has made him a subject of frequent biographies that try to unlock the key to his personality. Like Hitler, Stalin seemed an unlikely leader, born the son of a shoemaker and the grandson of serfs, a Georgian who became a fervent Russian nationalist. He dropped out of theological seminary and joined the Bolshevik movement in 1900, when he changed his name from Josef Djugashvili to Stalin, which meant "man of steel." Like Hitler, as well, Stalin was no intellectual, not a great mind with original ideas, nor a cultured man, educated in the West, as were most of his Bolshevik contemporaries. He seemed to be the consummate bureaucrat, taking on the job of party secretary in 1922 and maneuvering among different factions of the party after Lenin's death until he was able to assert his leadership in 1928–1929. After this point, he developed an increasingly megalomaniacal view of his relationship to the revolution, the Russian state, and the Bolshevik Party, but it was perhaps his simple understanding of the world that allowed him to stay so brutally focused.

Mao Tse-tung (1893–1976). Like many 20th-century revolutionaries, Mao came from peasant origins; unlike many revolutionaries, Mao made his humble past an integral component of his political philosophy and his personal style. His first encounter with Marxism came at Peking University, and he was one of the founding members of the Chinese Communist Party in 1921. His ideology rapidly alienated him from more traditional Chinese nationalists; he also became increasingly alienated from mainline communism as he developed the idea that it was the peasantry—not the urban proletariat—that needed to be the revolutionary vanguard in overthrowing the capitalist system. By 1934, the nationalist forces under Chiang Kai-Shek were overthrowing the communist bases of power in southern China; Mao assembled his forces and led them on a year-long, 6,000-mile *Long March* to a remote northern stronghold. Although the majority of those who began the journey never completed it, the Long March solidified the party and made Mao the undisputed leader of the Chinese communists. Mao fought against the Japanese in World War II and resumed his struggle with the nationalists after that, taking full control of China in 1949. Mao's ideology paid little attention to industrialization, and his first attempt to modernize China—the Great Leap Forward of 1958—failed, weakening his power. He re-solidified his control under the Cultural Revolution (1966–1969), which purged Mao's opponents and attacked all nonconformist elements in society. Mao's final major initiative was to reopen ties with the United States, a move that helped China's subsequent modernization.

Emiliano Zapata (c. 1879–1919). Zapata's social origin was in the relatively narrow band of the Mexican peasantry that owned some land, and part of the explanation for his later revolutionary activity may arise from the confiscation of his family's orchards while he was still quite young. It was the plight of similar peasants, forced off their subsistence holdings and into working for large landowners, that prompted Zapata's initial foray into local politics. His opposition to the policies of the Porfirio Diaz regime prompted the government to draft him into the army in 1910. Zapata returned to politics the following year, siding with Francisco Madero's challenge to the Diaz government; however, when Madero gained power, he ignored Zapata's call to confiscate the holdings of large landowners and redistribute them more equitably among the peasants. By 1912, Zapata was in revolt against all the various political factions in Mexico as a way of accomplishing his land reforms (the Plan de Ayala). In 1914, Zapata joined forces with Pancho Villa and occupied Mexico City in order to force acceptance of his plan across the country. But by the following year, the forces of Alvaro Obregón had forced him out of the capital and into a guerilla revolt based in northern Mexico that lasted until Zapata's assassination in an ambush in 1919. This did not end his influence, however, and the

Obregón government used the ideas in the Plan de Ayala to institute its own agrarian reforms.

Bibliography

Essential Reading:

M.E. Chamberlain, *Decolonization: The Fall of the European Powers*. 2nd ed. Oxford: Blackwell Publishing, 2000. ISBN 0631216022. This book provides a good survey of the entire process of decolonization.

Larry Diamond and Juan Linz, eds., *Democracy in Developing Countries*. Vol. 4, *Latin America*. 2nd ed. Boulder, Colorado: Lynne Rienner, 1999. ISBN 1555870392. Written from the perspective of comparative democratization studies, this book provides a political-science oriented analysis of recent Latin American history.

Carol Fink, et al., eds. *1968: The World Transformed*. Cambridge: Cambridge University Press, 1998. ISBN 0521646375. This is one of the few books that provides a truly international interpretation of the impact of 1968, as well as articles dealing with protest movements in the U.S.A., Europe, Eastern Europe and the third world.

John Lewis Gaddis, *We Now Know: Rethinking Cold War History*. Oxford: Clarendon Press, 1997. ISBN 0198780710. Less a narrative of the Cold War than a series of essays on particular problems, like the division of Europe, conflicts in Asia, the question of origins, and so on. Gaddis has written numerous books on American foreign policy, all of which present a set of arguments laying most of the blame on the USSR.

Eric Hobsbawm, *Age of Extremes: A History of the World, 1914-1991*. New York: Vintage, 1994. ISBN 0679730052. Most scholars agree that this synthesis by one of the most important historians of the 20th century is an excellent narrative account, but one that leaves out many things that do no fit into his rather gloomy assessment of the century's trajectory.

Michael Howard and William Roger Lewis, eds. *The Oxford History of the 20th Century*. Oxford: Oxford University Press, 1998. ISBN 0192853708. This collection of articles takes the analytical approach, with excellent independent articles on specific topics, like urbanization, the end of imperialism and so on.

Paul Kennedy, *Preparing for the 21st Century*. Part 1. New York: Random House, 1993. ISBN 0517153017. A thought-provoking analysis of where the world is headed in the next century, it includes chapters on general trends and specific regions of the world.

William Keylor, Ch. 14, "Africa: From Independence to Dependency" in *The Twentieth Century World: An International History*. 4th ed. Oxford: Oxford University Press, 2000. ISBN 0195136802. This chapter provides an excellent general introduction to the initial stages of independence and the problems faced by the new nations.

Henry Munson, *Islam and Revolution in the Middle East*. New Haven: Yale University Press, 1988. ISBN 0300046049. This book provides a general survey of fundamentalist ideology and influence in different Middle Eastern countries in the 1970s and 80s, and asks why only in Iran did they take power.

Stanley Payne, *A History of Fascism, 1914-1945*. Madison: University of Wisconsin Press, 1995. ISBN 0299148742. This is the best overall history of the fascist movements and regimes, including his careful definition of the movement in the introduction. The rest of the book includes chapters on the various national variants, plus a section on differing interpretations of fascism.

Stephen White, *Communism and Its Collapse*. New York: Routledge, 2001. ISBN 0415244234. This book provides the most acclaimed broad interpretation of why the communist system collapsed.

Supplementary

Acton, Edward, et al. *A Critical Companion to the Russian Revolution*. Bloomington: Indiana University Press, 1997. This book contains a wide range of articles by both Western and Russian scholars, plus an introduction summarizing recent debates. The articles are organized thematically, including sections on the major actors, the revolution as event, and social groups.

Allen, William Sheridan. *The Nazi Seizure of Power*. 2nd ed. Danbury, CT: Franklin Watts, 1984. This book provides an excellent grassroots view of how the combination of consent and coercion worked at the local level to put the Nazis into power.

Lisa Anderson, ed. *Transitions to Democracy*. New York: Columbia University Press, 1999. This collection of articles provides an excellent window into recent scholarly theorizing on "transitology," i.e.: on what factors contribute to the creation and consolidation of democracies.

Anderson, Terry. *The Movement and the Sixties: Protest in America from Greensboro to Wounded Knee*. Oxford: Oxford University Press, 1995. A comprehensive survey of the different types of protest movements that constituted the phenomenon we call the "sixties."

Andrea, Alfred, and James Overfield, eds. "The Way of Subjects" (Japanese pamphlet, 1941). In *The Human Record: Sources of Global History*, vol. 2. Boston: Houghton Mifflin, 1994. This pamphlet gives a good sense of the anti-imperialist rhetoric that lay behind the Japanese government's vision of a new order in Asia.

Andrews, George Reid, and Herrick Chapman, eds. Part 4, "Democracy and the Welfare State, 1930–1990." In *The Social Construction of Democracy, 1870–1990*. New York: New York University Press, 1995. Chapters in this section consider the relationship between democratic practice and welfare policies in the United States, France, Germany, and Brazil.

Apollonio, Umbro. *Futurist Manifestos*. Boston, MA: MFA Publications, 2001. This collection of primary documents relating to the futurist movement includes the original manifesto written by Marinetti in 1909.

Auden, W. H. "The Unknown Citizen." In *Collected Poems*. New York: Vintage, 1991.This poem, about an average man whose tastes and habits conform so closely to the norm that he has no individual identity, sums up the fears of "mass man."

Barnhart, Michael. *Japan Prepares for Total War*. Ithaca: Cornell University Press, 1987. Barnhart provides a short, readable survey of the prewar period, focusing on the economic problems that pushed Japan toward imperialist policies.

Bayly, C. A. *Indian Society and the Making of the British Empire*. Cambridge: Cambridge University Press, 1988. For a more specialized and in-depth analysis of the relationship between the indigenous population and the colonial power, this book is an excellent source.

Jan Bazant, *A Concise History of Mexico from Hidalgo to Cardenas, 1805–1940*. Cambridge, U.K.: Cambridge University Press, 1977. An excellent general history of Mexico from independence to the 1940s.

Beasley, W. G. *Japanese Imperialism, 1894–1945*. Oxford: Clarendon Press, 1987. Beasley provides the most detailed account of Japan's expansionist policies.

Beckett, Samuel. *Waiting for Godot*. New York: Grove Press, 1959. The quintessential existentialist play, with a plot that defies logic, characters that don't develop, and a frustrating lack of resolution experienced by both the audience and the characters themselves.

Boemeke, Manfred, et al. *The Treaty of Versailles: A Reassessment after 75 Years*. Cambridge: Cambridge University Press, 1998. This book provides an up-to-date review of recent literature and debates.

Breton, André. "Manifesto of Surrealism." 1924. In *Manifestos of Surrealism*. Ann Arbor: University of Michigan Press, 1969. See Lecture Five for description.

Judith Brown, *Gandhi: Prisoner of Hope*. New Haven, CT: Yale University Press, 2003. The best contemporary biography of Gandhi, which effectively delves into his complex character and the diverse influences that helped shape him.

Browning, Christopher. *The Path to Genocide: Essays on Launching the Final Solution*. Cambridge: Cambridge University Press, 1992. *Ordinary Men: Reserve Police Battalion 101 and the Final Solution in Poland*. New York: Harper Collins, 1992. These two books, by one of the foremost scholars of "perpetrator" history, provide both a broader analytic view and a close-up personal view of the mindset that made the final solution happen. The second book is a chilling look at a battalion of "ordinary men" who committed unspeakable crimes and an attempt to understand their motives.

Bunch, Charlotte. "Prospects for Global Feminism." In *Passionate Politics*. New York: St. Martin's Press, 1987. Bunch discusses the need for transcending Western-based feminism and presents ideas for the construction of a global feminism.

Burkholder, Mark, and Lyman Johnson. *Colonial Latin America*. 4th ed. Oxford: Oxford University Press, 2000. This book is the best recent survey of colonial Latin America for those who want a broader and more detailed overview of the period of Spanish occupation.

Burleigh, Michael. *The Third Reich: A New History*. New York: Hill & Wang, 2000. An excellent, recently published survey of the Nazi regime by an author who has published extensively on Nazism, with an emphasis on racism.

Bushnell, David, and Neil Macaulay. *The Emergence of Latin America in the 19th Century*. 2nd ed. Oxford: Oxford University Press, 2000. This book provides an excellent recent treatment of the neo-colonialist experience, arguing that Latin America's economic problems originated in unfavorable trade relationships with more powerful nations.

Chan, Anita, Richard Madsen, and Jonathan Unger. *Chen Village under Mao and Deng: The Recent History of a Peasant Community in Mao's China*. Rev. ed. Berkeley: University of California Press, 1992. This classic local study provides an excellent view of the rural transformation in Chinese society from the perspective of a single farming collective.

Conquest, Robert. *Stalin: Breaker of Nations*. New York: Viking, 1991. The best Western biography, written by a staunch anti-communist.

Cook, Haruko, and Theodore Cook. *Japan at War: An Oral History*. New York: New Press, 1992. This book provides an excellent view of the war from the perspective of Japanese citizens, covering a wide range of experiences, from victims of the Allied bombings to soldiers who perpetrated atrocities.

Cott, Nancy. *The Grounding of Modern Feminism*. New Haven: Yale University Press, 1987. One of the best classic theoretical discussions of the Western feminist tradition.

Cronin, Anthony. *Samuel Beckett: The Last Modernist*. New York: Harper Collins, 1997. Of the many biographies of Beckett, this one is both elegantly written and directed at a general audience. It is admiring of Beckett without treating him as some sort of god-like figure.

Daniels, Robert, ed. *The Stalin Revolution*. 4th ed. Boston: Houghton Mifflin, 1997 (out of print). A number of articles provide opposing perspectives on the major debates about the regime.

Dawidowicz, Lucy, ed. *A Holocaust Reader*. New York: Berhman House, 1976. Hermann Goering's memo, July 31, 1941; minutes of the Wannsee Conference, January 20, 1942; memos from Generals

Gienanth and Himmler on the conflict between war aims and the final solution; memos from the death camps (pp. 72–82, 101–120). Primary documents that illustrate points made in Lecture Twenty-Five.

Derfler, Leslie, and Patricia Kollander, eds. *An Age of Conflict: Readings in 20th Century European History*, chapter 8, "The Holocaust." 3rd ed. San Diego: Harcourt, 2002. This collection of essays provides an accessible summary of major, scholarly debates on central themes of the 20th century, with excerpts from prominent historians who have made major contributions to those debates.

———. Chapter 10, "The End of European Empire." The Smith, Lijphart, and Grimal selections focus on the patterns of decolonization from different perspectives.

———. Chapter 12, "The End of the Cold War and the Collapse of the USSR."

———. Chapter 13, "Nationalism Resurgent: The Break-Up of Yugoslavia." The essays in the section on Yugoslavia provide an excellent short introduction to the problems of ethnic nationalism in post-communist Yugoslavia.

Diamond, Larry. *Class, Ethnicity and Democracy in Nigeria*. Syracuse: Syracuse University Press, 1988. This book provides an excellent introduction to Nigeria's colonial and post-colonial history, in the context of its struggle to democratize. It includes a clear understanding of the parameters and meaning of ethnic and geographical divisions.

Dore, Ronald. *Taking Japan Seriously*. Stanford: Stanford University Press, 1987. Dore's book focuses on Japan's economic policies and how they compare and contrast with European and American conceptions of how to manage the capitalist economy.

Dower, John. *War Without Mercy: Race and Power in the Pacific War*. New York: Pantheon Books, 1987. A powerful and controversial history of the war in the Pacific that puts racism at the center of the hostilities.

Eisenhower, Dwight D. "Eisenhower's T.V. Address on the Situation in Little Rock, Sept. 24, 1957." In *Debating the Civil Rights Movement*, Steven Lawson and Charles Payne, eds. Lanham, MD: Rowman and Littlefield, 1998. President Dwight D. Eisenhower explains in this public address why he has chosen to send in federal troops to calm the rioting in Little Rock over the attempts to desegregate local schools.

Engels, Friedrich. "The Origin of the Family, Private Property and the State." In *The Marx-Engels Reader*. 2nd ed., Robert C. Tucker, ed., pp. 734–759. New York: Norton, 1978. This essay, written in the 1880s, set the terms for all future formulations of Marxist feminism by setting out the economic foundations of women's oppression.

Esposito, John L. *The Islamic Threat: Myth or Reality?* 3rd ed. Oxford: Oxford University Press, 1999. This book provides a sympathetic account of Islamic fundamentalism, which tries to deflate some of the common myths held in the West.

Fieldhouse, D. K. *The Colonial Empires*. 2nd ed. London: Macmillan, 1982 (out of print). This book gives a general account of the actual process of decolonization and the different models followed by the colonial powers.

Fitzpatrick, Sheila. *The Russian Revolution: 1917–1932*. 2nd ed. Oxford: Oxford University Press, 1994. See chapters 1–2. This is the best and most balanced short history of the revolution.

Freud, Sigmund. *Civilization and Its Discontents*. New York: Norton, 1989. Written in 1930, this book represents Freud's efforts to apply insights gained from individual patients to society at large.

Fukuyama, Francis. "The End of History and the Last Man." In *The National Interest: Special Edition*, Summer 1989. See Lecture Forty-Six for description.

Fussell, Paul. *The Great War and Modern Memory*. Oxford: Oxford University Press, 1975. Fussell's classic book is still the best analysis of the postwar mood as expressed in British literature.

Gandhi, Mohandas. *An Autobiography: The Story of My Experiments with Truth*. Boston, MA: Beacon Press, 1993. This autobiographical account of Gandhi's life provides an excellent window into his motivations, his philosophy and his activism.

Garrow, David. *Bearing the Cross: Martin Luther King and the Southern Christian Leadership Conference, 1955–1968*. New York: William Morrow, 1986. This book focuses on the leadership of the civil rights movement and, in particular, offers a sympathetic biography of King.

Garton Ash, Timothy. "Ten Years After." *The New York Review of Books*, November 18, 1999. One of the most important journalistic chroniclers of the 1989 revolutions in Eastern Europe, Garton Ash wrote a follow-up essay on where these countries were 10 years after the end of communism.

―――. *The Magic Lantern: The Revolution of 1989 Witnessed in Warsaw, Budapest, Berlin and Prague*. New York: Random House, 1990. *History of the Present*. New York: Random House, 1999. These books present an on-the-ground analysis of the 1989 revolutions and what happened to them over the first decade since the end of communism, written by the most important journalist of the events.

Gay, Peter. *Freud: A Life for Our Time*. New York: Norton, 1988. This is the best short biography of Freud.

―――. *Weimar Culture: The Outsider as Insider*. New York, N.Y.: Harper & Row, 1968. A classic and masterful short study on avant-garde culture in post-war Germany.

Gros, Jean-Germain, ed. *Democratization in Late Twentieth-Century Africa: Coping with Uncertainty*. Westport, CT: Greenwood Press, 1998. This book includes national case studies, written by a number of different authors, from the perspective of struggling democratization at the end of the century.

Hart, John. *Revolutionary Mexico: The Coming and Process of the Mexican Revolution*. Berkeley: University of California Press, 1987. One of the best one-volume introductions to the revolution. The early chapters include a fine analysis of the long-term problems that set the terms for the revolution.

Havel, Vaclav. "Kosovo and the End of the Nation-State." *New York Review of Books*, June 10, 1999. See Lecture Forty-Eight for description.

Harvey, Neil. *The Chiapas Rebellion: The Struggle for Land and Democracy*. Durham, NC: Duke University Press, 1998. Harvey draws the connection between the Zapatistas of the early 20th century and the Chiapas Rebellion, with the resurgence of demands for indigenous rights and land.

Held, David, ed. *Globalization/Anti-Globalization*. Oxford: Blackwell Pub., 2002. This book provides a brief, balanced discussion of the arguments for and against globalization, both in the sense of its existence and whether it is "good" or "bad."

Held, David, et al. *Global Transformations: Politics, Economics and Culture*. Stanford: Stanford University Press 1999. The articles in this book offer an in-depth analysis of the globalization phenomenon and its repercussions.

Herken, Gregg. "The University of California, the Federal Weapons Labs and the Founding of the Atomic West." In *The Atomic West*, Bruce Hevly and John Findley, eds., pp. 119–135. Seattle: University of Washington Press, 1998. Herken's article provides a case study of the relationship between the state and scientists during the Manhattan Project, in which he argues for the detrimental impact on scientific integrity.

Herman, Arthur. *Joseph McCarthy: Reexamining the Life of America's Most Hated Senator*. New York: Free Press, 1999. In contrast to Pessen's book, Herman's offers a spirited defense of McCarthyism as a necessary response to a real and present danger.

Herring, George. *America's Longest War*. 4th ed. Boston: McGraw-Hill, 2002. Herring provides a good introduction to the American phase of the Vietnam War.

Hibbert, Christopher. *The Dragon Wakes: China and the West, 1793–1911*. New York: Penguin, 1989 (1970). Hibbert's book offers a traditional narrative account of the evolving relationship between China and the West and its impact on internal political stability.

Hitler, Adolf. *Mein Kampf*. Boston: Houghton Mifflin, 1998. See vol. 1, chapter 9, "Nation and Race," and vol. 2, chapter 11, "Propaganda and Organization." Hitler's incoherent, rambling, two-volume work is not worth wading through, but a couple of chapters will give you the crux of his ideas and his fanatical tone.

Hughes, H. Stuart. *Consciousness and Society*. Rev. ed. New Brunswick: Transaction Publishers, 2002 (1977). This classic work is still one of the best introductions to the broader philosophical revolution of the late 19th and early 20th centuries.

———. *Between Commitment and Disillusion: The Obstructed Path and the Sea Change*. Middletown, CT: Wesleyan University Press, 1987 (out of print).

Johnson, Chalmers. *Japan: Who Governs?* See "Japan: Who Governs?" and "Social Values and the Theory of Late Economic Development in East Asia." New York: Norton, 1995. In these essays, Johnson explains the different role of the state in Japanese capitalism and discusses the power of non-elected bureaucratic institutions in running the country.

Joll, James. *Intellectuals in Politics: Three Biographical Essays*. New York: Harper & Row, 1960 (out of print).

Judt, Tony. "The Story of Everything." *The New York Review of Books*, Sept. 21, 2000. Both the Judt and the Wills reviews try to make sense of the spate of books published at the end of the century.

Keegan, John. *The First World War*. New York: Knopf, 1999. Written by the foremost military historian of the First World War, this is one of the best and most up-to-date accounts of the war itself.

———. *The Second World War*. New York: Penguin, 1990. The best one-volume history of the war, it synthesizes a large amount of material in a chronological narrative that also highlights central themes.

Kevles, Dan. *The Physicists*. New York: Random House, 1997. Kevles is a renowned expert in the field, and this book provides the best survey of the topic. It is also a readable and compelling description of the establishment of "big science."

King, Martin Luther. "Letter from a Birmingham Jail." In *Documentary History of the Modern Civil Rights Movement*, Peter B. Levy, ed., pp. 110–115. Westport: Greenwood Press, 1992. Written after King's arrest during a peaceful demonstration, the letter is a classic statement of the "fundamentalist" nature of the civil rights movement's framework.

Kishlansky, Mark, ed. *Sources of World History*, vol. II. Belmont, CA: Wadsworth, 1998. A collection of primary documents for world civilization courses; volume 2 covers the 17th through 20th centuries.

Kollantai, Alexandra. "Sexual Relations and the Class Struggle." In *The Selected Writings of Alexandra Kollantai*, Alix Holt, ed., pp. 237–249. New York: Norton, 1977 (out of print). Kollantai was a Marxist feminist, but she went beyond the limited analysis of women's oppression to imagine how true equality would be constructed.

LaFeber, Walter. *Inevitable Revolutions: The United States in Latin America*. 2nd ed. New York: Norton, 1993. A critical view of the relationship between the United States and Latin America, focused on four Central American revolutions.

Leffler, Melvin. *The Specter of Communism*. New York: Hill & Wang, 1994. This book takes the more revisionist perspective, arguing that both sides shared responsibility for the Cold War but placing special emphasis on making the United States a willing partner, rather than an innocent defender of democracy. Reading both Gaddis and Leffler will provide a good sense of how historical debates play out in practice.

Lenin, V. I. "April Theses." In *Lenin Anthology*, Robert Tucker, ed., pp. 295–300. New York: Norton, 1980. With this document, Lenin made his pitch for an independent Bolshevik strategy that would abandon the provisional government and move toward a socialist revolution.

———. *State and Revolution*. New York: Penguin, 1993 (1917). In this pamphlet, written between the February and October Revolutions, Lenin laid out his argument in favor of the violent seizure of power by the vanguard party.

Lewin, Moshe, and Ian Kershaw, eds. *Stalinism and Nazism: Dictatorships in Comparison*. Cambridge: Cambridge University Press, 1997. This book, edited by two prominent historians of their fields, contains interpretive essays more fully developing the idea that the two regimes shared a new style of dictatorial rule, while allowing for differences.

Lewis, Bernard. "The Roots of Muslim World Rage." *Atlantic Monthly*, September 1990. This article, by a prominent scholar of Islam, discusses the historical roots of conflict between Islam and Christianity and the general phenomenon of Islamic fundamentalism.

Lindemann, Albert. *A History of European Socialism*. New Haven: Yale University Press, 1983. An older but excellent survey of the evolution of socialist thought and practice, from a historical rather than philosophical perspective. Chapter 3 focuses on Marx in the 1850–1870 period; chapter 4, on the building of the socialist movement before 1914; and chapter 5, on the emergence of communism and Lenin's contributions.

Lippman, Walter. *Public Opinion*. New York: Free Press, 1997 (1922). This book raises the fear that irrational public opinion polls would sway politicians from doing the right thing and argues that professionals should help organize public opinion.

Lukacs, J. *The End of the Twentieth Century and the End of the Modern Age*. New York: Ticknor & Fields, 1993. A thought-provoking general interpretation and prognosis of where the world is headed in the next century.

Lynd, Robert S., and Helen Merrell Lynd. *Middletown*. San Diego: Harvest Books, 1959. This classic local study brings the changes wrought by mass forms of leisure to life through its examination of a single community.

Marinetti, F. T. "The Founding and Manifesto of Futurism 1909." In *Futurist Manifestos*, Umbro Apollonio, ed., pp. 19–23. Boston: MFA Publications, 2001. See Lecture Five for description.

Marshall, T. H. *Citizenship and Social Class and Other Essays*. Cambridge: Cambridge University Press, 1950 (out of print). Marshall's classic essay on citizenship and social class provided the theoretical underpinnings for the expansion of state responsibility toward individual welfare.

Marx, Karl, and Friedrich Engels. *The Communist Manifesto*. New York: Signet, 1998 (1848). This is Marx's most famous pamphlet, which still provides one of the best statements of his theory of history.

McDaniel, Tim. *The Agony of the Russian Idea*. Princeton: Princeton University Press, 1996. This book provides an excellent analysis of why the Soviet Union and the communist system collapsed.

McMahon, Robert, and Thomas G. Paterson, eds. *The Origins of the Cold War: Problems in American Civilization*. 4th ed. Boston: Houghton Mifflin, 1999. This book is a collection of essays that nicely lays out the debates about the Cold War and includes a wide range of articles written by authors with different positions.

Mill, John Stuart. "The Subjection of Women." In *On Liberty and Other Essays*, pp. 471–582. Oxford: Oxford University Press, 1998. Mill's classic essay, written in the 1860s, is still one of the best encapsulations of the liberal argument for women's equality.

Mohanty, Chandra, Ann Russo, and Lourdes Torres, eds. *Third World Women and the Politics of Feminism*. Bloomington: Indiana University Press, 1991. The articles in this book discuss women's movements in the non-Western world and their conflicts with Western feminist movements.

Moon, J. Donald, ed. *Responsibility, Rights and Welfare: The Theory of the Welfare State*. Boulder, CO: Westview Press, 1988 (out of print). The articles in this book discuss the theoretical justifications for the welfare state in the context of Western liberalism.

Moore, Barrington. *Social Origins of Dictatorship and Democracy*. Boston: Beacon Press, 1993. In chapter 5 of this classic work, "Asian Fascism: Japan," Moore makes the argument that Japan and Germany created a new modernization model in which industrialization is accomplished without democratic government.

Morris-Suzuki, Tessa. *The Technological Transformation of Japan*. Cambridge: Cambridge University Press, 1994. This book provides the best recent analysis of Japan's economic modernization.

The New York Times Magazine, February 18, 1996. Special issue: "China Booms: The World Holds Its Breath." The articles in this special section focus on the changes prompted by the new economic policies and their consequences for the future.

Nicolson, Harold. *Peacemaking, 1919*. New York: Simon Publications, 2001 (1933). From one of the participants at the table, Nicolson's memoirs provide a close-up view of the negotiations.

Nietzsche, Friedrich. *Beyond Good and Evil*. New York: Vintage, 1989. In this book, Nietzsche lays out his critique of Christian morality and the need for a "transvaluation of values"

Nitze, Paul. "NSC-68." In *The Cold War*, Katherine A. S. Sibley, ed., pp. 150–153. Westport: Greenwood Press, 1998. See Lecture Twenty-Seven for description.

Obasanjo, Olusegun. "The Country of Anything Goes." *The New York Review of Books*, Sept. 24, 1998. Writing just before the new democratic elections that made him president in 1999, Obasanjo gives a good sense of the corruption that arises from competition over state resources.

Ortega y Gasset, Jose. *The Revolt of the Masses*. New York: Norton, 1994. Ortega argues that the masses had taken leadership away from the "superior minorities" without having the necessary qualities to lead.

Orwell, George. *The Road to Wigan Pier*. San Diego: Harvest Books, 1958 (1937). Orwell was commissioned to write a documentary account of the impact of the Depression in the worst-hit industrial areas of northern England.

———. *1984*. New York: Signet, 1990 (1949). Orwell's classic novel explored a terrifying totalitarian world in which "Big Brother" had a television/monitor in every room that made it impossible to have a private life.

Owen, Wilfred. *The Collected Poems of Wilfred Owen*. London: Chatto & Windus, 1965. See Lecture Two for description.

Overy, Richard. *Why the Allies Won*. New York: Norton, 1995. This book examines the various reasons—material, psychological, and moral—that the Allies defeated the Axis powers.

Perry, Elizabeth, and Li Xun. *Proletarian Power: Shanghai in the Cultural Revolution*. Boulder: Westview Press, 1997. This book provides a grassroots look at the Cultural Revolution and its impact on one of China's most vibrant intellectual urban centers.

Pessen, Edward. *Losing Our Souls: The American Experience in the Cold War*. Chicago: I.R. Dee, 1993. This book provides a critical assessment of the Cold War's impact on American life and politics.

Polachek, James. *The Inner Opium War*. Cambridge: Harvard University Press, 1992. This is the best specialized study on the important turning point of the Opium War, in which the author asks why this major military defeat did not spark an overhaul of China's foreign policy.

Ponting, Clive. *The 20ᵗʰ Century: A World History*. New York: Henry Holt, 1999. This book takes an analytic approach, along with criticizing Hobsbawm for what Ponting calls "Eurocentrism." Ponting tries to put the "periphery" of the world at the center of his analysis. He divides his book into three topic areas: social history, international affairs, and national politics.

Reed, John. *Ten Days That Shook the World*. New York: Viking Press, 1990 (1919). A memoir written by an American communist observer, this book provides an excellent view of the excitement generated by the revolution and was the basis for the movie *Reds*, starring Warren Beatty.

Reeves, Thomas. *The Life and Times of Joseph McCarthy*. Lanham, MD: Madison Books, 1997. The definitive biography of MacCarthy.

Reischauer, Edwin. *The Japanese Today: Change and Continuity*. Cambridge: Belknap Press, 1988. A good general survey of Japanese society, politics, and culture and how they have evolved since World War II.

Remarque, Erich Maria. *All Quiet on the Western Front*. New York: Fawcett, 1995. This is probably the most famous World War I novel and one that gives an excellent sense of the disillusionment and despair felt by battlefield soldiers.

Ridley, Jasper. *Mussolini: A Biography*. New York: St. Martin's Press, 1998. Of the many biographies of Mussolini, this one is the most readable and accessible for the general reader.

Rothermund, Dietmar. *The Global Impact of the Great Depression*. New York: Routledge, 1996. This book provides the best account of the broader impact of the Depression outside the West, while still including the conventional Western narrative.

Sartre, Jean-Paul. "Existentialism." In *Jean-Paul Sartre: Basic Writings*, Stephen Priest, ed., pp. 20–57. New York: Routledge, 2001. This essay, directed toward a broad audience, explains the principles of existentialism in straightforward laymen's terms. It was this ability to write for a broader public that made Sartre such a successful popularizer of the philosophy.

Sassoon, Donald. *One Hundred Years of Socialism*. Chapter 6, "Building Social Capitalism." New York: The New Press, 1996. In the context of an excellent history of social democratic parties in Europe, this chapter places the welfare state in the context of postwar consensus politics and the social democratic agenda.

Sen, Amartya. "How Is India Doing?" *The New York Review of Books*, December 16, 1982, and "How Has India Fared?" *Frontline*, August 22, 1997. Written by the Nobel Prize–winning Indian economist, these articles examine India's shortcomings in reducing poverty.

Sen, Sun Yat. "Fundamentals of National Reconstruction." In *Sources of World History*, vol. 2, Mark Kishlansky, ed. New York: Harper-Collins, 1995. In this program, Sun Yat-Sen defines the Nationalist platform, with its mixture of liberal values and anti-Western nationalism.

Shapira, Anita. *Land and Power: The Zionist Resort to Force, 1881–1948*. Oxford: Oxford University Press, 1992. Shapira's book on Zionism, in contrast to Sternhell's, accepts Zionists' nationalist claims as a given in telling the history of the same period.

Sitkoff, Harvard. *The Struggle for Black Equality: 1954–1992*. 2nd ed. New York: Hill & Wang, 1992. An excellent overview of the civil rights movement, placed in the context of the longer-term struggle for racial equality in the United States.

Skidmore, Thomas, and Peter Smith. *Modern Latin America*. 5th ed. Oxford: Oxford University Press, 2000. The best general introduction to 20th-century Latin American history.

Smith, Charles. *Palestine and the Arab-Israeli Conflict*. Boston: Bedford/St. Martin's, 2001. By most accounts, this is the best and most balanced survey of the origins of the Arab-Israeli conflict and of their competing nationalist claims. It includes primary documents, such as the selections below, from the "founding" documents of Arab and Jewish nationalism.

———. *Palestine and the Arab-Israeli Conflict*. Naguib Azoury, "The Awakening of the Arab Nation." 1905.

———. *Palestine and the Arab-Israeli Conflict*. Theodor Herzl, "The Jewish State." 1896.

Smith, Tony, ed. *The End of European Empire: Decolonization after World War II*. Lexington: D.C. Heath, 1976 (out of print). Part 5, "The Question of Neo-Colonialism." The articles in this section present opposing views on neo-colonialism and whether Third World poverty can be blamed on colonialism and its legacies or not.

Snow, Edgar. *Red Star over China*. New York, Grove Press, 1973 (1938). See especially part 4, "Genesis of a Communist." This book was written by a Western reporter who covered the revolution and gives a fascinating firsthand account of Mao and his followers during the years of civil war.

Snowden, Frank. *The Fascist Revolution in Tuscany*. Cambridge: Cambridge University Press, 1990. To get a better understanding of exactly who was attracted to fascism and under what conditions, it is essential to read one of the excellent local studies on the origins and rise of fascism in Italy.

Sorlin, Peter. *The Mass Media*. New York & London: Routledge, 1994. This book provides a short, reliable guide to the role played by the mass media in distributing information and forming public opinion in modern societies.

Spector, Ronald. *Eagle against the Sun*. New York: Free Press, 1985. The most readable account of the war in the Pacific.

Spence, Jonathan. *The Search for Modern China*. New York: Norton, 1999. This is the best scholarly survey of modern China by one of the preeminent scholars in the field. The 1999 edition comes with a companion volume, *Modern China: A Documentary Collection*, with primary documents to go along with each of the chapters.

—————. *Mao Zedong: A Penguin Life*. New York: Viking, 1999. Written by one of the premiere China specialists, this is a short and readable biography.

Stalin, Josef. "Economic Problems of Socialism in the USSR" In *The Essential Stalin*, Bruce Franklin, ed., pp. 467–473. Garden City: Anchor Books, 1972 (out of print). In this essay, Stalin makes clear his fears of the USSR being "encircled" by an expansionist and warlike capitalism.

Sternhell, Zeev. *The Founding Myths of Israel: Nationalism, Socialism and the Making of the Jewish State*. Princeton: Princeton University Press, 1998. Sternhell provides a skeptical view of Zionist nationalist claims.

Stone, Roger. *The Nature of Development*. New York: Knopf, 1992 (out of print). This book addresses the more general problem of what factors encourage and slow down the process of development in the Third World.

Students for a Democratic Society. "The Port Huron Statement." In *The New Radicals*, Paul Jacobs and Saul Landau. New York: Random House, 1966 (out of print). Written in 1964 as the mission statement of the SDS, this document provides an excellent introduction to the origins of student radicalism in the United States.

Suny, Ronald. *The Soviet Experiment*. Oxford: Oxford University Press, 1998. Suny examines the entire Soviet project, from the Bolshevik Revolution to the collapse of the USSR in 1991.

Susman, Warren. *Culture as History*. New York: Pantheon Books, 1994 (out of print). Part 3 outlines the parameters of an emerging American mass culture in the 1920s and 1930s.

Swingewood, Alan. *The Myth of Mass Culture*. London: Macmillan, 1977 (out of print). This book provides an excellent overview of critics of mass society, from Tocqueville to the Frankfurt school.

Terkel, Studs. *Hard Times*. New York: New Press, 2000 (1970). This oral history of the Depression in the United States provides a poignant account of its economic and psychological impact on ordinary Americans.

Tocqueville, Alexis de. *Democracy in America*. New York: Signet, 2001. This classic book, written by an aristocratic European, prefigures the later critiques of the dangers of democracy as the celebration of mediocrity.

Tzara, Tristan. "Dada Manifesto 1918." In *Seven Dada Manifestos and Lampisteries*, pp. 3–14. London: John Calder, 1977. See Lecture Five for description.

Vidal, Gore. "Pearl Harbor: An Exchange" in *The New York Review of Books*, May 17, 2001.

von Laue, Theodore. *The World Revolution of Westernization: the 20th Century in Global Perspective*. Oxford: Oxford University Press, 1987.This is a general history of the 20th century, written from the perspective of the increasing "westernization" of the world.

Wills, Gary. "A Reader's Guide to the Century." *The New York Review of Books*, July 15, 1999. Both the Judt and the Wills reviews try to make sense of the spate of books published at the end of the century, and it was Wills who organized them into narratives, analytical accounts, or chronologies. These essays are an excellent place to start for considering the bigger question of how to approach the subject itself.

Wilson, E. O. "Is Humanity Suicidal?" *The New York Times Magazine*, May 30, 1993. Written by a prominent socio-biologist, this article presents a biological interpretation of world environmental problems.

Wilson, Woodrow. "14 Points." In *Sources of World History*, Mark Kishlansky, ed., vol. 2, pp. 257–260. New York: Harper-Collins, 1995. See Lecture Three for description.

Wiseman, John. *Democracy in Black Africa: Survival and Revival*. New York: Paragon House, 1990 (out of print). See especially "The Conditions for Democracy?" In this chapter, Wiseman offers a theoretical discussion of the different arguments setting forth conditions for democratization. The other chapters in his book treat individual case studies and the progress made toward democratization in the 1980s.

Wolpert, Stanley. *A New History of India*. Oxford: Oxford University Press, 2000. The best overall survey of Indian history.

Wurfel, David, and Bruce Burton, eds. *Southeast Asia in the New World Order: The Political Economy of a Dynamic Region*. New York: St. Martin's Press, 1996. Written from a primarily economic and security perspective, this collection of articles discusses developments in the region since the end of the Cold War.

Zapata, Emiliano. "Plan de Ayala" and "Agrarian Program." In *Zapata and the Mexican Revolution*, John Womak, Jr., ed., pp. 393–412. New York: Knopf, 1969. These documents provide the essence of the Zapatista program and clarify the extent to which their demands go back to the legacy of Spanish imperialism and the hacienda system.

Internet Resources

http://www.fordham.edu/halsall/mod/modsbook.html.